Understanding Intellectual Disability

T0386421

Understanding Intellectual Disability supports professionals and parents in understanding critical concepts, correct assessment procedures, delicate and science-infused communication practices and treatment methods concerning children with intellectual disabilities.

From a professional perspective, this book relies on developmental neuropsychology and psychiatry to describe relevant measures and qualitative observations when making a diagnosis, and explores the importance of involving parents in the reconstruction of a child's developmental history. From a parent's perspective, the book shows how enriched environments can empower children's learning processes, and how working with patients, families, and organizations providing care and treatment services can be effectively integrated with attachment theory. Throughout seven chapters, the book offers an exploration of diagnostic procedures, new insights into the concept of intelligence and the role of communication and secure attachment in the mind's construction. With expertise from noteworthy scholars in the field, the reader is given an overview of in-depth assessment and intervention practices illustrated by several case studies and examples, as well as a lifespan perspective from a Human Rights Model of disability.

Understanding Intellectual Disability is an accessible guide offering an up-to-date vision of intellectual disability and is essential for psychologists, health care professionals, special educators, students in clinical psychology, and parents.

Things are connected through invisible bonds:
you cannot pluck a flower without disturbing a star.
Galileo Galilei

Margherita Orsolini is a Professor of Developmental and Educational Psychology. She was the Director of the Centre for the Learning Disabilities in the Department of Developmental and Social Psychology at Sapienza University of Rome, Italy.

Ciro Ruggerini is a specialist in Child Neuropsychiatry and Psychiatry and a psychotherapist. He is the past president of the Italian Society of Neurodevelopmental Disorders and was the Coordinator of the Section of Neuropsychology of the Italian Society of Child and Adolescent Neuropsychiatry from 2008 to 2011.

Understanding Atypical Development

Series editor: Alessandro Antonietti, Università Cattolica del Sacro Cuore, Italy.

This volume is one of a rapidly developing series in Understanding Atypical Development, published by Routledge. This book series is a set of basic, concise guides on various developmental disorders or issues of atypical development. The books are aimed at parents, but also professionals in health, education, social care and related fields, and are focused on providing insights into the aspects of the condition that can be troubling to children, and what can be done about it. Each volume is grounded in scientific theory but with an accessible writing style, making them ideal for a wide variety of audiences.

Each volume in the series is published in hardback, paperback and eBook formats. More information about the series is available on the official website at: https://www.routledge.com/Understanding-Atypical-Development/book-series/UATYPDEV, including details of all the titles published to date.

Published Titles

Understanding ADHD: A Guide to Symptoms, Management and Treatment
By Anna Maria Re and Agnese Capodieci

Understanding Dyscalculia: A Guide to Symptoms, Management and Treatment
By Daniela Lucangeli

Understanding Non-Verbal Learning Disability: A Guide to Symptoms, Management and Treatment
By Irene C. Mammarella, Ramona Cardillo and Jessica Broitman

Understanding Intellectual Disability: A Guide for Professionals and Parents
By Margherita Orsolini and Ciro Ruggerini

Understanding Intellectual Disability

A Guide for Professionals and Parents

Edited by
Margherita Orsolini and
Ciro Ruggerini

Routledge
Taylor & Francis Group

LONDON AND NEW YORK

Cover image: © Getty Images

First published 2022
by Routledge
4 Park Square, Milton Park, Abingdon, Oxon OX14 4RN

and by Routledge
605 Third Avenue, New York, NY 10158

Routledge is an imprint of the Taylor & Francis Group, an informa business

© 2023 selection and editorial matter, Margherita Orsolini and Ciro Ruggerini; individual chapters, the contributors

The right of Margherita Orsolini and Ciro Ruggerini to be identified as the authors of the editorial material, and of the authors for their individual chapters, has been asserted in accordance with sections 77 and 78 of the Copyright, Designs and Patents Act 1988.

British Library Cataloguing-in-Publication Data
A catalogue record for this book is available from the British Library

Library of Congress Cataloging-in-Publication Data
A catalog record has been requested for this book

ISBN: 978-1-032-11541-2 (hbk)
ISBN: 978-1-032-11539-9 (pbk)
ISBN: 978-1-003-22036-7 (ebk)

DOI: 10.4324/9781003220367

Typeset in Sabon
by Taylor & Francis Books

Contents

Illustrations

Figures

Tables

Boxes

Preface

Statistical data support the notion that the incidence of developmental disorders, and more generally the presence of atypical behaviors in childhood and youth, is increasing in the population around the world. This does not necessarily depend on the fact that pathological conditions are wide spreading; It might be the outcome of increased interest toward the conditions of children and adolescents, greater diffusion of knowledge about the features of atypical development, or higher levels of sophistication and implementation the diagnostic procedures have reached. In any case, adults who have to accompany and drive the growth of the young generations are challenged to find effective ways to manage situations which require peculiar attention. Specialists who take care of children and adolescents with special needs can do a part of this work. But another part is in the charge of people who live with those children and adolescents and interact with them outside the therapeutic setting. The contribution of parents, teachers, and trainers in extra-school domains (such as sport, art, hobbies, edutainment, religious education, social activities) can be relevant. But those people should be knowledgeable about the proper way of communicating, engaging, instructing, monitoring, and tutoring atypically developing children and adolescents in order to support their growth efficiently. This book series tries to fit this need.

The series aims to be a set of basic, concise guides on various developmental disorders or issues of atypical development. The books focus on providing insights into the aspects of the condition that can be troubling to children and adolescents and suggesting ways in which to support them. Each volume follows a basic structure and is grounded in scientific theory but written very accessibly for the target audience. Typically, each book faces the following issues:

- Signs and symptoms of the disorder
- What causes the disorder

- Available treatments and therapies
- Living with the condition produced by the disorder
- Practical ways to help children with the disorder and to support caregivers
- Communicating the diagnosis to peers
- Cultural differences and sensitivities.

The books include the description of case-studies, practical examples, and tasks and exercises to be proposed to children and adolescents, as well as check-lists and suggestions to improve the quality of life of children and their family, to support school achievement, and to enhance adaptation and inclusion in social life.

The series is addressed to parents, caregivers, and professionals, with particular emphasis on health, social care, and education. The books are of value to practitioners in clinical and educational psychology, counselling, mental health, nursing, teacher training, child welfare, social work, and youth work as well. Professionals and trainees involved in relevant medical disciplines – including midwives, health visitors, school nursing, and public health professionals – and those in general practice, as well as those involved in education including teachers, classroom assistants, and all those concerned with Early Years can benefit from the books.

Alessandro Antonietti
Department of Psychology – Catholic University of the Sacred Heart,
Milan, Italy
Editor of the series Understanding Atypical Development

Contributors

Margherita Orsolini is a Professor of Developmental and Educational Psychology. She has been the Director of the Centre for the Learning Disabilities in the Department of Developmental and Social Psychology at Sapienza University of Rome, Italy. Her research focuses on language and reading development, the role of adult-child interaction in the development of discourse and cognition, and the assessment and treatment of cognitive impairment in mild intellectual disabilities. *Discovering thought and reasoning in children with intellectual disabilities* is the theme of her lectures in several Italian University master's degree courses.

Ciro Ruggerini, Child Neuropsychiatrist, Psychiatrist and Cognitive Psychotherapist, is a Lecturer at the Department of Education and Human Sciences (University of Modena and Reggio Emilia) and the Institute of Science for Education and Training *Giuseppe Toniolo* (Modena) affiliated with the Pontifical College of Education *Auxilium*. He is the Director of the Mental Health department of the *Cooperativa Sociale Progetto Crescere* (Reggio Emilia) and a consultant of the ASP Charitas (Modena). He has been the President of the Italian Society of Neurodevelopmental Disorders, and the Scientific Coordinator of the Section of Neuropsychology of the Italian Society of Child and Adolescent Neuropsychiatry.

Sara Conforti is a Psychologist and holds a PhD in Behavioral Neuroscience acquired from the Sapienza University of Rome. She is a lecturer in Specific Learning Disorders and an honorary research fellow at the Department of Psychology, Sapienza University of Rome. Her current research is primarily concerned with the evaluation and intervention of learning difficulties for children and young adults.

Marilena Fatigante is an Associate Professor in Social Psychology at Sapienza University of Rome, Italy. She is an expert in the study of social interaction in natural settings carried out using ethnography, recording, and transcription practices. Research interests include the study of language socialization practices and Conversation Analysis of interaction in ordinary and institutional contexts such as family, classroom, healthcare and psychodiagnostic settings.

Francesca Federico is an Associate Professor at the Department of Developmental and Social Psychology, Sapienza University of Rome, Italy. She is the current director of the Centre for the Learning Disabilities in the same department. Her research interests include cognitive development with a focus on executive functions and their relationship with cultural and environmental contexts. Recent publications include "Natural Environment and Social Relationship in the Development of the Attentional Network" in *Frontiers in Psychology.*

Furio Lambruschi, a Psychologist and Psychotherapist, is the Director of Cognitive Therapy Center Forlì and School of Cognitive Psychotherapy in Bologna. He is a Lecturer and Supervisor of the Italian Society of Behavioral and Cognitive Therapy and a lecturer in several Italian schools of cognitive psychotherapy. He is the author of numerous publications in developmental psychopathology, attachment theory, and cognitive psychotherapy.

Sergio Melogno is an Associate Professor at the "Niccoló Cusano" Telematic University of Rome, where he teaches Developmental Cognitive Neuroscience and Developmental Neuropsychology. His research interests range from neuropsychological profiles of children with Neurodevelopmental Disorders, Klinefelter Syndrome and Agenesis of the Corpus Callosum, to the figurative language competencies of children with typical and atypical development. He carries out a clinical activity at the Department of Human Neuroscience and the Department of Developmental and Social Psychology, of the Sapienza University of Rome.

Aldo Moretti, Psychologist and Pedagogist, is the President of the Coordinators of the Regional Agencies for People with Disability (Genova), the Scientific Director of a foundation for families of children with intellectual disability associated with genetic syndromes (CEPIM Foundation, Genova) and the Scientific Director of the *Boggiano Pico Opera Don Orione* Rehabilitation Centre (Genova).

Stefania Musci, Psychologist and Psychotherapist is specialized in psychotherapy with adolescents. She is a consultant at the *Cooperativa*

Sociale Progetto Crescere (Reggio Emilia) and a trainer for executive functions. She works as a coordinator in Erasmus Projects focused on Special Education Needs, and as a trainer in European projects.

Antonina Pellegrino, a Psychologist and Psychotherapist, is a Consultant of the Libera Università di Lingue e Comunicazione IULM (Milano). She worked at the *Cooperativa Sociale Progetto Crescere* (Reggio Emilia). She acquired a Mphil in Strategies for a correct and Good Quality of Nutrition in the Developmental Age. Her clinical and research interests are in neurodevelopmental disorders, such as Nonverbal learning disabilities, Autism spectrum disorders, and Learning Disabilities.

Melvin Piro, a Psychologist and Psychotherapist, is a Lecturer at the Cognitive Therapy Center of Forlì and the School of Cognitive Psychotherapy in Bologna. He is a member of the Italian Society of Behavioral and Cognitive Therapy. His clinical activity focuses on evaluating and treating several psychopathological areas, with particular reference to parenting support interventions and teacher training.

Samantha Salomone is a consultant child and adolescent psychologist. She acquired a Master's degree in Learning and Cognitive Development Disorders. She has extensive experience in working with children who have neurodevelopmental disorders and collaborated with the Centre for the Learning Disabilities of the Department of Developmental and Social Psychology at the Sapienza University of Rome. Currently, she carries out private clinical activity in Rome.

Chapter 1

A rose is a rose but what is intellectual disability?

Ciro Ruggerini and Antonina Pellegrino

Language allows us to communicate about reality, but reality can be a fact of nature – as a rose is – or a fact of culture, as are the constructs developed by psychiatry. When we use the term intellectual disability (ID), we must be conscious that it indicates a construct and not a fact of nature. The construct of ID does not express any permanent quality from which the set of attributes of a person derives. People who receive a diagnosis of ID possess their own uniqueness/peculiarities that must be discovered and understood in both the clinical evaluation process and in common social relationships. The ID construct is periodically updated by several international organizations. The AAIDD uses the term disability, conceiving ID as the manifestation of a state of functioning in which a discrepancy exists between a person's abilities and limitations, and his or her life context. The ICD and DSM systems, on the other hand, conceive of ID as a disorder, i.e., the expression of a neurobiological alteration that hinders intellectual functioning and learning. Once their purposes are differentiated, the two constructs of disability and disorder can coexist. The second part of this chapter provides an overview of the diagnosis of intellectual disability (ID) that has its own specificities: in the methods – since it requires the involvement of several professionals – and in the purpose, because the main goal is not healing, but the promotion of development. For ID, multiple types of diagnoses are required, which describe different aspects of the condition.

1 Some historical considerations

The history of assistance to people with intellectual disability showed constant changes that were related to the different social representations of the human conditions underlying the psychiatric categorizations. According to Boekhoff (1996), at the beginning of the last century there was a medical frame labelling persons with disabilities as patients: "big institutions were set up: hospitals. Their goal was to cure ... so treatment was the most

DOI: 10.4324/9781003220367-1

important thing, but besides that they were also important to provide food and clothes ... medical doctors and psychiatrists were the most important staff member for many years ..." (50). In the 60s a pedagogical model considered persons with mental handicap as "life span pupils" who were assisted by psychologists, pedagogues and medical doctors and attended special schools. The underlying assumption was that "professionals know what is best for you" (Boekhoff, 1996).

Eventually an age without models began as people with disabilities started to be considered, Boekhoff carries on, as "citizens with the same rights and duties as any of us". They need support for "living in the society with normal housing; making their own choices; having their own network of friends; working in the open labor market; getting respect from other people... " (50). After the Convention on the Rights of Persons with Disabilities (UN, 2006) we have a *Human Rights Model*, that is a Model based on respect for human rights (Comitato Sammarinese di Bioetica, 2013).

The beginning of our century was characterized by new important changes. Starting with scientific research, the neurosciences made us more aware of the importance of neurodevelopment whereas the Human Genome Project and the Human Connectome Project, with a new style of collecting, analysing, and sharing data (Van Essen and Glasser, 2016), allowed us to better conceptualize the intertwined working of genetic, environmental, and developmental factors as underlying human individual differences. In parallel with this turbulent progress, the need for a critical use of scientific knowledge emerged. It was clearer that scientific knowledge cannot be developed outside a perimeter defined by ethical conceptions. Respect for difference and acceptance of human diversity (as stated by the Convention on the Rights of Persons with Disabilities UN, 2006) are ethical principles that cannot only be derived from scientific knowledge (Gelb, 2002).

The organization of assistance systems for people who have the need to receive support for the entire life span (WHO, 2002) also started to be guided by new concepts. It is now assumed that care and support require a network formed by the individual and his family, the health system, and the community agencies, including the school. Such network can effectively work if relevant concepts are constantly negotiated and shared. An example of a concept to be shared concerns intelligence. Researchers interested in individual differences, specialists on typical and atypical development, teachers who adapt programs to individual learning profiles, parents who plan autonomy for their children, all these figures may use the notion of intelligence with radically different meanings.

Sharing a scientifically updated concept of intelligence, along with observations on how different contexts may elicit flexible vs more rigid concepts and behaviors in a person with intellectual disability, can make the difference for care and support.

A crucial new assumption is also that people with disabilities must actively participate in the organization of care. Although specialists have more information on the general aspects of the condition, the individual and his/her family are the truly experts on the peculiarities of their personal history and condition (Ruggerini et al., 2010). Prepared, informed, and motivated family members are formidable allies of specialists and operators.

This chapter is guided by the coordinates that we have outlined so far. The overriding objective is to share concepts that foster in the reader a critical attitude towards scientific knowledge. Such attitude, in our opinion, will facilitate the professional encounter with the person whose functioning can be categorized as deficient. In our professional experience, and not only in our everyday life we meet people and not categorized entities.

2 The construct of intellectual disability

2.1 A rose is a rose is a rose is a rose

From time to time, poets express profound insights that create a synthesis of themes that concern disparate fields of knowledge. For instance, Gertrude Stein wrote the phrase "Rose is a rose is a rose is a rose" in her poem "Sacred Emily" in 1913 to indicate that "things are what they are". In other words, if the name of the thing that we call a "rose" evokes different images and emotions in each of us (e.g., beauty, youth, femininity, etc.), a rose is nothing but itself according to the principle of identity.

The theme of the relationship of words with entities of the world also exists in psychiatry. When we use the term intellectual disability (ID), are we referring to the same, unique, and permanent entity?

The answer, of course, is no.

The entity of the rose belongs to the world of nature, in which entities possess physical, tangible, and permanent dimensions. The expression *intellectual disability*, on the other hand, refers to a construct, i.e., to an elaboration that belongs to the world of culture. It is a nonmaterial entity in constant evolution and, like all constructs, is a product of its time and circumstances.

Essentially, the rose is a thing, an entity of nature, whereas, intellectual disability is a construct, an entity of culture.

2.2 What is a construct?

We use the authoritative definition of *construct* given by Schalock et al. (2007). A construct is an idea literally created to represent an observable behavior. A construct arises in the context of a theory of human functioning, it is not directly observable as are certain other constructs, such as motivation or intelligence. It is only possible, therefore, to make inferences about its presence.

There are two types of constructs:

- Theoretical definitions (or constitutive constructs) that define the relationship of a construct to other constructs. Specifically, since 1959, the construct of mental retardation of the American Association on Mental Retardation (AAMR) refers to the constructs of intellectual functioning, maturation, learning, and social adaptation, whereas the construct of intellectual disability in the 2012 manual of the American Association on Intellectual and Developmental Disabilities (AAIDD) refers to the constructs of disability, intellectual functioning, and adaptive abilities.
- Operational definitions (or operational constructs), which define the operations or criteria by which constructs can be defined or measured. In our field, for example, operations or criteria are the evaluation of results in standardized tests of intellectual and adaptation efficiency.

According to Berrios (2013), classification systems (e.g., the ICD and DSM systems) belong to a hybrid science because elaboration of the categories that they define involves both human and natural sciences (e.g., neurobiology). It is necessary, Berrios states, to keep the correct sequence of involvement clearly in mind. The human sciences (e.g., sociology) indicate the subject of the investigation; once this is done, the natural sciences strive to understand the problem that is being posed. No discovery of nature can produce a definition of mental disorder by itself. In addition, no neurobiological data themselves can support a construct in our field. A construct originates only from a request that arises from an existing social context.

For instance, in the established diagnostic manuals of our time, the definition of the constructs of neurodevelopmental disorders (or disabilities) aims to identify the people to whom to address adequate supports for their development and inclusion.

Constructs, both constitutive and operational, necessitate continuous updating (a "periodic calibration", according to Berrios) to reflect new knowledge that is shared in society. Currently, the scientific knowledge shared by scientific societies and/or associations serves an ideal of justice shared by nations.

2.3 Which philosophy of knowledge is the foundation of the constructs: are the constructs valid or useful?

Since constructs are a representation of reality, a question naturally arises: How good are constructs? Or, in other words, how loyal are the constructs to reality?

To answer this question, we will take two relevant points from Kendler (2016). The first is the notion that a mental disorder emerges from "clusters of properties", consisting of interactions between symptoms and neurobiological connections involving the mind and the brain. Disorders, therefore, have a neurobiological basis, which confirms that they are a part of reality.

The second is the notion of validity as consistency. The more a disorder is consistent with currently available knowledge, the more valid it is. In this way, the notion of validity as coherence departs from the conventional idea of truth (according to the assertion that what is true corresponds to something in the world that can be easily verified) in favor of a pragmatic orientation (according to the belief that what is useful is valid).

In summary, diagnostic categories are the reflection of "property clusters" of the mind and its neurobiological counterparts (realistic perspective of knowledge). They are also, however, the consequence of perpetually ongoing scientific work that produces an increasingly coherent definition, i.e., one that is more useful, for understanding the different conditions (pragmatic perspective).

Kendler's (2016) observations concerning the condition of intellectual disability have the following implications:

*The intellectual disability construct is only a generic attribute of the person. People with typical development meet each other without presuming to know each other just because they are typical; it is commonly assumed that knowledge requires experiences of interpersonal relationships. People with typical development also meet people with intellectual disabilities for whom the same attitude should be applied. In fact, people with intellectual disabilities are not "essences" whose particularities are, in some way, predictable a priori based on the diagnostic category assigned to them. Similar considerations are valid for people with typical or atypical development who meet a specialist psychologist or psychiatrist. The discovery of the attribute of typical or atypical development is only one of the moments of the diagnostic process (see the following section).

*If a disorder is a cluster of properties, a dissertation on the symptoms of intellectual disability and their connection with neurobiological characteristics is relevant to a diagnostic context and its practices, obviously including communication with the person receiving the diagnosis and his or her family. *The construct "intellectual disability" and those connected to it, such as intelligence and adaptation, are, in terms of scientific knowledge, a permanent work in progress. While this is known to researchers, it is likely that it is unknown to the families and the operators who do not belong to a technical culture. This indicates the need for these social groups to have explicit knowledge of the relevant scientific references of the historical moment in which they work.

2.4 Who updates the construct of intellectual disability?

As mentioned previously, constructs are revised over time. However, who proposes and carries out this work regarding the intellectual disability construct? Below, the main working groups are given.

- American Association on Intellectual and Developmental Disabilities (AAIDD),

The American Association on Intellectual and Developmental Disabilities (AAIDD), founded in 1876, is an American non-profit association of professionals who deal with intellectual disabilities and related developmental disabilities (AAIDD, 2019). It should be noted that its first president was Edouard Sèguin, a teacher and physician, who came from France, and collected and expanded the cultural heritage of Jean Marc Gaspard Itard (1801–1807). Itard was the physician who developed for Victor, the wild boy of Aveyron, the very first method of education/treatment for people with intellectual disabilities in the history of assistance.

The name of this association has changed five times to adapt to the different ways of conceptualizing this condition:

- 1876: Association of Medical Officers of American Institutions for Idiotic and Feebleminded Persons.
- 1906: American Association for the Study of the Feebleminded.
- 1933: American Association on Mental Deficiency.

- 1987: American Association on Mental Retardation.
- 2007: American Association on Intellectual and Developmental Disabilities.

The AAIDD's (2019) mission is to "promote advanced policies, research capable to have resonance in society, effective practices and the enjoyment of universal human rights for people with intellectual and developmental disabilities". This predominantly (but not exclusively) humanistic orientation maintains the approach of the founder, who derived his physiological and educational method (Sèguin, 1846) from an anthropological statement common to all men, irrespective of the characteristics of their functioning. Since 1910, the AAIDD has published a text on the definition of the condition every 10 years; the latest edition (the eleventh) is from 2010, and is entitled "Intellectual Disability: Definition, Classification and Support System". Of these manuals, in our discussion, we will refer to that of 2002 (Luckasson et al., 2002) and 2010 (Schalock et al., 2010).

- International Classification of Diseases (ICD)

The ICD (International Classification of Diseases) is the international classification of diseases and related conditions established by the World Health Organization (WHO). It is used as a standard classification for statistical and epidemiological studies, and as a public health management tool (i.e., to clarify which services must be provided for a nation or territory, and for which diseases and related conditions).

The eleventh revision (ICD-11), which was approved by the World Health Assembly of the WHO in May 2019, will be adopted and implemented on January 1, 2022 (Girimaji and Pradeep, 2018).

The condition of intellectual disability has been included in the ICD since the inception of its compilation, although with different expressions ("mental deficiency" in the ICD-6 of 1948; "mental retardation" in the ICD-8 of 1965).

The statement of the General Director of the WHO at the time of the approval of ICD-11 should be emphasized: "… the ICD is a product that allows us to understand a lot about what makes people sick … and to act (editor's note: in a one-direction organization) to prevent suffering … " (Lindmeier, 2018). This statement is relevant to our discussion because it reiterates the purpose of this classification system as essentially aimed at the planning of health services.

- The Diagnostic and Statistical Manual (DSM)

The Diagnostic Statistical Manual of Mental Disorders (DSM) is compiled by the American Psychiatric Association (APA). The term "statistical" should be noted because it indicates the philosophy that undergirds the system: mental disorders are identified based on the frequency with which certain symptoms co-occur. The authors define their system as "atheoretical", since it is independent of any paradigm of understanding the aetiology of the symptoms themselves; it is a system that allows a substantially descriptive categorical diagnosis.

The condition of mental retardation/intellectual disability has been included in all the versions of the DSM, although it was described in a separate guide in the 1952 manual.

3 Intellectual disability as a type of disability

As mentioned in the previous sections the construct with which we are dealing is a cultural product and, for this reason, subject to periodic updating. In the following sections, we consider the most recent updates found in the AAMR (2002), AAIDD (2010), DSM-5 (2013), and ICD-11 (2022) manuals. We will attempt to illustrate the logic behind the more recent changes by drawing on some of the documents, which are the core of the debate that preceded publication of the manuals.

We will present the position of the AAIDD and that of the working groups that developed the DSM and ICD classifications separately because these have progressively reached, over the last decade, overlapping concepts. Three paths of change will be considered: the name; the theoretical definition (constitutive construct); and the operative definition (operative construct).

3.1 Theoretical definition (constitutive construct)

The terms "mental retardation" and "intellectual disability" also express different ways of conceptualizing the same condition. For a descriptive summary of the difference, we refer to the work of Wehmeyer et al. (2008). The mental retardation construct assumes that "the disability lives in the individual". Having "mental retardation" thus means being imperfect. The place where that deficit resides is the mind; the nature of that deficit of the mind (mental deficiency) is a lower mental performance.

The construct intellectual disability assumes, instead, that disability "is the manifestation of a state of functioning in which there is a discrepancy between the abilities and limitations of a person and the context in which the person functions" (Wehmeyer et al., 2008, p. 313). The term "mental retardation" therefore refers to a static and permanent condition inside of the person (i.e., slowness of the mind); the term "intellectual disability", on the other hand, denotes a state of functioning that can vary according to the level of facilitation of the context.

The AAIDD (2010) definition of intellectual disability is related to five assumptions.

The definition presented is: "Intellectual disability is a condition characterized by significant limitations in both intellectual functioning and adaptive behavior (see Box 1.1), that appear in conceptual, social and practical domains. This disability occurs before the age of 18" (Schalock et al., 2010, pp.7–8).

The five assumptions are as follows:

1   Limitations in present functioning must be considered within the context of community environments typical of the individual's age, peers, and culture.
2   Valid assessment considers cultural and linguistic diversity, as well as differences in communication, sensory, motor, and behavioral factors.
3   Within an individual, limitations often coexist with strengths.
4   An important purpose of describing limitations is to develop a profile of needed support.
5   With appropriate personalized support over a sustained period, the life functioning of the person with intellectual disability generally tends to improve.

Support is defined as "… resources and strategies that promote development, education, interests and personal well-being and that enhance individual functioning …" (Schalock et al., 2010).

Box 1.1 Intellectual functioning and adaptive behavior in the AAIDD system

The most adequate concept for explaining and defining intellectual functioning for diagnostic purposes is, according to the AAIDD manual, "a general mental ability that includes reasoning, planning, solving problems, thinking, comprehending complex ideas, learning quickly, and learning from experience". Although highly imperfect, IQ scores are still the measure that best represents intellectual functioning.

Adaptive behavior is the set of skills that are learned and expressed by people in daily life. It includes the following:

• Conceptual skills: language, reading and writing, the concept of money, time, and numbers.

- Social skills: interpersonal skills, social responsibility, self-esteem, deceivability (likelihood of being deceived or manipulated), a lack of naivety (for example, caution in dealing with novelty), an ability to follow rules, showing respect for laws, an ability to avoid victimization, and an ability to solve problems related to social life.
- Practical skills: activities of daily living   (personal care), occupational skills, schedules/routines, safety, use of money, use of the telephone.

3.2 Operational definition (operational construct)

A limitation in intellectual functioning and adaptive behavior is considered significant when scores on the standardized tests that describe them (for intellectual functioning: the IQ score) are at least two standard deviations below the mean of the peer age. It is necessary to emphasize that this operational definition assumes that a correlation exists between intellectual functioning and adaptive behavior, but a causal link does not. Both intellectual functioning and adaptive behavior are important for the diagnosis. They also have the same weight for the diagnosis (equal weight) and must be considered together (joint consideration) (Tassè et al., 2016).

The intellectual disability (ID) construct is part of the constructs that make up the developmental disability (DD)/developmental disabilities (DDs). ID is a scientific definition based on research with a long, stable definitional history, whereas DD and DDs constitute administrative definitions. The definitions of operational constructs are reported in the following (Box 1.2, from Schalock and Luckasson, 2021).

Box 1.2

Table 1.1 Disability-related constructs

	Operational definition
Disability	A significant functional limitation that (a) reflects an inability or constraint in human functioning; (b) represents a substantial disadvantage to the individual; (c) is influenced by contextual variables; and (d) can be mitigated (i.e., reduced or alleviated) through interventions and supports or by reducing barriers that preclude opportunities, equity, and inclusion (Schalock and Luckasson, 2021).
Intellectual disability (ID)	Significant limitations both in intellectual functioning and in adaptive behavior, as expressed in conceptual, social, and practical adaptive skills; this disability originates during the developmental period.

	Operational definition
Developmental disability (DD)	Severe, chronic disability of an individual that (a) is attributable to a mental or physical impairment or combination of mental and physical impairments; (b) is manifested before the individual reaches the age of 22; (c) is likely to continue indefinitely; (d) results in substantial functional limitations in three or more of the following areas of major life activity: (I) self-care; (II) receptive and expressive language; (III) learning; (IV) mobility; (V) self-direction; (VI) capacity for independent living; (VII) economic self-sufficiency; and (VIII) reflects the individual's need for a combination and sequence of special, interdisciplinary, or generic services, individualized supports, or other forms of assistance that are of lifelong or extended duration and are individually planned and coordinated (Developmental Disabilities Assistance and Bill of Rights Act Amendments of 2000, Sec. 102. (8)(A).
Developmental disabilities (DDs)	A broad term used to refer to "a group of conditions due to an impairment in physical, learning, language, or behavior areas. These conditions begin during the developmental period, may impact day-to-day functioning, and usually last throughout a person's lifetime" (Centers for Disease Control and Prevention, 2017).
Intellectual and developmental disabilities (IDDs)	The broader, combined field of intellectual disability and developmental disabilities.

The developmental disabilities construct is used to study prevalence trends in the general population. Zablotsky et al. (2019), for example, considered 10 conditions (i.e., attention-deficit/hyperactivity disorder (ADHD), autism spectrum disorder, blindness, cerebral palsy, intellectual disability, learning disability, moderate to profound hearing loss, other developmental delay, seizures, and stuttering or stammering) in a population of 3–17-year-olds in the U.S. It was found that the frequency of the 10 conditions increased significantly from 2009–2017, i.e., 16.2% to 17.8%. During the same time, frequency of the intellectual disability condition increased from 0.93% to 1.17%.

4 Intellectual disability as a disorder

4.1 The name

The publication of the DSM-5 (2013) and ICD-11 (2022) was preceded by an extensive debate within the Psychiatry Section of Mental Retardation/ Intellectual Disability of the World Psychiatric Association (WPA) and the Working Group on the Classification of Intellectual Disability of the World Health Organization (WHO)(Salvador-Carulla and Bertelli, 2008; Salvador-Carulla et al., 2011; Girimaji and Pradeep, 2018).

Essentially, different groups of psychiatrists considered it appropriate to replace the term "disability" with that of "disorder". The term "intellectual developmental disorder (IDD)" was adopted by the DSM-5 in 2013, and the term "disorders of intellectual development (DID)" was approved in the revision of the ICD-11 in 2020. The essential motivation for this change was health strategy. People with intellectual disabilities express a very high frequency of medical, neurological, and/or psychiatric health needs; if their condition is assigned to the disability field (a field in which social categories of definition of needs prevail), there is a risk that health needs will be overshadowed if not entirely overlooked. The term "disorder" is consistent with the location of the condition within a medical classification system.

It is worth noting that, just prior to the publication of the DSM-5, both the AAIDD and the ARC (Association for Retarded Citizens of the United States) expressed opposition to the adoption of the term "disorder" (Gomez and Nygren, 2012; Berns, 2012) in favor of retaining the term "disability", which is shared by international movements and is consistent with the professional activities of action on contextual factors. Based on these social pressures, the writers of the DSM-5 choose to keep both the names "intellectual disability" and "developmental disorder".

4.2 Theoretical definition (constitutive construct)

The key to comprehending the condition is a neurobiological alteration that hinders intellectual functioning; intellectual functioning hinders adaptation skills assumed as a set of conceptual, social, and practical skills. The construct predicts, according to the DSM-5, a cause-and-effect relationship (not just a close correlation) between intellectual and adaptive functioning. The DSM-5 states: "... to meet diagnostic criteria for intellectual disability, the deficit in adaptive functioning must be directly related to the intellectual impairment...". This type of causal relationship is considered by esteemed authors such as Tassè et al. (2016) not provable. The need for this causal relationship is not explicit in the ICD-11.

The alteration of cognitive functioning is often part of a multiplicity of syndromic pictures. The term Intellectual Disability therefore indicates a set of syndromes: it is a "meta-syndrome".

The construct emphasizes two aspects of the condition: the multiple aetiology and the fact that the IQ value is not so helpful if not accompanied by other assessments of cognitive functioning, so to have a complete understanding of the difficulties of adaptation. There is, therefore, the need to deepen the study of cognitive functions which, in individual cases, are crucial for adaptation.

4.3 Operational definition (operational construct)

The operative construct of Intellectual Disability / Intellectual Development Disorder is substantially like the one approved by the AAIDD and it refers to deficits in intellectual functions, deficits in adaptive functions and an onset during the developmental period. The DSM-5 and the ICD-11 emphasize to those who formulate the diagnostic classification a "critical" use of the results of the standard assessments of cognitive and adaptive functioning when there are non-homogeneous scores in multicomponent tests such as the Wechsler Scale and when there is a co-occurrence of other neurodevelopmental disorders (such as language disorders or Autism Spectrum Disorders).

People whose cognitive or adaptive function deficits are described by scores ranging between one and two standard deviations below the mean are included in the DSM-5 in the section, Other Conditions That May be a Focus of Clinical Attention; the ICD-11 uses the term "borderline intellectual functioning" for the same condition. This construct refers to an individual characteristic and does not correspond to a disorder (Ruggerini and Manzotti, 2021).

5 Disability and disorder: two terms, two conceptualizations, two complementary objectives

The positions of the AAIDD, and the classification systems of the ICD and DSM, have different definitions of the constitutive construct, and this translates into use of the terms "disability" and "disorder". The theme of the two conceptualizations, discussed since 2008 in the WPA Section of Psychiatry of Mental Retardation/Intellectual Disability (Salvador-Carulla and Bertelli, 2008), has led to the recognition that they possess different purposes.

The disorder construct permits, as stated previously, to keep the condition in the range of medical assistance. Specifically, it solicits adequate training of professionals to satisfy physical and mental health needs; urges the organization of adequate services; and recalls the need for dedicated research.

The construct of disability, on the other hand, urges adaptation of social contexts to the principles of inclusion and the fulfilment of human rights.

The two constructs and terms (disability and disorder) can therefore coexist once their purposes are distinct. In the specialized literature, this coexistence is indicated with the term "polysemic – polynomious approach" to the condition.

In summary, as a disorder, the condition is listed in the DSM-5 and ICD-11 systems; as a way of functioning, the condition can be described in terms of its characteristics by the ICF and/or by the AAIDD classification system (it is important to note that these classification systems allow a description of areas of functioning, and the result is not a nosological/diagnostic classification, but a description of the human functioning) (Box 1.3)

Box 1.3

Table 1.2 Keywords of the disability and disorder constructs

Intellectual disability	*Disorder of intellectual development*
- **state of functioning (or existential condition)**: which recalls the need for recognition of every citizenship right. - **disability**: which underlines the strong relation between personal development and opportunities offered by the context (presence of support). - **improvement**: which highlights the error of any conceptualization of the present limitations as being "fixed".	- **disorder/health condition**: which emphasizes the need to have access to appropriate treatments for disorders or co-occurring diseases. - **syndrome**: which underlines the importance of researching the etiological factors to understand the multiplicity of symptoms that may involve other biological systems, in addition to the brain. - **key role of the cognitive functions**: which requires a detailed description of the cognitive functions to understand the difficulties in adaptation.

6 Crucial aspects common to both conceptualizations (disability and disorder)

Two crucial and common aspects to both conceptualizations must be emphasized:

Definition of intelligence

Both the AAIDD system and the DSM and ICD systems currently consider IQ scores (see Box 1.4) to be a useful index of intelligence. In fact, this is a pragmatic position: while waiting for a more comprehensive definition of intelligence shared by the scientific community, a useful index is the IQ. Both systems, however, recognize that IQ is not a completely satisfactory measurement. For this reason, these systems argue that the assessment of cognitive functions should be completed with other assessments. The choice of assessments should be guided by data from psychology and developmental neuropsychology related to new insights on the precise meaning of intelligent and adaptive. These topics are developed in chapter 2 (Is intelligence a general mental capacity?) and in chapter 3 (Assessments of children with developmental delays and intellectual disability).

Modifiability of adaptability

Both the AAIDD system and the DSM and ICD systems emphasize that adaptability can improve over time. The AAIDD system asserts that this depends on the presence of adequate supports. The DSM and ICD systems, on the other hand, indicate the importance of medical and genetic factors, and early and continuous interventions, that can improve adaptive and intellectual functioning. Since the improvement may be such that a diagnosis of intellectual disability may no longer be appropriate, intellectual disability is thus a dynamic condition.

Box 1.4 The notion of IQ and the Wechsler test

The term Intelligence Quotient (IQ) originally indicated the relationship between mental age and chronological age and was coined soon after the construction of Binet's first intelligence test in 1905. Currently, the term "IQ" indicates the position of a subject's score on an intelligence test on the Bell curve (also known as the Gauss curve) compared to the scores of subjects of the same age. A score of 100 indicates that this position ranks exactly on the average. The most widely used intelligence test globally is the Wechsler test, published in 1939 and periodically revised (Wechsler, 2014). The version currently in use in Italy is from 2003 (the Italian translation is from 2012). It is made up of 15 subtests that give rise to the following five composite measures of IQ:

Global skills: Full scale IQ.

Lower-order composite scores: Verbal Comprehension Index (VCI), Perceptual Reasoning Index (PRI), Working Memory Index (WMI), and Processing Speed Index (PSI).

The 15 subtests are supported by different skills (specified in parentheses): 1. block design (spatial relations); 2. similarities (language development); 3. digit span (memory span); 4. picture concepts (inferential reasoning); 5. coding (pace of time execution); 6. vocabulary (lexical knowledge); 7. letter-number sequence (working memory); 8. matrix reasoning (inferential reasoning and general sequence reasoning); 9. comprehension (general information); 10. symbol search (perceptual speed); 11. picture completion (general information); 12. cancellation (perceptual speed); 13. information (general information); 14. arithmetic (achievement in mathematics); and 15. word reasoning (lexical knowledge) (Flanagan and Kaufman, 2009).

In the case that the IQ of the composite scores VCI, PRI, VMI, and PSI are homogeneous, the total IQ is a valid indicator of general intellectual abilities. The statistical correlation among the scores of the different subtests is an expression of a general factor of intelligence (Factor G). A strong criticism of this interpretation is presented in chapter 2.

A lack of homogeneity through the scores of the four indices could be understood in terms of the connectome theory (see section 9.1), according to which genes guide the development of the different parts of the cerebral cortex that support the different functions, including those solicited by the Wechsler test. This is clear in certain genetic syndromes, in which similar values of the total IQ correspond to profiles of functioning with significantly different VCI, PRI, VMI, and PSI composite scores (section 5.4).

7 Where is the person?

The definitions and the operational constructs included in the AAIDD, DSM, and ICD systems refer to dimensions of the mind supported by its own neurobiological basis (brain).

Then, what consideration is given in these diagnostic systems to being a "person"?

Indeed, any specialist in the field is involved in this question. The nosographic/nosological systems classify states of functioning/disorders/diseases, whereas specialists meet people with states of functioning/disorders/diseases.

At the beginning of this chapter, when discussing Kendler's conceptions, we stressed that no disorder refers to an "essence". We also assume that this implies that the nosographic/nosological identity does not in any way summarize the concept of personal identity. This statement leads to the question mentioned above: are the brain, the mind, and the person different entities?

In the manuals of the AAIDD (since at least 2002), the term "person" appears explicitly: the person is the entity to which the supports should be addressed, which is the final goal of an evaluation process.

Moreover, the manuals assume that the main quality of being a person is the ability to "desire" and create one's own "life project". Being a person is, therefore, at the center of the AAIDD construct when used in terms of assistance.

In the ICD and DSM systems, the term "person" does not appear explicitly. However, one of the preliminary works of the DSM-5 (Salvador-Carulla and Bertelli, 2008) indicate the need to integrate the diagnostic classifications of intellectual disability into person-centered approaches, such as those included in the Guidelines for Diagnosis in Psychiatry, drafted for the WPA by the International Guidelines for Diagnostic Assessment (IGDA, 2003).

This document suggests that a complete diagnosis should consist of a diagnostic classification and an assessment carried out according to an idiographic approach which considers the point of view – in terms of expectations and desires – of the person. This again centers the attribute of being a person on the ability to function as a "desiring subject".

In conclusion we will refer to a metaphor that can assist in making a distinction between the brain, the mind, and the person. An explicit distinction is necessary to prevent clinical or evaluation data related to the brain and the mind from becoming irrelevant to those related to being a person.

We can compare the brain to the building structures of a room; the mind to pieces of furniture within the room that have distinct functions; and the person to the owner of the room and the furniture, who chooses the use of the room according to his or her goals or wishes.

The characteristics of the brain can be described with imaging tools (focusing on structural neuroimaging measures of brain morphology and tissue properties); the characteristics of the mind can be described with indexes of cognitive functioning; and the "meanings" of the person can be obtained through a listening and dialogue relation. In fact, the "meanings" of the person are at the center of assistance.

In the AAIDD system, the "meanings" of the person guides the programming supports aimed at the "life project" (see chapter 7) in the ICD and DSM systems and is included in the complete diagnostic formulation (see the following sections).

8 Conceptualizations underlying diagnostic labels matter

Eleonora is a 22-year-old girl with Down syndrome. Her intellectual efficiency, as evaluated by psychometric tests, gives a lower value (on the

Wechsler Scale, her QIV and QIP are equal to 45), but she neither has other associated impairments nor physical or mental disorders. Eleonora's parents are in good health. Eleonora was taken for a psychiatric consultation when she was in the third year of high school. After the first months of the third year of high school, Eleonora refused to do the homework given to her by her remedial teacher, lost all interest in school, and started to spend the afternoon watching television and neglecting her social relationships. This change was the consequence of two factors at school. The first was that the new remedial teacher had little expertise, and gave Eleonora homework that was boring, repetitive, and difficult to understand. The second was that a class teacher misinterpreted a message – with affective and sexual contents – that Eleonora had written to a classmate and reprimanded her in front of her classmates.

Within a few months after a new consultation, Eleonora made great progress (see Box 1.5). Her parents identified the cause of the changes in the added information about her intellectual impairments during the psychiatric consultation. All the previous consultation reports had been disappointing enough to make the parents pessimistic about their daughter's future perspectives. In one of the reports, written at the end of the fifth year of elementary school, Eleonora was described in the following way: "the girl shows a moderate – severe mental retardation that significantly influences learning at school and makes it necessary to help her with everyday activities". However, the current information given to the parents – in accordance with the AAMR 2002 definition – was markedly different:

> The IQ 45 is a score on a psychometric test suggesting that there is a cognitive delay. This score will be considered to offer supports to school learning and social activities but is not an indication of what Eleonora will learn both as a student and, more generally, as a human being. The developmental level of every aspect of Eleonora's personality will be the outcome of her neurobiological potential and the opportunities offered by the environment.

This is how Eleonora's parents described the effects that this information had on them:

> ... until that consultation, no specialist had ever proposed an attainable perspective; we've had the opportunity of looking at our daughter from a different perspective ... in the past because the catastrophic perspective we were given, anything extra that she did meant a little miracle to us ... .

The new perspective of the parents is passed onto their relatives, the teachers, and Eleonora's friends; every one of them has changed his or her view on her potential and offers her matching opportunities (Ruggerini et al., 2008).

Box 1.5 Changes in Eleonora's behavior before and after her parents acquired a new concept of her intellectual impairment

Before
After
1
She rarely helps in the household – she does not set the table or make the bed
She sets the table every night; helps in the house and dusts; puts the cutlery in the dishwasher without asking; she offers to help spontaneously
2
She does not know how to cook
She learns to make pizza dough and pasta; she writes down the recipes of the foods that she is making
3
She does not want to do her homework; she copies down parts of a book that are written in dialect; every weekend, she gets homework from the same book
There is a drastic change in the teaching: she is asked to write a biography of her friends in a music group; she interviews them, writes down their stories; she writes down the lyrics of her favourite songs; she is passionate about her homework
4
She does not know basic math, such as addition and subtraction
After 15 lessons by an elementary teacher, she can add and subtract
5
She does not know how to use money
After 15 lessons, she recognizes Euro coins and uses them for purchases up to 10 Euro
6
She does not know how to tell time
She has learned to tell time
7
She does not know how to use a camera properly
She becomes the photographer of the musical group and learns how to take pictures
8
She does not know how to ski

In less than a week's time, she learns the technique of the "snow shovel" and how to use the ski lift, so that she can go skiing with her friends

9

She cannot dance

She takes dancing classes and learns steps of ballroom dancing and Latin-American dances; in the evenings with her group, she dances without making any mistakes; she wears the same uniform as her friends in the music group

10

She does not phone her friends to go out, but waits for them to call her

It is now her who calls her friends to see if they are going out, saying: "I'm free tonight. If you're organizing anything let me know."

11

She used to work at a barber's shop once a week – she cleaned the floor and passed out the rollers; she was not very enthusiastic

She works in an office a couple of hours a week and uses a computer, numbers page and gives them headings, and photocopies documents. To the question "What kind of work would you like to do?" her answer is: "secretary work!"

12

She does not care much about personal hygiene

She wants to have highlights and a perm; she epilates her body by herself using a cream and she goes to the beautician to have her face waxed; she has started to use make up

9 Explain and describe differences in development

In the first part of this chapter, we used the nosographic culture in terms of defining the construct of intellectual disability, which collects what is shared by the scientific community.

In this second part, we must answer, as a premise, the following question: which theory do we refer to in explaining individual differences in development?

9.1 The connectome theory

In this exposure we use Seung's connectome theory (2012) and subsequent scientific works that have verified it using innovative study methods (Oldham and Fornito, 2019; Arnatkeviciute et al., 2020). The term "connectome" created by Sporns et al. (2005) indicates the totality of connections between neurons and centers (hubs) of the cerebral cortex.

In every human being, the brain is comprised of the same parts (the cerebral cortex, the basal ganglia, the cerebellum, etc.). How can it then be explained that, in different ages of human life, endowed with the same brain structure, human beings develop different cognitive and adaptive capacities so that they become competent in a very wide range of activities?

Nature has invented an ingenious way of accomplishing this. Over the course of foetal life, genes guide the distribution of neurons in the cerebral cortex, in the same way as a commander disposes his or her army using orders. Genes produce proteins which, like orders given by a commander, lead every single neuron to its assigned position in an overall plan. The same genes also determine the predisposition of individual neurons to connect with the closest and furthest neurons once they reach their location. The network that builds gradually has points – or centers (hubs) – where neurons become more abundant, and they connect, preferably, with those of other centers. At this stage, the connections are superabundant in every possible direction.

After birth, the network begins to change, and models itself based on experiences. The connections and their most used circuits are strengthened (increasing the number of synapses that constitute them and the thickness of the connections between the centers; these events are defined as "reweighing" and "rewiring"). The connections and circuits that are less or not used at all thin out their connections until they disconnect (an event that is termed pruning).

The brain of every human being is made of a set of parts sculpted by the genetic heritage that is common to all human beings, but also personalized both by the individual genetic characteristics and by the particularity of life experiences. The stratagem of nature therefore consists of the fact that, from an original network of widespread and superabundant connections, a personalized network is derived, which is also modelled by experiences.

We know that there are at least 180 centers of the cerebral cortex and that, in adulthood, the connections between the centers, expressing both action of genes and the stimulations linked to experience, possess an extreme inter-individual variability (measurable based on dimensions of the bundles of association). In fact, the uniqueness of each connectome is so strong that we can consider the characteristics of each single connectome the same as the uniqueness of human fingerprints.

The connectome theory therefore clearly explains the origin of individual differences in cognitive abilities supported by a neurobiological substrate.

This theory has important implications for our discourse on intellectual disability:

The notion of normality

If each connectome is unique, the norm is the existence of differences in cognitive functioning between one individual and another. The distinction between cognitive ability and disability is therefore challenging, and makes the continual discussions present in nosographic systems understandable. The same notion also allows us to predict that people of the same diagnostic category may have radically dissimilar ways of cognitive functioning.

Typical and atypical development

In typical development, children achieve distinct functions, such as walking, expressive verbal language and reading skills according to ages showing broad inter-individual variability. For instance, walking is possible between 10 and 16 months; the production of a simple sentence ("baby eats food") takes place between 20 and 29 months; and some children achieve the ability to blend single phonemes after a few months of being taught how to read, and in others this occurs after two years. In atypical development, the trajectory of the development of one or more functions occurs in times that are not included in the interindividual variability of typical development, or it is disrupted in one of the points of the sequence. The number of functions affected, and the quality of their developmental atypia, affects the variety of cognitive functioning in people with intellectual disabilities.

The effect that the context has on cognitive functioning

The connectome theory highlights the role of context in strengthening or disengaging the brain circuits that support cognitive functions. Every moment of our experience activates the circuits of our brain and is present to our consciousness. Indeed, each moment of this activation modifies our connectome, just as the water of a river slowly sculpts the bed in which it flows. We, explained Seung, are our connectome. Realizing this relationship prompts interest in the type and quality of experiences lived both in the past and in the present. The connectome theory describes brain development as a dynamic event resulting from a relationship between genetic heritage and a wide range of biological or relational environmental factors.

9.2 Diagnosis in intellectual disability: different paths

A person should receive a diagnosis, a path of knowledge drawn up from a specialist in a health care or assistance system with the aim of achieving a physical and mental well-being goal. Since the condition of intellectual disability can be conceptualized both as an existential condition and as a disorder, the diagnosis requires the support of specialists from different fields. Any diagnosis, in fact, is oriented by the setting in which it occurs. Intellectual disability requires multiple types of diagnosis. All types of diagnosis aim to identify the factors that hinder or promote development.

Diagnostic classification (or categorical diagnosis)

Diagnostic classification answers the following question: does the functioning of this subject correspond to types of the category of intellectual disability?

The reference culture is that of psychiatric nosography. The diagnostic manuals mentioned in the first part of this chapter (AAIDD, DSM-5, ICD -11) gather the consensus of the scientific community regarding what these characteristics are.

The reported prevalence of intellectual disability is 1% globally and varies from 1% to 3% by country with a male to female ratio of 2:1 (Patel et al., 2020).

What is the usefulness, for the subject, of receiving this classification?

First, the subject is recognized to have the legitimate need (and the right) to receive support for his or her development and appropriate treatment for co-occurring diseases when present. Second, the subject, his or her family, and his or her treating system can beneficially use the information shared by the scientific community about the general attributes of the category. In a diagnostic process, classification constitutes a starting point, and other types of diagnoses must follow to describe the specificity of the individual.

The diagnostic manuals underline that the interpretation of scores on intellectual functioning tests and on adaptive functioning questionnaires must consider a wide range of variables: age, socio-cultural background, sensory or motor impairments, communication ability, behavioral factors, associated medical or mental disorders, examiner factors, test environment, etc. (Patel et al., 2020). For this reason, the interpretation of the scores requires a "clinical judgment".

The diagnosis of mild intellectual disability should be given particular attention. In a study of a series of 46 adult patients diagnosed with intellectual disability who had contact with a psychiatry department, only two of the nine subjects with a mild intellectual disability kept the diagnosis. This was also based on the assessment of adaptation. The first diagnoses, made in childhood, were based only on IQ value (Ruggerini et al., 2008).

A diagnosis of intellectual disability is not reliable under the age of five years. The DSM-5 uses the term "global developmental delay" for children under the age of five years who exhibit a delay in two or more areas of development. The ICD-11 uses the category of "provisional disorder of intellectual development" for children under the age of four years if there is evidence of developmental delay. It also uses the same term in situations in which it is not possible to conduct a reliable assessment due to sensory or physical damage or when a mental disorder exists.

Describing individual characteristics in assessments

What are the peculiarities of the cognitive and adaptive functioning of a person to whom the diagnostic category of intellectual disability is attributed?

The DSM-5 and ICD-11 systems indicate four levels of severity of disability (mild, moderate, severe, profound) based on the level of inefficiency of the adaptive functions and, therefore, of the intensity of the requisite supports. The mild level comprises 85% of people diagnosed with ID, the moderate one 10%, the severe one 3–4%, and the profound one 1–2%.

To describe these levels, we must consider that each of the adaptive abilities indicated in Box 1.1 ranges from a slight or minimal impairment in mild intellectual disability, to a maximum impairment in profound severity.

Regarding conceptual skills, verbal language, for example, can reach – even if late – the typical developmental milestones, but it can be insufficient at school age in understanding and describing the cultural information of school curricula. In contrast, verbal language can also be completely absent and can coexist with a profound deficit in symbolic capacity.

Regarding social skills there may be, for instance, good skills in maintaining interpersonal relationships but excessive naivety in understanding the intentions of others. It could also be possible that only non-verbal and non-symbolic communication exists. In terms of practical skills, in the mild level there may be, for example, the ability to perform an independent job if it does not require high cognitive skills. In contrast, support for every aspect of daily life may be required.

The levels of severity in intellectual disability include conditions in which the needs of supports in development are, therefore, markedly dissimilar. The description of these levels of severity has an administrative utility (e.g., to allocate economic resources) and/or value in the context of research.

In planning an individual intervention program, we cannot derive the needs for supports based only on fitting one of these levels. We illustrate an assessment describing the characteristics of intellectual and adaptive functioning oriented to an individual intervention in chapter 3. In chapter 5, we propose that the quality of relational development in the light of attachment theory is a necessary completion of the description of each of the levels.

Etiological diagnosis

Etiological diagnosis answers the following question: is it possible to recognize the cause of intellectual and adaptive inefficiency?

Relevant cultural references are those of medicine, neurobiology, and genetics. In a significant part of the cases, we cannot identify the causes, and especially at the mild level.

The identification of a cause is more frequent in moderate, severe, or profound intellectual disability. The causes can be (see Purugganan, 2018):

- Genetic syndromes: chromosomal disorders, e.g., Down syndrome; contiguous gene deletions, e.g., Williams syndrome, Angelman syndrome; and single-gene deletions, e.g., Fragile X syndrome, Rett syndrome.
- Environmental causes: alcohol and other teratogens; prenatal infections; early childhood central nervous system infections; and traumatic brain injury.
- Central nervous system disorders/malformations
- Inborn errors in metabolism
- Nutritional deficits (e.g., severe malnutrition, chronic iron deficiency)
- Unknown causes

The connectome theory enables us to understand how these causes act. Specifically, alterations in genetic heritage can lead to an atypical disposition of neurons and/or their reduced propensity to build circuits. Toxic or infectious causes can hinder this organization, and injurious causes can destroy it. Furthermore, environmental causes can, in each of the listed causes, facilitate or impede the development of the neural network.

The reasons for seeking an etiological diagnosis are as follows:

- Identify treatable cause (as in the case of errors in metabolism).
- Implement surveillance and treatment programs for co-occurring diseases (e.g., heart complications in Williams syndrome and hypothyroidism in Down syndrome, as shown in Table 1.3).
- Provide genetic counselling to family members.

- Facilitate parents' contacts with groups of other parents who, especially in the case of rare diseases, can provide more information on clinical settings than those present in the literature.
- Facilitate access to health services.
- Facilitate research.
- Currently, 800 genetic syndromes have been identified.

Table 1.3 (adapted from Purugganan, 2018) describes the genetic anomaly, frequency, cognitive profile, and physical aspects of the most common genetic syndromes.

The very rapid progress of the technologies used in the study of genetics (Cardoso et al., 2019), and epigenetic factors that can turn the expression of DNA on or off without altering its sequence (Panisi and Burgio, 2021), makes any list of etiological causes obsolete. In any situation, therefore, paediatric, and genetic counselling are critical (Moeschler and Schevell, 2014; AHRQ, 2020).

- Diagnosis of co-occurring disorders

People with intellectual disabilities can present the full range of internal and neurological diseases, and mental disorders, of the general population. The frequency of mental disease and mental disorders can be remarkably different depending on the aetiology. In cases of genetic aetiology, the frequency of co-occurring diseases and/or mental disorders can be particularly high.

People's difficulties in communicating their symptoms or, in the case of mental disorders, the contents of their emotional states, hinder the diagnosis of diseases and disorders. This explains the need to use questionnaires that use caregivers' observations in the diagnosis of mental disorders (Siegel et al., 2020).

Behavioral alterations can appear in certain genetic syndromes (see Table 1.3). It is necessary to emphasize that, in general, even if a behavior has its roots in biology (is organically-driven), this does not mean that it is independent from the context in which it appears.

If we consider the variable levels of severity of intellectual disability, aetiology and difficulty in diagnosis, we must conclude that the data on the frequency of internal and neurological diseases and mental disorders in the general population with intellectual disabilities should be considered with caution. This is the case even if agreement exists regarding whether it is higher or, at times, much higher, than in the general population.

In terms of the area of mental health, it is essential to differentiate situations in which a symptom or a disorder is present, with the full set

Table 1.3 A synthetic overview of the most common genetic syndromes

SYN-DROME	Frequency	GENETIC ABNORM-ALITY	DEVELOP-MENTAL PROFILE	COMMON PHYSICAL FINDINGS
Down	1/800	Trisomy 21 (95%) Translocation (4%) Mosaicism (1%)	Mild to moderate ID (Verbal low) Hypotonia Early Alzheimer's disease	Down facies Congenital heart disease Hypothyroidism Gastrointestinal abnormalities
Fragile X	1/4000	CGG trinucleotide repeat (>200)	ID (typically moderate) Learning disorders Autism spectrum disorder	Elongated face Macrocephaly Prominent ears Hyperextensible joint Enlarged testes (post puberty)
Rett	1/10000	MECP2 deletion	ID Stereotypic hand mannerisms Language regression	Deceleration in head growth Gait abnormalities
Williams	1/10000–20000	7q11 deletion	Mild to moderate ID (non-verbal – low)	Elfin-like facial features Cardiac issues (e.g., supra-valvular aortic stenosis) Renal abnormalities Hypertension
Angel-man	1/10000–20000	Maternally-derived deletion 15q (or paternal disomy)	Severe to profound ID Atypical hand mannerisms	Microcephaly Prognathism
Prader-Willi	1/10000–15000	Paternally-derived deletion 15q (or maternal disomy)	ID (variable levels) Psychiatric conditions	Neonate: hypotonia/feeding difficulties Toddler: obesity, excessive appetite

of symptoms that identify it, from behavioral problems that usually express communicative, but non-adaptive, behaviors to an environmental situation (Royal Collage of Psychiatrists, 2001).

A crucial concept is that people with intellectual disabilities may present multiple vulnerability factors that can lead to non-adaptive behaviors or mental disorders.

Simonoff (2015) lists the following vulnerability factors: genetic factors that favor the co-occurrence of intellectual disability, Autism Spectrum Disorder, and ADHD; the presence of medical or neurological diseases; and adverse psychosocial conditions. Chapter 5 describes the cultural framework of developmental psychopathology that allows us to understand how these factors can act, mediated by the superordinate factor of attachment quality.

Values and expectations of the subject and his or her family (idiographic formulation)

The patient and his or her family's point of view are an essential part of the assessment. According to IGDA document 8 (2003), it expresses itself in different moments of the evaluation.

First, the subject and his or her family must face the evaluations of specialists. We must underline that, in the field of intellectual disability, we often use definitions or concepts that are not easy to understand. For example: the distinction between disability and disorder; the meaning of the term "diagnostic classification" versus "diagnosis"; understanding the fact that belonging to a condition of neurodevelopment does not mean a fixed state in cognitive or adaptive functioning; the distinction between growth and development; and the need to identify a developmental goal and the promotion of personal identity through concrete experiences. The comparison should lead to a shared comprehension (joint understanding) of the data, which is a crucial element of the therapeutic alliance.

A second step is describing the positive factors of the subject, which include personality traits, personal and spiritual strengths, and aspirations. In a third step, the point of view of the subject and his or her family appears in the formulation of expectations about the quality of his or her life. This aspect of the assessment allows the individual to actively participate in his or her therapy and development project.

A diagnostic formulation is synonymous to a complete diagnosis, and includes all of the previous ones. The goal is to respond to the medical, psychological, existential, and social needs of the whole person.

The expected outcomes are clinical (when the treatment of a co-occurring disease is necessary), functional (when the goal is an increase in adaptive skills), and personal (when the goal is to orientate towards what is important for the person himself or herself, i.e., his or her values)

10 Caring (care) and cure (cure)

Intellectual disability, which constitutes both an existential condition and a disorder, questions us as citizens and as professionals of the field. As citizens, it requires us to reflect on our contribution to recognizing the human rights of vulnerable people. As professionals, it reminds us of the enormous power of scientific knowledge in defining assistance. We must recognize that this knowledge is in progress, and that the starting point of any improvement is recognition of the weaknesses of the current culture. The construct of intelligence is an exemplar of this weakness, as we have attempted to point out in this first chapter. Although this construct is poorly defined, questioned, and contested, it remains a central part of currently used diagnostic manuals when they refer to diagnoses with which we are concerned. What, then, is to be done?

As professionals we have three work tracks:

The first is to re-examine an immense volume of data from developmental psychology and neuropsychology to obtain a new vision of the intelligent act which breaks with long-established habit and convention. The second is to search for the person hidden by definitions that are peremptory and uncertain and take care (Care) of their development. The third is to propose an appropriate therapy (Cure) of co-occurring medical conditions as recognition of a common right of citizenship. The next chapters of the book will deepen the first two lines of work.

References

AAIDD (2019). *About AAIDD*. Author. http://www.aaidd.org.

AHRQ – US Department of Health and Human Services, Agency for Health Care Research and Quality (2020). *Genetic Testing for Developmental Disabilities, Intellectual Disability, and Autism Spectrum Disorder*. Content last reviewed March 2021. Effective Health Care Program, Agency for Healthcare Research and Quality, Rockville, MD. https://effectivehealthcare.ahrq.gov/p roducts/genetic-testing-developmental-disabilities.

American Psychiatric Association. (2013). *Diagnostic and statistical manual for mental disorders (5th ed.)*. American Psychiatric Publishing

Arnatkeviciute A., Fulcher B. D., Oldham S., Tiego J., Paquola C., Gerring Z., Aquino K., Hawi Z., Johnson B., Ball G., Klein M., Deco G., Franke B., Bellgrove M., and Fornito A. (2020). *Genetic influences on hub connectivity of the human connectome*. doi:10.1101/2020.06.21.163915

Berns, P. V. (2012). DSM-5 Draft diagnostic criteria for "Intellectual Developmental Disorder" and "Autism Spectrum Disorder"https://studylib.net/doc/7315299/read-the-arc-s-letter-here.

Berrios, G. E. (2013). *Per una nuova epistemologia della psichiatria*. Roma: Giovanni Fioriti Editore.

Boekhoff, B. (1996). A paradigm shift in care for people with a mental handicap. In M. Sala et al. (Eds.), *La persona adulta con ritardo mentale nelle istituzioni: cura e riabilitazione*. (pp. 50–55). Milano: Ghedini Editore.

Berrios G. E. (2015), The history and epistemology of the neurodevelopmental disorders, *Spazi e Modelli*, 12 (N°1), pp. 47–48.

Bolte, S. and Richman, K. (2019). Editorial. Hard talk: does autism need philosophy? *Autism*, 23 (1), 3–7. doi:10.1177/1362361318808181journals.sagepub.com/home/aut

Borthwick-Duffy, S. A., Buntinx, W. H. E., Coulter, D. L., Craig, E. M., Reeve, A., Schalock, R. ... Tassé, M. J. (2002). *Mental retardation: Definition, classification, and system of supports* (10th ed.). American Association on Mental Retardation.

Cardoso, A. R., Lopez-Marques, M., Silva, R. M., Serrano, C., Amorim, A., Prata, M. J., and Azevedo L. (2019). Essential genetic findings in neurodevelopmental disorders. *Human Genomics*, 13, 31. doi:10.1186/s40246-019-0216-4

Centers for Disease Control and Prevention. (2017). *Facts about developmental disabilities*. https://www.cdc.gov/ncbddd/developmentaldisabilities/facts.html#ref

Comitato Sammarinese di Bioetica (CSB). (2013). *L'approccio bioetico alle persone con disabilità*. http://www.superando.it/files/2013/05/san-marino-approccio-bioetico-persone-con-disabilita-25-febbraio-20131.pdf.

Developmental Disabilities Assistance and Bill of Rights Act Amendments of 2000, PL 106–402, 42 U.S.C SS6000 et seq.

Gelb S.A. (2002). The dignity of humanity is not a scientific construct . *Mental Retardation*, 40 (1), 55–56.

Flanagan, D. P., and Kaufman, A. S. (2009). *Essentials of WISC-IV Assessment* (2nd ed.).(Trad. It. Fondamenti per l'assessment con la WISC-IV. Firenze: Organizzazioni Speciali, 2012).

Girimaji, S. C., and Pradeep, A. J. (2018). Intellectual disability in International Classification of Diseases – 11: a developmental perspective. *Indian Journal of Social Psychiatry*, 34, S68–74.

Gomez, S., and Nygren, M. A. (2012). *DSM-5 Draft diagnostic criteria for "Intellectual Developmental Disorder"*www.aaidd.org.

International Guidelines for Diagnostic Assessment (IGDA) (2003). IGDA. Introduction. *British Journal of Psychiatry*, 182 (suppl. 45), s 37 –s39.

International Guidelines for Diagnostic Assessment (IGDA) (2003). IGDA. 8: Idiographic (personalized) diagnostic formulation. *British Journal of Psychiatry*, 182 (suppl. 45), s55–s57.

Kendler K. S. (2016). The nature of psychiatric disorders. *World Psychiatry*, 15 (1), 5–12.

Lindmeier, C. (2018), *WHO releases New International Classification of Diseases (ICD 11)*, Communication Officer WHO

Luckasson, R., Borthwick-Duffy, S., Buntinx, W. H. E., Coulter, D. L., Craig, E. P. M., Reeve, A., ... Tasse, M. J. (2002). *Mental retardation: definition, classification, and system support* (10th ed.). Washington, DC: American Association on Mental Retardation

Medeghini, R. (2015). *Norma e normalità nei disability studies – Riflessioni e analisi critica per ripensare la disabilità*. Trento: Erickson.

Moeschler, J. B. and Shevell, M. (2014). Comprehensive evaluation of the child with intellectual disability or global developmental delays. *Pediatrics*, 134, 903–918.

Oldham S. and Fortino A. (2019). The development of brain network hubs. *Developmental Cognitive Neuroscience*. https://doi.org/10.1016/j.dcn.2018.12.005.

Panisi C. and Burgio E. (2021). Dalla genetica alla epigenetica: cosa cambia nella pratica clinica dell'ASD. *Area Pediatrica*, 22, 127–133.

Patel D. P., Cabral M. D., Ho A., and Merrick J. (2020). A clinical primer on intellectual disability. *Translational Pediatrics*, 9 (Suppl 1), S23–S35. http://dx.doi.org/10.21037/tp.2020.02.02.

Purugganan, O. (2018). Intellectual disabilities. *Pediatrics in Review*, 39 (6), 299–310. doi:10.1542/pir.2016-0116.

Royal Collage of Psychiatrists (2001). *DC-LD, Diagnostic criteria for psychiatric disorders for use with adults with learning disabilities/mental retardation*.

Ruggerini C., Vezzosi F., Solmi A., and Manzotti S. (2008). Narrative based medicine in genetic syndromes with intellectual disability. In A. Verri (Ed.), *Life span development in genetic disorders* (pp. 195–211). Waltham: Nova Biomedical Books.

Ruggerini C., Vezzosi F., Villanti F., Guaraldi G.P. (2008). L'esperienza di un Dipartimento Integrato di Psichiatria di Modena, In C. Ruggerini, A. Dalla Vecchia and F. Vezzosi (Eds.), *Prendersi cura della disabilità intellettiva* (pp. 177–199). Trento: Erickson.

Ruggerini, C., Dalla Vecchia, A., Manzotti, S., and Vezzosi, F. (2010). Una esperienza di applicazione del documento OMS "Innovative Care for Chronic Conditions (ICCC)" alla condizione della disabilità intellettiva: metodo e risultati. *Psichiatria dell'infanzia e dell'adolescenza*, 77, 193–210.

Ruggerini, C., and Manzotti S. (2021). Funzionamento intellettivo limite: caratteristica cognitiva individuale e non categoria nosografica. In A. Canevaro, R. Ciambrone, S. Nocera (Eds.), *L'inclusione scolastica in Italia, Percorsi, riflessioni, prospettive* (pp. 377–391). Trento: Erickson.

Salvador-Carulla, L., and Bertelli, M. (2008). "Mental retardation" or "intellectual disability": time for a conceptual change. *Psychopathologia*, 41, 10–16. doi:10.1159/000109950.

Salvador-Carulla, L., Reed, G. M., Vaez-Azizi, L. M., Cooper, S. A., Martinez-Leal, R., Bertelli, M., ... Saxena, S. (2011). Intellectual developmental disorders: towards a new name, definition and framework for "mental retardation/intellectual disability" in ICD-11. *World Psychiatry*, 10, 175–180.

Schalock, R. L. (2002). What's in a name? *Mental Retardation*, 40 (1), 59–61.

Schalock, R. L., Luckasson, R. A., Shogren, K. A., Borthwick-Duffy, W. S., Bradley, V., Buntinx, ... Yeager, M. H. (2007). The renaming of mental retardation:

understanding the change to the term Intellectual Disability, *Intellectual and Developmental Disabilities*, 45 (2), 116–124.

Schalock, R. L., Borthwick-Duffy, S. A., Bradley, V. J., Buntinx, W. H. E., Coulter, D. L., Craig, E. … Yeager, M. (2010). *Intellectual disability: Diagnosis, classification, and systems of supports* (11th ed.). American Association on Intellectual and Developmental Disabilities.

Schalock, R. L., and Luckasson, R. (2021). Intellectual disability, developmental disabilities, and the field of intellectual and developmental disabilities. In M. G. Glidden (Editor-in-chief), *APA Handbook of Intellectual and Developmental Disabilities: Vol. 1. Foundations*, pp. 31–45. American Psychological Association. doi:10.1037/0000194–0000002.

Séguin, E. (1846). *Traitement moral, hygiene et éducation des idiots et des autres enfantes arriérés*. Paris: Baillière

Seung, S. (2012). *Connectome. How the brain's wiring makes us who we are.* Boston: Houghton Mifflin Harcourt.

Siegel, M., McGurie, K., Veenstra-VanderWeele, J., Stratigos, K., King, B, and the American Academy of Child and Adolescent Psychiatry (AACAP) Committee on Quality Issues (CDI) (2020). Practice parameter for the assessment and treatment of psychiatric disorders in children and adolescents with intellectual disability (Intellectual Developmental Disorder). *Journal of the American Academy of Child and Adolescent Psychiatry*, 59 (4), 468–496.

Simonoff E. (2015). Intellectual disability. In A. Thapar, D. S. Pine, J. F. Leckman, S. Scott, M. J. Snowling, E. Taylor (Eds.), *Rutter's Child and Adolescent Psychiatry*. Hoboken: John Wiley and Sons.

Sporns, O., Tononi, G., and Kotter, R. (2005). The human connectome: a structural description of the human brain. *PLoSComput. Biol.* 1, 245–251. doi:10.1371/journal.pcbi.0010042

Tassè, M. J., Luckasson, R., and Schalock R.L. (2016). The relation between intellectual functioning and adaptive behavior in the diagnosis of intellectual disability. *Intellectual and Developmental Disabilities*, 54 (6), 381–390. doi:10.1352/1934-9556-54.6.381.

United Nations (2006). *Convention on the rights of persons with disabilities.* http://www.un.org/disabilities/convention/conventionfull.shtml

Van Essen, D. C. and Glasser M. F. (2016), The human connectome project: progress and prospects. *Cerebrum.* https://www.ncbi.nlm.nih.gov/pmc/articles/PMC5198757/.

Zablotsky, B., Black, L. I., Maenner, M. J., Schieve, L. A., Danielson, M. L., Bitsko, … Boyle, C. A. (2019). Prevalence and trends of developmental disabilities among children in the United States: 2009–2017. *Pediatrics*, 144 (4). e20190811.

Wechsler, D. (2014). *Wechsler Intelligence Scale for Children (5th ed.; WISC-V): Administration and scoring manual.* San Antonio: Pearson Clinical Assessment.

Wehmeyer, M. L., Buntinx, W. H. E., Lachapelle, Y., Luckasson, R. A., Schalock, R. L., Verdugo, M. A., … Yeager, M. H. (2008). The intellectual disability construct and its relation to human functioning. *Intellectual and developmental disabilities*, 46 (4), 311–318.

World Health Organization (WHO). (2002). Innovative care for chronic conditions: building blocks for action. *New challenges*. https://www.who.int/chp/knowledge/publications/icccglobalreport.pdf.

World Health Organization (WHO). (2015). *Draft of ICD-11 clinical description and diagnostic guidelines: Disorders of intellectual development* (January 16, 2015).

World Health Organization (WHO). (2019). *ICD-11: International classification of diseases* (11th revision). Retrieved from https://icd.who.int/.

Chapter 2

Is intelligence a general mental capacity?

Margherita Orsolini, Francesca Federico, and Sergio Melogno

The notion that general intelligence is a neurobiological "entity" underlying IQ had several negative consequences in terms of assessment, intervention, and educational practices. Each difficulty of a person with intellectual disabilities tended to be interpreted as an expression of low intelligence, rather than analysed with the specific and scientifically grounded constructs of developmental cognitive psychology and neuropsychology. Assuming that general intelligence is the common factor involved in IQ tests generated lively disputes by several researchers (Cornoldi, 2011; Gardner, 2011; Sternberg, 2004; van der Maas et al., 2017; Zigler, 1986) but did not help us to identify the mechanisms that need to be stimulated and enhanced to *become* intelligent in all human beings, including children whose development shows some atypical trends.

This chapter explores how low development of attention and inhibitory control, working memory and language can generate important, though individually variable differences in reasoning, knowledge acquisition, and adaptive skills of people with intellectual disabilities.

In the present chapter we argue that clinicians' attitudes should change from a type of assessment that only takes a static picture of the IQ level of a child, to a more dynamic perspective that looks for the specific abilities and motivational factors allowing development to move ahead.

I How Intelligence has been defined

The concept of intelligence is part of people's common sense and is used in the literature of different cultures. Cunning is the greatest trait of Odysseus, a quality that made him triumph over the giant Polyphemus and other threatening characters through lies, disguises, language tricks. Problem solving and creativity seem to be the key characteristics of

DOI: 10.4324/9781003220367-2

intelligence in Odysseus but other intelligence traits are attributed to special heroes or gods in different world cultures. Knowledge and wisdom, sometimes associated with learning skills often characterize idealized qualities of humanity across world mythologies (as for Seshat, goddess of wisdom, knowledge and writing in ancient Egypt).

From the 20th century onwards, psychologists have defined intelligence in slightly different ways, focusing on judgment, practical sense, and initiative (Binet and Simon, 1916), global capacity to think rationally (Wechsler, 1940), or an ability to adapt to the environment (Neisser et al., 1996; Sternberg, 2021). Learning new concepts, solving problems, inductive and deductive reasoning are other intelligence characteristics common to different theories (Spearman, 1923; Sternberg, 2018, 2020).

Although intelligence can be conceived of as a key characteristic of all human beings and one that allowed Homo Sapiens to invent and use symbols and boost a dramatic cultural evolution, such a human quality has been more studied to measure differences between human beings than to scientifically analyse the different, culturally grounded forms of intelligence (but see Sternberg, 2004, 2018, 2021).

To analyse how people differ in acquiring concepts, learning from experience, and inferring new solutions for problems, applied psychology started to measure intelligence assuming that such complex and heterogeneous human quality could be treated as a general mental entity. Such measurement started a century ago and continues to be used – mainly in the western world – for a wide range of practical aims such as granting access to higher education, identifying intellectual talent, issuing diagnoses of dementia in aged people, and of neurodevelopmental disorders such as learning or intellectual disabilities.

Despite the success of its practical applications, the scientific construct of intelligence is still the object of much disagreement among researchers in psychology and neuropsychology (see Wilhelm and Engle, 2005; Sternberg, 2020). The tasks that make up intelligence batteries have been often selected because they work well as predictors of success at school or as indicators of general learning disabilities. However, such tasks are not derived from a cognitively grounded analysis of what characterizes human intelligent behaviours, they do not target the skills that support effective problem-solving and make reasoning more consistent. For such reasons, intelligence has been defined as *a diva and a workhorse* (Wilhelm and Engle, 2005): its measures have been widely and sometimes usefully applied, but we do not have yet a scientifically grounded definition of intelligence.

1.1 Underneath the IQ measure

When 3-year-old children present a delay in the development of language or show some clumsiness, parents often ask whether such delays might indicate that the child would not become "intelligent" as other typically developing children. The same worrying question is sometimes asked by parents whose school-aged children presented consistent difficulties in learning to read, write, or use arithmetic procedures. After decades of developmental research, we now know that language or motor delays, and difficulties in academic learning are often related to specific and circumscribed weaknesses that do not undermine a child's general cognitive development. However, how can parents be sure that their child's persistent delays are not expressions of a general cognitive impairment? There is an obvious answer: an assessment of the child's IQ can clarify whether intelligence is at the level typically expected from the child's age.

IQ tests, as well as other popular instruments (e.g., Kaufman and Kaufman, 2004; Naglieri, Das, and Goldstein, 2014), have a mean of 100 and a standard deviation of 15. A score of 100 places an individual in the 50th percentile, meaning that one's score is higher than 50 per cent of the other people taking the test (and lower than 50 per cent of the other people). An IQ score of 70 is in the second percentile with only 2 per cent of people scoring lower. If a child's performance in an IQ test corresponds to the second percentile this low score tends to be interpreted as an intellectual deficit. But are we sure that such low performance is a deficit of intelligence? Could it not be a composite and heterogeneous outcome of developmental delay or impairment of more specific skills?

The theory of general intelligence – which originates from more than a century ago (Binet and Simon, 1916) relies on the observation that performances in the tasks included in intelligence tests tend to correlate with each other. For instance, children who are good at defining words tend to be good also in reproducing models using coloured blocks. Thus, performance in tasks involving different cognitive processes and different domains (i.e., verbal vs visuo-constructive) correlate with each other, aligning toward the high, medium, or low levels. They do so irrespectively of the participants' age, ethnic characteristics, or socio-cultural background. How can we explain such positive correlations? One answer has been provided by statistical techniques that identified a unique common "factor" that could mathematically predict the correlations among the scores of intelligence tests. Such a common predictor, known as the "g" factor (see next section), has been interpreted as the expression of general intelligence (Spearman, 1927).

Thus, the majority of psychologists assumed that the different tasks included in intelligence tests all involve a general intelligence factor. On this basis IQ scores have been used as reliable indicators of an individual's general intelligence and considered evidence grounding a diagnosis of what was once called *mental retardation*. From such assumption derived several cascade effects, from interpreting an individual as incapable of complex learning and reasoning skills to oversimplified academic curriculum proposed when such diagnosis occurred.

In our University clinic, we could observe all these negative consequences in several families whose children had a history of cognitive developmental delays. For instance, Damiano's parents told us in an interview the change that a diagnosis of *mental retardation* had induced in the school's teachers. For the first two years of primary school, the teachers saw Damiano as rich in "potentialities" but in grade 3, after he was diagnosed with *mental retardation*, the teachers started to say that the child's difficulties prevented him from complex learning, especially if abstract concepts were involved. Damiano, despite being included in a mainstream class – though with a special needs teacher – became the object of social stigma and the parents of some children started to say that he was sick. In sum, what could be defined as an atypical developmental history became labelled as sickness and generated Damiano's fear, shame, and social isolation.

A further consequence results from interpreting atypical cognitive development with a simplified concept of low intelligence. Such consequence was clearly explained by the teachers of Lorenzo, a 9-year-old child who had been diagnosed with a mild intellectual disability. When a psychologist in our clinic proposed that problem-solving should be included in Lorenzo's intervention plan, his mathematics teacher saw this as an unrealistic objective: "you can teach multiplication tables, you can make him practice simple math, but he never will solve a problem. Problem-solving requires logic and abstract thinking". It was clear that teaching mathematics to Lorenzo required a relevant adaptation of objectives and longer times to train new skills and teach concepts. However, Lorenzo could learn problem-solving strategies when adequate, individually tuned teaching, was proposed to him (Orsolini et al., 2009). As teachers imagined Lorenzo deeply impaired in reasoning skills, school activities only engaged the child with highly simplified tasks that made him practice memory rather than active thinking.

Claiming that a child with intellectual disability can never solve problems and form abstract concepts requires the comment that Binet wrote more than a century ago:

> Never! What a momentous word. Some recent thinkers seem to have given their moral support to these deplorable verdicts by affirming that

an individual's intelligence is a fixed quantity, a quantity that cannot be increased. We must protest and react against this brutal pessimism; we must try to demonstrate that it is founded upon nothing.

(1909, p.100–101, this quotation is drawn from the book of Gould, 1985).

Thus, if teachers think that children with intellectual disabilities cannot learn and develop reasoning skills, such abilities will be less and less practised at school (or even in family activities) and therefore become progressively weaker. In other words, a wrong interpretation of cognitive atypical development generates poor educational stimulation and poor developmental outcomes. Reasoning can show mild or severe developmental delays but assuming that this skill is neither accessible nor improvable for children with a diagnosis of intellectual disability is not scientifically grounded.

1.2 General intelligence (g) as a statistical factor

Statistical factorial analyses of psychometric approaches identify intelligence as a single factor that can explain the joint variation among a series of variables. A statistical factor, however, does not imply a psychological mechanism or a process underlining it.

Other approaches, grounded on cognitive psychology, try to analyse the component mechanisms that affect an individual's performance in complex tasks and explore individual differences in terms of such mechanisms. For example, studying reading comprehension in children and adults, the research identified the role of several processes and knowledge components that generate differences in reading comprehension. These include fluency in the process of decoding written words, semantic knowledge of a text's written words, inferential skills, and working memory (Babayiğit and Shapiro, 2020; Carretti et al., 2009; Kim, 2015). It was thus observed that the weight of such skills can change across development (i.e., reading as decoding skill has a more important role in the first three years of primary school) and that basic skills, such as richness in the semantic representation of words, influence higher abilities such as drawing inferences in text comprehension (Nation and Snowling, 1998).

This line of scientific reasoning has been set out also in terms of longitudinal trajectories of atypical cognitive development (D'Souza, D'Souza and Karmiloff-Smith, 2017). The central idea is that one or more basic cognitive mechanisms (e.g. *gaze following* to detect the direction of a person's eyes) have longitudinal effects on complex processes (e.g., associating objects and words in episodes of adult-child communication). Impairments of basic cognitive mechanisms, such as visual attention, can drive a fragile and delayed development of more complex skills. Moreover, a basic-level deficit affecting one functional domain (e.g., visual attention) may constrain functions in other domains (e.g., language) because development is deeply interactive (Thomas et al., 2009). In sum, assuming that general intelligence is the common factor involved in IQ tests generated lively disputes by several researchers (Cornoldi, 2011; Gardner, 2011; Sternberg, 2004; van der Maas et al., 2017; Zigler, 1986) but did not help us to identify the mechanisms that need to be stimulated and enhanced to *become* intelligent in all human beings, including children whose development shows some atypical trends.

2 Intelligence as reasoning skills

Engaging in various forms of reasoning is a key aspect of what is commonly called intelligence. We can observe the use of reasoning skills already in preschool children whenever they infer a rule from experience. Showing children a set of objects and asking them which will sink or float if put on a basin of water, children will draw on their experience to infer a relationship between buoyancy and some property such as being round or being light.

When children or adults are assessed for reasoning skills through cognitive tests, the tasks usually ask them to find out some relationship among the task's materials with no previously known rule that can be directly applied to the situation. For instance, they may be asked to complete a series of related concepts, such as *leg-foot/xxx?-hand* or to fill an image's empty slot with a part that fits the image's pattern (see Figure 2.1). Reasoning skills have been conceptualized in terms of fluid intelligence and their correlation with IQ has been interpreted through the common relationship with the "g" factor. However, again we ask whether forms of reasoning are merely an expression of general intelligence or if they have a more specific nature.

2.1 Two basic skills underlying reasoning

In a widely used reasoning task, the Raven's Matrices (Raven et al., 1992), participants are asked to identify the missing element in a complex pattern (see item A10 in Figure 2.1) or in a matrix (as in item B9 of Figure 2.1). In the matrices, participants should consider the characteristics that change both in the rows and in the columns to infer the rules that can be satisfied by the missing element.

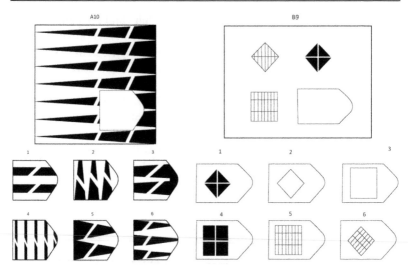

Figure 2.1 Examples of items in the style of the Raven's Matrices test

Neuroscience studies have used magnetic resonance techniques (fMRI) to analyse the brain areas that are involved when tasks require participants to infer rules, as in the Raven Matrices, or in relations (e.g., Anna is taller than Julia, Mary is shorter than Julia, who is the tallest?).

Areas in the lateral prefrontal cortex (PFC) and posterior parietal cortex (PPC), are reported in such studies as associated with different forms of reasoning (Prado et al. 2011; Krawczyk 2012). Wendelken and collaborators (2016) analysed the patterns of connectivity between specific nodes of the PFC and PPC, asking if the patterns of connectivity related to reasoning were stable in development or underwent some change. The authors observed that between the age of 10 and 14 there is a steady increase in communication between specific prefrontal and parietal nodes, those same areas that have been found involved with adults' reasoning.

In the Wendelken and collaborators' study (2016) a further issue was whether processing speed (e.g., the time individuals employ in simple tasks requiring to match visually identical stimuli) and working memory (that is the capability to keep active in short-term memory some verbal or visual stimuli whereas, at the same time, they are elaborated) were related to reasoning development as other studies suggest (Demetriou et al., 2014; Kail et al., 2016). It turned out that in the youngest age group (6–8 years) processing speed had the strongest relation to reasoning ability whereas neither functional connectivity between PFC and PPC nor working memory had a significant role. In the middle age group (9–11 years), in contrast, working memory was a key factor mediating the relationship between prefrontal-parietal connectivity on the one hand and reasoning skills on the other. In older children and adolescents (12–18 years), there was a direct relationship between fronto-parietal connectivity and reasoning ability that interacted with neither processing speed nor working memory.

The findings of the Wendelken and collaborators' study are particularly relevant to the question of whether intelligence is a general mental capacity. First, they show that a key aspect of intelligence, reasoning skills, involves more specific brain areas than IQ. Whereas the total IQ is associated with a "global efficiency" of functional brain networks (see Li et al. 2009), reasoning skills recruit functional connectivity of specific nodes in the frontoparietal network. Second, they suggest that reasoning develops because basic cognitive mechanisms such as processing speed and working memory boost its functioning.

2.2 Processing speed in persons with intellectual disability

Low IQ, along with below age-expected adaptive skills, occur in several genetic disorders such as Fragile X, Down or Williams syndromes, to mention just a few. They also occur in persons who do not present any syndrome-based brain dysfunction but have a diagnosis of intellectual disability. Maintaining our focus on reasoning skills we may ask whether processing speed, which turned out to be a basic requirement for the development of reasoning (see the previous section) shows an atypical developmental pattern in persons with intellectual disability (ID).

Processing speed can be observed through reaction time tasks where, for instance, participants press a button underneath an illuminated target. In other tasks, processing speed is measured considering the time of visual inspection needed to correctly judge which of two lines presented on a computer screen is longer. In such types of tasks, persons with low IQ show slow response patterns whereas in typically developing children processing speed increases with age and is associated with progressively higher reasoning skills (Demetriou et al., 2014; Kail et al., 2016).

A recent study (Kaat et al., 2021), involving one group of persons with Fragile X, another with Down syndrome, and the third group of idiopathic ID (that is an ID of unknown origin), used a computer-administered task in which participants are shown a target picture (e.g. a cat) above a line and have to press a button to select, among four pictures below the line (e.g., a dog, a horse, a pig and a cat), the one that is identical to the target.

The study found that processing speed, in the three groups with ID, correlated with mental age and that such correlation did not differ from that shown by a group of typically developing individuals whose chronological age corresponded to the mental age of the ID groups (see Box 2.1 for an explanation on mental age). Thus processing speed in persons with ID seems to be consistent with the extent of their developmental delay.

Some researchers considered slow processing in very simple tasks the main indicator of atypical brain development in persons with ID (Anderson, 2001; Deary et al., 2010). The idea is that underlining such slow processing there is some abnormality in the nerve conduction (Vernon and Mori, 1992) and myelin integrity (Miller, 1994) that slows down signals transmission in the brain. However, a different hypothesis considers whether an alternation between relaxation and activation brain states shows a typical pattern in persons with ID. In typically developing persons a slowdown in cerebral activity occurs in the brain's resting states whereas the brain's activation suddenly increases when engagement is required. In persons with low IQ, the brain is somehow active even in the resting states as if the alert system was always overactivated (see Palix et al., 2020). Keeping evenly high general arousal in the nervous system would undermine the deployment of additional resources when sudden activity is needed, as in reaction time tasks (Deary et al., 2010; Palix et al., 2020). Therefore, the slow reaction times, rather than being an outcome of general abnormalities in the nerve conduction, would be related to an atypical regulation of the neural threshold, with a tendency to keep evenly high cortical activation (Palix et al., 2020). In sum, the underlying nature of slow processing in persons with an intellectual disability is not clear yet and is unlikely that such a unique factor can explain by itself the developmental delay of persons with ID.

An important contribution of developmental psychology is identifying the basic skills (e.g., oculomotor control) that aliment a more complex acquisition in specific domains (e.g., face recognition, visual exploration of task materials). Analysing which basic skills are particularly weak or are strength points can suggest anchorage points to construct compensatory strategies and design intervention. Important basic skills, such as phonological memory, attention, and oculomotor control, tend to correlate and support each other in a typically developing 3–4-year-old child. However, each of such skills may have developed at different paces in persons with syndromes or in individuals whose developmental delay has an unknown origin. Comparing individual development of correlated basic skills to mental-age norms (see Box 2.1) allows researchers and clinicians to consider the relative functioning of basic cognition within a system that has developed in atypical ways. Thus, going back to reasoning and problem-solving, we do expect that such complex cognitive abilities are delayed in persons with a diagnosis of ID.

However, analysing the more basic skills that support reasoning, and the conditions that undermine or facilitate their application in academic tasks or everyday life contexts, research can help identify what needs to be particularly stimulated to aliment reasoning in children with atypical cognitive development.

Box 2.1 Comparing the behavioural characteristics with chronological age and mental age groups

Cognitive deficits in persons with neurodevelopmental disorders are assessed by interpreting scores through age-expected norms. If behavioural performances are in the extreme low-end of the age's typical distribution this suggests that the assessed characteristics are impaired compared to individuals' with the same chronological age. Researchers often undergo a second type of comparison using the individuals' non-verbal reasoning score to estimate mental age. For instance, a 15-year-old in a group of persons with intellectual disability may show a non-verbal reasoning score that would fall within the mean limits in a scores distribution of 8-year-old typically developing children. Repeating the same operation for each person of the group allows researchers to estimate the group's mental age means, and select younger typically developing individuals (e.g., children who are 8 years old) to form a mental-age control group. Researchers can then ask which cognitive mechanisms of the group with ID tend to be at a similar level as the mental-age controls. Mechanisms or skills that are consistent with a mental age level can be considered relative strength points, potential anchorages to boost learning processes and cognitive development in persons with ID.

Another method of investigating cognitive profiles of persons with ID is investigating developmental trajectories (Thomas et al., 2009) with growth curves (that is trends in increasing levels of performance) to assess whether specific skills increase with age at a pace that resembles that of mental-age controls. Analysing patterns of change in response to intervention, or simple correlations between basic-level skills, and comparing them to those shown by mental-age controls are other ways to look for relative strength points in persons with ID (Thomas et al., 2009).

Traditionally, when behaviours do not exhibit delay compared to a mental-age group, the skills that have been assessed are considered *only delayed* rather than exhibiting an atypical development. It is clear, however, that similarity to a mental-age group cannot be considered an "only delayed" development as if within some time the expected developmental progression could be restored. Brain development, as determined by a highly complex interaction between genes' expression and environmental resources, is unfolding in an atypical though extremely variable way in persons with a diagnosis of ID (see chapter 1 in this book and Levy, 2018 for a critical discussion on the concept of developmental delay).

The individual's sensory-motor, cognitive, and socio-affective behavioural characteristics are affected by the brain's developing structure but changes in this structure and characteristics are also deeply affected by environmental resources (including the parents' interactive style) through extremely complex and reciprocally affecting processes.

2.3 The role of cognitive strategies and attention control in reasoning

We can ask whether participants addressing the Raven's Matrices use some strategies that facilitate the detection of a rule and the selection of the target among the bottom alternatives shown by each item. Vigneau and collaborators (2006), explored with eye-tracking methods whether correct responses with Raven's Matrices task were more likely when specific visual attention strategies were applied.

Two different strategies could be identified by analysing the participants' eye fixations and saccades. In *constructive matching*, the participant first anchors visual attention on the top matrix from which a target part is lacking (see Figure 2.1 in section 2.1), then visually explores its parts, and eventually looks for the target element among the bottom alternatives. This strategy sounds as if the participant first explores the regularities presented by the matrix and then looks for the alternative that can fit them. Other participants use a *response elimination* strategy, starting with an inspection of each bottom alternative and evaluating whether it might correctly fill the matrix slot. Such a strategy is likely to be more based on a visual completion process that is recursively applied to each alternative using a trial-and-error method. The first strategy is more often used by participants with high performance, the second is observed in low-scoring individuals but is occasionally used even by the former participants when the problems are particularly difficult (Vigneau et al., 2006).

Curie and collaborators (2016) explored with eye-tracking methods the correctness and speed of performance with a simplified, computer-administered, Raven's Matrices task (see Figure 2.2). Involving persons with typical cognitive development or with an intellectual disability the authors hypothesized that two factors were likely to negatively affect the participants' correctness and speed. The first is the items' complexity: the more rules are involved in a test item, the more difficult it is to find a solution. For instance, to identify the target in 1b, only one shape rule is involved whereas target 1d involves two rules (shape and size). The second factor affecting the

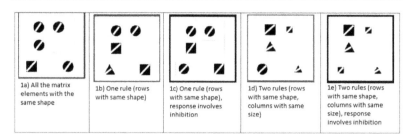

| 1a) All the matrix elements with the same shape | 1b) One rule (rows with same shape) | 1c) One rule (rows with same shape), response involves inhibition | 1d) Two rules (rows with same shape, columns with same size) | 1e) Two rules (rows with same shape, columns with same size), response involves inhibition |

Figure 2.2 Example of the different conditions of the task used by Curie et al. (2016). The participants are asked to select one of the two small bottom images that can complete the top matrix. Items are adapted from the original

participants' performance is inhibitory control: some items require to inhibit suggestions from irrelevant alternatives. For instance, in item 1e (see Figure 2.2) the small square at the bottom is identical to one of the squares in the matrix and can work as an irrelevant suggestive cue. In item 1d the irrelevant alternative has a completely different shape than those of the matrix and can thus be easily discarded without the need for inhibition.

The results of such a study showed that both adults and typically developing children had longer times of response and made more errors for items involving more than one rule. In other words, the items' complexity affected both processing time and correctness. Only in children, there was a remarkable effect of inhibition that for errors was significantly greater than the effect of items' complexity until participants were 6 year olds. Inhibition also affected children's response time except for the youngest age groups (4–5 and 6–7 years) who gave quicker and more impulsive responses when items had suggestive cues.

When we examine the results of persons who have been diagnosed with intellectual disability (ID), we expect that they will be lower compared to chronological age (CA=control group of typically developing individuals (see box 2.2)). However, we do not know whether such performance will be undermined by specific types of impairments. To clarify this point, the Curie and collaborators' study (2016), similarly to many other studies, compared people with ID also with a mental-age (MA) control group consisting of younger individuals who had a similar level of performance on a non-verbal reasoning task test (i.e., the classic form of the Raven's Matrices).

The results of such a comparison showed that the performance of people with ID was affected by a matrix complexity effect similarly to both CA and MA groups: errors and response times were longer with matrices involving more than one rule.

People with ID were less correct and had longer response times than the CA group whereas comparison with the MA group showed that there were no significant differences in response time. By contrast, there was a significant difference with MA for both the number of errors (higher for individuals with ID) and the stronger influence of inhibition on errors. Persons with ID were particularly sensitive to irrelevant suggestive cues: they made more errors solving a simpler condition requiring inhibition than a more difficult condition not involving inhibition, showing that the negative effect of inhibition was greater than the matrix complexity effect.

The eye-tracking analysis showed that persons with ID shifted their gaze toward the responses much earlier than MA who looked longer at the matrix before looking at the responses.

We can ask at this point what the Curie and collaborators' study (2016) adds to our understanding of reasoning skills in people who have been diagnosed with intellectual disability. These persons can infer rules, they do have the ability to reason, as we have seen that there are conditions in which they can solve complex items involving two rules. However, the Curie and collaborators' study (2016) shows that their reasoning –even at an adult age – is quite unsteady because is highly sensitive to interference from irrelevant cues that are not effectively inhibited. Thus, visual attention of persons with ID seems to be less controlled, and more often automatically triggered by some irrelevant stimulus, as may happen to 6-year-old children or younger.

The eye-tracking analysis of the Curie and collaborators' study (2016) also suggests that visual attention's anchorage in people with ID is not driven by an awareness of which parts of the task materials are important to explore. This suggests that persons with intellectual disabilities tend to be also particularly weak in constructing, while they are addressing a new task, a strategy that can facilitate finding a solution. Metacognition, in the two distinct components of awareness and self-regulation (Flavell, 1979) of the actions accomplished to address tasks or everyday life situations, is less likely to be spontaneously used by persons with ID or developmental delays (Campione and Brown, 1984). When children with developmental delays or typical development were involved in training focused on the rules under-lying Raven-like problems, their initial learning was at the same level as the mental-age matched typically developing peers. However, in a second testing phase, when problems were presented in a random order, children with delays had more difficulties in recognizing the types of problems and apply-ing the learned rules (Campione and Brown, 1984). In a sense, their learning appeared more anchored to a specific presentation sequence and therefore less flexible and prone to self-regulation.

We have so far reviewed how specific factors – inhibitory control and metacognitive strategies – make reasoning skills weaker and more unstable in persons with intellectual disabilities. Such factors should therefore become a privileged target of intervention to enhance cognitive development in persons with ID.

3 Intelligence as acquired knowledge

According to Cattell (1963), the wide set of concepts, rules and word meanings that are acquired through everyday life and academic learning, is a peculiar type of intelligence (defined *crystallized*) developing from reasoning and problem-solving skills (defined *fluid intelligence*). Fluid intelligence drives the acquisition of domain-specific concepts and procedures and determines individual differences in knowledge acquisition. It is on these premises that clinicians often interpret tests asking to define words, provide "general information" (e.g., *what comes after March?*) or show comprehension of social situations (e.g., *what would you do if you see thick smoke coming out of a neighbour's window?*) as taxing a child's general intelligence. This assumption, however, disregards three main types of evidence. First, even Cattell (1971) recognized the relative specificity of knowledge acquisition that in adulthood is maintained into old age whereas fluid intelligence declines after young adulthood. The second type of evidence is that both reasoning and acquired knowledge rely on one basic cognitive function, working memory, that determines an important part of individual differences in the typical development of fluid and crystallized intelligence (Kuhn, 2016; Tourva et al., 2016). Dependence on such basic cognitive function, rather than general intelligence, is likely to underly the tight correlation between fluid and crystallized intelligence. Finally, the greater dependency of acquired knowledge, compared to reasoning skills, on language learning and motivational factors points to the important role of cultural tools, along with affective processes, driving the development of crystallized intelligence.

3.1 Working memory and knowledge acquisition

Initial learning of rules, concepts, and procedures, require assistance from cognitive functions that have been defined *executive* for their common characteristic of recruiting voluntary attention to organise actions. Executive functions coordinate, organise, and supervise physical and mental actions when there is a new task, or when strategies must be generated to pursue a new goal or adjust to a new situation.

The executive function of working memory (Diamond, 2013) has a central role in complex learning as it allows controlling attention on task-relevant content, keeping information active in memory and monitoring its manipulation. When we explain to a five-year-old child that *an aunt is your mother's or father's sister*, each of the concepts should remain active in short-term memory whereas, at the same time, the relationship between them is elaborated. Imagine that a child is presented with a short text: *John was on the beach, stepped on broken glass, he is now in the hospital.* To understand this text the mind keeps active in memory the meaning of each sentence, but also uses long-term memory knowledge about real-world events (e.g., we are often barefoot on the beach). Such knowledge is integrated with the text content through inferences (e.g., stepping barefoot on broken glass can hurt). Thus, working memory is at the same time the necessary support of the mind's reasoning and a resource enhancing attention on task-relevant information.

Research on the typical and atypical development of WM has largely adopted the Baddeley's model (Baddeley and Hitch, 1974) that describes a system in which a central attentional component selects and coordinates mental operations keeping a constant interaction with verbal and visuospatial short-term memory stores. The efficiency of the verbal store is evaluated with tasks asking to repeat verbal stimuli (i.e., digits) keeping the sequential order in which they have been heard. It has thus been observed that the verbal store increases in its capacity from 4 to 15 years (Gathercole et al., 2004) also for the mediation of the articulatory rehearsal mechanism – a subvocal repetition of the verbal information along as it enters the verbal store. Visuospatial short-term memory is typically evaluated with tasks asking to reproduce the ordered tapping of blocks that have been shown by the evaluator. Such type of short-term memory levels off at 12–16 years depending on whether the task requires a visual or a spatial encoding (Gathercole et al., 2004). Whereas tasks evaluating the short-term memory components of working memory involve relatively passive processing of stimuli, the more complex structure of working memory is assessed by tasks requiring to actively elaborate information whereas stimuli are kept active in short-term memory. In the verbal domain, participants hear a sequence of verbal stimuli and are asked to repeat them in the reverse order, whereas in the visuospatial domain, the ordered tapping of blocks shown by the evaluator must be reproduced in the reverse order. Working memory increases its capacity with age and protracts its development even at adult age (Swanson, 1999). Visuospatial and verbal domains of working memory are both tightly related to the development of fluid and crystallized intelligence in typically developing children (Swanson, 2011).

Research on working memory in persons with intellectual disabilities revealed some similarities and differences with typical development. Keeping active in short-term memory verbal-phonological information tends to be more difficult than visual-spatial information for people with idiopathic ID in the comparison with both chronological age (CA) and mental age (MA) controls (Van der Molen et al., 2009; Schuchardt, 2010). Persons with Down syndrome are also more impaired in verbal than visuospatial short-term memory when they are compared to MA controls (Godfrey and Lee, 2020; Jarrold et al., 1999; Edgin et al., 2010). Lanfranchi et al. (2009) provided evidence that verbal short-term memory deficit in individuals with DS cannot be attributed to general language impairment, as the MA control groups in this study were selected through an accurate matching, individual by individual, based on vocabulary level or verbal IQ. The low verbal short-term memory was found to be a primary deficit and a major determinant of individual differences in IQ for persons with Down syndrome (Edgin et al., 2010).

Individuals with William syndrome are more impaired in visuospatial short-term memory when the comparison with MA relies on language development but not when is made with non-verbal mental age (Jarrold et al., 1999; Edgin et al., 2010). People with Williams syndrome also show notable impairments in tasks asking them to retrieve, after a delay of 10 minutes, words or visual stimuli that have been associated through a previous learning experience. Such performance in associative memory was found to be a major determinant of individual differences in IQ in such a group (Edgin et al., 2010).

Working memory, assessed by tasks asking to keep active in mind and, at the same time, elaborate verbal or visuospatial stimuli, is lower in persons with idiopathic ID in comparison with CA controls whereas comparisons with MA controls show contrasting results. Schuchardt (2010) finds no significant differences with MA controls, whereas Van der Molen et al. (2009) finds that working memory is lower than MA only when is evaluated with verbal tasks. In individuals with idiopathic ID, similarly to children with typical development, working memory increases with age but, unlike typical development, does not explain individual differences in academic learning (reading and mathematics in the study of Van der Molen et al., 2009).

For persons with Down syndrome, lower performances on working memory tasks, in comparison with MA controls, has been observed in both the verbal and visuospatial domains (Lanfranchi et al., 2004; 2009). When typical verbal and visuospatial WM tasks are administered to adults with Down or Williams syndromes their performance tends to be at the floor (Edgin et al., 2010) showing a degree of impairment that exceeds that found with short-term memory tasks.

For male individuals with Fragile X syndrome (FXS) both verbal and visuospatial working memory was significantly impaired compared to MA controls even in tasks asking a relatively simple elaboration as remembering the first word from each of two different five-word lists (see the review of Schmitt et al., 2019). An analysis of the learning trends (i.e., growth curves) demonstrates a relatively flat change rate from 6–12 years, followed by a rapid increase in performance beginning around 12 years. This suggests that working memory tends to increase in the adolescent years in this population. In female individuals with FXS, working memory in the verbal domain is at a similar level than MA controls whereas is more impaired in the visuospatial domain (Schmitt et al., 2019).

Involving two groups of children and adolescents with ID or borderline intellectual functioning (≥70 IQ ≤ 84) of heterogenous origin (both idiopathic nature and people with syndromes), Erostarbe-Pérez and collaborators (2021) found that working memory tasks, both in the verbal and visual domain, show moderate but statistically significant correlations with fluid and crystallized intelligence.

Thus, research suggests some conclusions that can orient the clinicians' assessment and intervention practices involving persons with intellectual disabilities. First, individual differences in fluid and crystallized intelligence, also for people with an intellectual disability or borderline intellectual functioning, are partly explained by working memory. Such important function can therefore be carefully evaluated to discover for each person the specific domain in which it can be more easily stimulated to support active comprehension processes in which regularities, cause-consequence or means-end relationships are elaborated.

The age at which working memory can be the focus of a training program should also be carefully considered. For idiopathic forms of ID, complex working memory tasks can be addressed by 9–10-year-old children, but stimulation with WM simple tasks could start even in the preschool years, especially in the visual domain. WM in the verbal domain seems to continue its development even in the adult age and stimulating this function in adolescents and young adults with ID can support knowledge acquisition in educational programs involving them.

Compensation strategies can be also suggested by the research findings reviewed above. As verbal short-term memory is particularly low in several forms of intellectual disability, such important function cannot facilitate language acquisition, unlike what occurs in typical development (Gathercole and Baddeley, 1990). Semantic familiarity, more than phonological rehearsal, is likely to enhance verbal memory in persons with ID (Numminem et al., 2002). Visual short-term memory, on the other hand, being of comparable level as mental age controls in most forms of syndrome-based ID, can be stimulated from a relatively young age and can be used as a resource to learn semantic categories.

3.2 Verbal abilities and motivational factors affecting knowledge acquisition

The pervasive role of learning in knowledge acquisition is evident from the changes that occur as a function of age. Although working memory affects the development of both fluid and crystallized intelligence, age has a direct effect only on crystallized intelligence in typical development (Kuhn, 2016; Tourva et al., 2016). As children grow older, they acquire more skills (e.g., reading, calculation procedures) and concepts by participating in school and other acculturation contexts. The influence of age is also clear for persons with ID as suggested by the study of Facon and Facon-Bollengier (1999) who involved 126 participants with intellectual disabilities to analyse whether crystallized intelligence was affected by age after controlling the influence of reasoning skills. The study found that age explains a substantial, statistically significant portion of individual differences in crystallized intelligence. Thus, as the time of exposure to formal and informal educational contexts increases with age, such a finding suggests that knowledge acquisition is positively affected by exposure to the learning experience in people with intellectual disabilities.

We may ask whether language skills are particularly important to support learning in persons with ID. Lifshitz et al. (2018) involved a group of 32 adults with mild ID in a post-secondary academic education project. All participants not only could read and write but were also independent in activities of daily living (e.g., could arrive at the university campus autonomously using public transportation). After two years of participation in specially adapted enrichment courses, the teachers realized that a subgroup of students, considering their level of understanding, could be involved in a fully inclusive program with a special education teacher who provided an hour of preparation before each academic lecture. To determine with a more objective method the eligibility for participation in the full inclusion versus the adapted program, each participant was assessed with two cognitive batteries evaluating several skills that could be broadly identified as fluid or crystallized intelligence. It was clear that a subgroup had in these tests higher total IQ, with vocabulary, knowledge (i.e., performance in the subtest asking general culture questions such as *Who is the president of Russia?*) and working memory showing the greater difference with the other participants. Thus, higher language abilities, concept acquisition, along with stronger working memory, allow persons with ID to acquire knowledge and participate in post-secondary academic programs.

Involvement in academic activities requires energy to face effort and contrast the fear of failure. Motivation provides such energy and has therefore a crucial role in feeding the students' intention to learn. Gottfried and Gottfried (2004) explored the predictive validity of early measures of *intrinsic* motivation (the pleasure involved in a situation, an orientation to succeed in a learning task) in a subgroup of children showing IQ levels particularly high. In this group of gifted participants, both measures of motivation and IQ contributed to explaining individual differences in academic achievement from early childhood to adolescence. Gilmore and Cuskelly (2009), in a longitudinal study involving 4 to 6-year-old children with Down syndrome, found that task persistence – an indicator of intrinsic motivation – was a longitudinally enduring characteristic that predicted, when children grew up as adolescents, a preference for challenging activities along with higher learning levels in reading and mathematics.

Similar findings emerged in a longitudinal study (Tracey et al., 2020) involving 11-year-old students with low cognitive ability (IQ<85) and exploring not only the role of motivation in providing support to learning mathematics but also the participants' motivation beliefs and the capacity to self-organize learning. Beliefs concerning one's own ability to learn (e.g., *It is easy for me to understand mathematics*) was the motivation component that, in the second observation (in middle adolescence), reliably predicted the class grades in mathematics after controlling the influence of the class grades in the early observation. Also self-regulated learning, in students with low cognitive ability or typical cognitive development, was predicted by self-beliefs about one's capacity to learn.

Awareness of the relevance of language and motivational factors on knowledge acquisition can change the attitudes of clinicians, from a type of assessment that only takes a static picture of the level of knowledge acquisition in a child, to a more dynamic perspective that looks for factors allowing development to move ahead. Asking whether language can be used by a child to construct meaning, whether learning is lived with pleasure, and self-concepts show a positive consideration of the personal learning capability, are crucial questions to explore when we assess persons with intellectual disability.

4 Adaptive functioning

The American Association on Intellectual and Developmental Disabilities defined adaptive behaviour as a set of skills that are learned by participating in informal contexts of everyday life and the more formal school context (Schalock et al., 2012). Adaptive functioning has been conceptualised in terms of conceptual, social, and practical domains that are in turn defined by a wide and heterogeneous set of more specific skills. For instance, the social domain includes the ability to communicate, use language, understand risk, following rules. The practical domain includes the capacity of personal care, using transportation, participating in age-appropriate daily living tasks. Although adaptive functioning correlates with IQ in typically developing individuals (see Johnels et al., 2021), evidence of such correlation is less clear for persons with intellectual disabilities.

When we consider adaptive functioning we are not always aware of its huge reliance on implicit learning. Although parents and other adults teach rules of behaving, explain to children what to say and not to say in certain situations, show how to accomplish new complex actions as eating spaghetti, or washing teeth, most informal skills of everyday life are acquired by participating in social life, observing others, imitating them, inferring other people's intentions and goals. In other words, there is implicit learning occurring without the explicit support and supervision of experts.

Such an informal learning process is likely to be a complex outcome of a wide range of environmental factors and basic functions (e.g., sensory-motor integration, visuo-constructive skills, communication and language, awareness of one's own and other people's intentions, goals, and emotions). Among basic cognitive functions, an important role is again played by executive functions and particularly by inhibitory control.

4.1 Inhibitory control and its role in adaptive functioning

We have seen in a previous section how difficulty in inhibiting attention to an irrelevant visual stimulus can undermine performance in a reasoning task. Inhibiting eye movement toward the site of an irrelevant cue to direct the eye toward the location of a relevant stimulus is a basic attention control function that starts to emerge in the first year of life (Cornish et al., 2013; Sherif et al., 2004).

Besides attention control, other different forms of inhibitory control can affect children's adaptive skills (see Box 2.2 with examples).

Inhibition of response is involved when there is a new response procedure that has a similar function as an already acquired one: this latter needs to be actively inhibited to produce the target new behaviour. In control of impulsivity, the new response requires resisting consolidated habits that are overused and deeply encoded in our brains. Both inhibition of response and control of impulsivity require effortful control to resist actions that are somehow related to the goal of the current situation or that urge to be implemented.

A further type of inhibitory control is resisting extraneous or unwanted mental representations, as when the mind resists wandering on memories or thoughts that are extraneous to our current goal. Suppressing proactive interference from mental content that has been elaborated earlier but that in the current situation is irrelevant is another form of inhibition. Resisting perseveration also requires inhibiting the tendency to continue a response or a procedure that is no more relevant in the current situation. Self-control is a form of inhibitory control on actions we have invested of emotional value but that conflict with other goals. When young children are shown an attractive toy and then asked not to touch it for a short while, self-control is involved in the capability of delaying gratification.

The experimental tasks used by psychologists to assess inhibitory control show that inhibition of attention (resisting attention to distractors) and inhibition of action (response inhibition) behave as a unique factor (Friedman and Miyake 2004) whereas self-control in delaying a gratification seems to be a more specific type of inhibition, in which motivational and emotive factors have a stronger role (Diamond, 2013).

Moffit and collaborators (2011) followed 1,000 children born in the same city and found that better forms of inhibitory control among ages 3 to 11 are predictive of broad adaptive skills. Children who had been less impulsive, less easily distracted, more able to cope with effort, were much more likely to have become teenagers who were still in school, made less risky choices, did not take drugs. Thus, inhibitory control is a complex basic skill that can longitudinally enhance cognitive and social learning and provide strong protective guidance in human development.

We can ask whether inhibitory control in children with ID shows a delay that is consistent with the level of cognitive development or, on the contrary, is an area of peculiar weakness.

The findings of several studies show heterogeneous trends, with differences related to the child's syndrome and to the forms of inhibitory control that are investigated. An inhibition deficit, mostly consisting of low resistance to a prepotent response and low interference control, emerged in a meta-analytic study (Bexkens et al., 2014) examining research work in which the performance of individuals with intellectual disability was compared only to a chronological age group. Comparing individuals with Down syndrome (10 to 19-year-olds) to a mental age group of typically developing children (3 to 6-year-olds), Borella and collaborators (2013) found that individuals with DS were lower than the mental age group in tasks assessing response inhibition, proactive interference and attention inhibition. Loveall et al. (2017) used the BRIEF – a parents' rating scale (Gioia et al., 2003) – to evaluate the use of executive functions in everyday contexts. Involving a large sample of parents of individuals with DS (3 to 35-year olds), Loveall et al. (2017) found that self-control – the inhibition component evaluated by the BRIEF – was lower than expected from age but was not an area of special weakness. It turned out that such inhibition component improved from preschool to mid-childhood, but gradually declined in the adults.

Studies involving persons with the Fragile X syndrome documented a reduced ability of response inhibition in young male children with FXS compared to both mental age and chronological age controls (see the systematic review of Schmitt et al., 2019). Perseverative errors are particularly frequent in persons with FXS, suggesting a specific weakness in inhibiting attention from responses that have been previously given.

Although response inhibition is a special weakness in individuals with FXS syndrome, there is evidence that such skill improves with age. Hooper et al. (2018) followed boys with the Fragile X syndrome for five years and compared them to a younger typically developing mental-age group. They found that response inhibition was always lower in children with Fragile X syndrome but increased with a similar rate of improvement as the mental age group.

In sum, inhibitory control is lower in persons with intellectual disabilities compared to typically developing individuals of the same age. However, as studies do not always have used comparison with mental-age controls, it is not clear whether inhibitory control is an area of special weakness. The extent of delay compared to chronological age controls seems to vary according to the form of inhibition that has been assessed, the age of the assessment, the type of genetic syndrome.

The absence of a genetic syndrome associated with the intellectual disability does not seem to make inhibition deficits lower, as shown by the study of Martin et al. (2016) who found that women with FXS had better inhibitory control compared to a group with idiopathic ID, of the same age and similar IQ level. This finding suggests that since an early diagnosis of intellectual disability is more likely when there is a genetic syndrome and is accompanied by early intervention, better longitudinal outcomes in inhibitory control may be observed in syndrome-based rather than idiopathic forms of intellectual disability.

What is clear from several studies is that inhibitory control is deeply related to the adaptive skills of persons with intellectual disabilities. For instance, the study of Gligorović and Đurović (2014) who investigated children (10 to 13-year-olds) whose intellectual disability was not associated with a genetic syndrome, shows that response inhibition was the main predictor of independent functioning, language skills, number, and time concepts, after the influence of IQ and age was controlled. In other words, taking IQ as a broad indicator of a child's cognitive level, inhibitory control is a factor that contributes to explaining individual differences in adaptive skills, beyond IQ related differences.

Box 2.2

Table 2.1 Different forms of inhibitory control

Inhibitory control	Examples
Inhibiting attention	Exploring pictures, pages of an illustrated book, maps, requires focussing attention on the parts that are relevant to a specific goal and inhibit attention to other irrelevant contiguous parts.
Inhibiting a response	When children are initially taught the sound corresponding to an alphabetic symbol they are often presented with a word that begins with that sound: *this is the /s/ of SUN.* The visual stimulus S initially work as a cue to recall the words that have been associated with it but this habit should then be inhibited in favour of recalling only the phonemic sound. Resisting an already acquired response in favour of a new one is crucial for adaptive skills and academic learning.
Control of impulsivity	Taking turns in playing, waiting before receiving a piece of cake at a party, not interrupting someone who is talking, require an effortful control of actions that urge to be implemented.
Resisting extraneous or unwanted mental representations	A child keeps thinking of her pet while the teacher explains the rules of a new game.
Suppressing proactive interference	A child learned the phone number of a person who then changed the number. Despite having learned the new number, the child often retrieves the old rather than the new number.
Inhibiting perseveration	A child may continue talking about a topic even when the conversation has moved on to other things. A child is asked to count forward from one to ten. When she is asked to count backward from ten to one, from time to time she resumes counting forward.
Self-control and delay of gratification	When we are on a diet and resist eating sweets. When we keep staying on a difficult task and do not give up on something more pleasant. When a child can wait half a minute before touching an interesting toy.

5 Conclusions

To create intelligent acts in our world, higher abilities need more basic abilities: developing complex cognition is an outcome of several more basic skills and their interaction. Such developmental outcome is affected by several factors, from genes to brain development, learning processes, affective and social relationships, cultural and educational contexts. All these factors interact between them in highly complex ways with continuous reciprocal influences.

We explored in this chapter how low development of attention and inhibitory control, working memory and language can generate important, though individually variable differences, in reasoning, knowledge acquisition, and adaptive skills of people with intellectual disabilities.

Thus, in our opinion, reasoning – a central attribute of intelligence – is not the core deficit of children with intellectual disabilities. Low reasoning is rather a consequence of impairment of other skills, such as attention and inhibitory control, working memory, and metacognition. When such skills are not highly challenged, children with ID can reason and draw inferences (see examples of reasoning and abstract thinking in the discourse of children with ID in chapters 3, 4, 7). If attention or inhibitory control, working memory and metacognition are empowered, the reasoning is also likely to make progress when evaluated with tests (Orsolini et al., 2019).

Recognizing that they can reason and act intelligently, within some favourable conditions (e.g., when attention control or working memory are not deeply challenged), means to people with intellectual disabilities that they can be attributed with a fundamental human quality. The key issue, from a person-centred perspective, is not if your reasoning skills are as effective as those shown by people of your same age. The question is whether you are recognized as a human being with the capacity for intelligence and reasoning. Starting from this recognition, an intervention can start with the most important assumption that will help a child to believe in her/himself.

To make a good concert, every instrument, from the horn to the first violin, is of great importance. The conductor has a wider view on how to interpret music, but only along with the good use of all the orchestra instruments can good music be performed. How might such deep, intense use of inner skills and qualities occur to people who are constantly receiving feedback of a supposed low or inexistent intelligence? But this is what happened and still happens to persons who have been diagnosed with intellectual disabilities.

References

Anderson, M. (2001) Annotation: conceptions of intelligence. *Journal of Child Psychology and Psychiatry, 42(3)*, 287–298.

Åsberg Johnels, J., Yngvesson, P., Billstedt, E., Gillberg, C., Halldner, L., Råstam, M., Gustafsson, P., Selinus, E. N., Lichtenstein, P., Hellner, C., Anckarsäter, H., Lundström, S. (2021). The relationship between intelligence and global adaptive functioning in young people with or without neurodevelopmental disorders. *Psychiatry Research*, 303, 114076. doi:10.1016/j.psychres.2021.114076.

Babayiğit, S., and Shapiro, L. (2020). Component skills that underpin listening comprehension and reading comprehension in learners with English as first and additional language. *Journal of Research in Reading, 43(1)*, 78–97. doi:10.1111/1467-9817.12291.

Baddeley, A. D., and Hitch, G. J. (1974). Working memory. In G. A. Bower (Ed.), *The Psychology of Learning and Motivation: Advances in Research and Theory* (pp. 47–89). New York: Academic Press.

Bexkens, A., Ruzzano, L., Collot D' Escury-Koenigs, A.M., Van der Molen, M. W., and Huizenga, H. M. (2014). Inhibition deficits in individuals with intellectual disability: a meta-regression analysis. *Journal of Intellectual Disabilities Research, 58(1)*, 3–16. doi:10.1111/jir.12068.

Binet, A. (Ed.) (1909). *Les idées modernes sur les enfants*. Paris: Flammarion

Binet, A., and Simon, T. (1916). *The Development of Intelligence in Children* (E. S. Kite, trans.). Baltimore, MD: Williams and Wilkins.

Borella, E., Carretti, B., and Lanfranchi, S. (2013). Inhibitory mechanisms in Down syndrome: is there a specific or general deficit? *Research in Developmental Disabilities, 34(1)*, 65–71. doi:10.1016/j.ridd.2012.07.017.

Campione, J. C., and Brown, A. L. (1984). Learning ability and transfer propensity as sources of individual differences in intelligence. In P. H. Brooks, R. Sperber, and C. McCauley (Eds.), *Learning and Cognition in the Mentally Retarded* (pp. 265–293). Hillsdale, NJ: Erlbaum

Carretti, B., Borella, E., Cornoldi, C., and De Beni, R. (2009). Role of working memory in explaining the performance of individuals with specific reading comprehension difficulties: A meta-analysis. *Learning and Individual Differences*, 19 (2), 246–251. doi:10.1016/j.lindif.2008.10.002.

Cattell, R. B. (1963). Theory of fluid and crystallized intelligence: a critical experiment. *Journal of Educational Psychology*, 54, 1–22.

Cattell, R. B. (1971). *Abilities: Their Structure, Growth, and Action*. Boston: Houghton Mifflin.

Cornish, K., Cole, V., Longhi, E., Karmiloff-Smith, A., and Scerif, G. (2013). Mapping developmental trajectories of attention and working memory in fragile X syndrome: Developmental freeze or developmental change? *Development and Psychopathology*, 25, 365–376. doi:10.1017/S0954579412001113..

Cornoldi, C. (2011). Le basi cognitive dell'intelligenza (The cognitive ground of Intelligence). *Giornale italiano di psicologia*, 2, 267–290.

Curie, A., Brun, A., Cheylus, A., Reboul, A., Nazir, T., Busy, G., et al. (2016) A novel analog reasoning paradigm: new insights in intellectually disabled patients. *PLoS ONE*, 11(2), e0149717. doi:10.1371/journal.pone.0149717.

D'Souza, D., D'Souza, H., and Karmiloff-Smith, A. (2017). Precursors to language development in typically and atypically developing infants and toddlers: the importance of embracing complexity. *Journal of Child Language*, 44, 591–627. doi:10.1017/S030500091700006X.

Deary, I.J., Penke, L., and Johnson, W. (2010). The neuroscience of human intelligence differences. *Nature Reviews Neuroscience*, 11(3), 201–211. doi:10.1038/nrn2793.

Demetriou, A., Spanoudis, G., Shayer, M., van der Ven, S., Brydges, C. R., Kroesbergen, E., Podjarny, G., and Swanson, H. L. (2014). Relations between speed, working memory, and intelligence from preschool to adulthood: structural equation modeling of 14 studies. *Intelligence*, 46, 107–121. doi:10.1016/j.intell.2014.05.013.

Diamond, A. (2013). Executive functions. *Annual Review of Psychology*, 64, 135–168. doi:10.1146/annurev-psych-113011–143750.

Edgin, J. O., Pennington, B. F., and Mervis, C. B. (2010). Neuropsychological components of intellectual disability: The contributions of immediate, working, and associative memory. *Journal of Intellectual Disabilities Research*, 54 (5), 406–417. doi:org/10.1111/j.1365–2788. 2010.01278.x

Erostarbe-Pérez, M., Reparaz-Abaitua, C., Martínez-Pérez, L., and Magallón-Recalde, S. (2021). Executive functions and their relationship with intellectual capacity and age in schoolchildren with intellectual disability. *Journal of Intellectual Disabilities Research*, doi:10.1111/jir.12885..

Facon, B., and Facon-Bollengier, T. (1999). Chronological age and crystallized intelligence of people with intellectual disability. *Journal of Intellectual Disabilities Research*, 43 (6), 489–496. doi:10.1046/j.1365–2788.1999.00224.x.

Flavell, J. H. (1979). Metacognition and cognitive monitoring: a new area of cognitive-developmental inquiry. *American Psychologist*, 34(10), 906–911. doi:10.1037/0003–0066X.34.10.906.

Friedman, N. P., and Miyake, A. (2004). The relations among inhibition and interference control functions: a latent variable analysis. *Journal of Experimental Psychology: General*. 133, 101–135. doi:10.1037/0096–3445.133.1.101.

Gardner, H. (2011). *Frames of mind: The theory of multiple intelligences*. New York:: Basic Books.

Gathercole, S. E., Pickering, S. J., Ambridge, B., and Wearing, H. (2004). The structure of working memory from 4 to 15 years of age. *Developmental Psychology*, 40(2), 177–190. doi:10.1037/0012–1649.40.2.177.

Gathercole, S.E., and Baddeley, A.D. (1990). The role of phonological memory in vocabulary acquisition: A study of young children learning new names. *British Journal of Psychology*, 81, 439–454. doi:10.1111/j.2044–8295.1990.tb02371.x.

Gilmore, L., and Cuskelly, M. (2009). A longitudinal study of motivation and competence in children with Down syndrome: early childhood to early adolescence. *Journal of Intellectual Disabilities Research, 53(5)*, 484–492. doi:10.1111/j.1365–2788.2009.01166.x.

Gioia, G.A., Espy, K.A., and Isquith, P.K. (2003). *Behaviour Rating Inventory of Executive Function-Preschool Version*. Lutz, FL: Psychological Assessment Resources.

Gligorović, M., and Buha Đurović, N. (2014). Inhibitory control and adaptive behaviour in children with mild intellectual disability. *Journal of Intellectual Disabilities Research*, 58(3), 233–242. doi:10.1111/jir.12000.

Godfrey, M., and Lee, N. R. (2020). A comprehensive examination of the memory profile of youth with Down syndrome in comparison to typically developing peers. *Child Neuropsychology*, 26(6), 721–738. doi:10.1080/09297049.2020.1721454.

Gottfried A. E. and Gottfried A. W. (2004) Toward the development of a conceptualization of gifted motivation. *Gifted Child Quarterly*, 48, 121–132. doi:10.1177/001698620404800205.

Gould, S.J. (1985). *The Mismeasure of Man*. New York: W.W. Norton and Company.

Hooper, S. R., Hatton, D., Sideris, J., Sullivan, K., Ornstein, P. A., and Bailey, D. B.Jr. (2018). Developmental trajectories of executive functions in young males with fragile X syndrome. *Research in Developmental Disabilities*, 81, 73–88. doi:10.1016/j.ridd.2018.05.014.

Jarrold, C., Baddeley, A. D., and Hewes, A. K. (1999). Genetically dissociated components of working memory: evidence from Down's and Williams syndrome. *Neuropsychologia*, 37(6), 637–651. doi:10.1e016/S0028–3932(98)00128–00126.

Kaat, A. J., McKenzie, F. J., Shields, R. H., LaForte, E., Coleman, J., Michalak, C., and Hessl, D.R. (2021). Assessing processing speed among individuals with intellectual and developmental disabilities: A match-to-sample paradigm, *Child Neuropsychology*. doi:10.1080/09297049.2021.1938987.

Kail, R.V., Lervåg, A., and Hulme, C. (2016). Longitudinal evidence linking processing speed to the development of reasoning. *Developmental Science*, 19 (6), 1067–1074. doi:10.1111/desc.12352.

Kaufman, A. S., and Kaufman, N. L. (2004). *Kaufman Assessment Battery for Children – Second Edition (KABC-II)*. Circle Pines, MN: American Guidance Service.

Kim, Y.-S. G. (2015). Language and Cognitive Predictors of Text Comprehension: Evidence From Multivariate Analysis. *Child Development*, 86(1), 128–144. doi:10.1111/cdev.12293.

Krawczyk, D.C. (2012). The cognition and neuroscience of relational reasoning. *Brain Research*, 1428, 13–23. doi:10.1016/j.brainres.2010.11.080.

Kuhn, J.-T. (2016). Controlled attention and storage: an investigation of the relationship between working memory, short-term memory, scope of attention, and intelligence in children. *Learning and Individual Differences*, 52, 167–177. doi:10.1016/j.lindif.2015.04.009.

Lanfranchi, S., Cornoldi, C., and Vianello, R. (2004). Verbal and visuo-spatial working memory deficits in children with Down syndrome. *American Journal on Mental Retardation*, 109, 456–466. doi:10.1352/0895–8017(2004)109<456:VAVWMD>2.0.CO;2.

Lanfranchi, S., Jerman, O., and Vianello, R. (2009). Working memory and cognitive skills in individuals with Down syndrome. *Child Neuropsychology*, 15 (4), 397–416. doi:10.1080/09297040902740652.

Levy, Y. (2018). "Developmental delay" reconsidered: the critical role of age-dependent, co-variant development. *Frontiers in Psychology*, 9, 503. doi:10.3389/fpsyg.2018.00503.

Li, Y., Liu, Y., Li, J., Qin, W., Li, K., Yu, C., and Jiang, T. (2009). Brain anatomical network and intelligence. *PLoS Computational Biology*, 5(5), e1000395. doi:10.1371/journal.pcbi.1000395.

Lifshitz, H., Verkuilen, J., Shnitzer-Meirovich, S., and Altman, C. (2018). Crystallized and fluid intelligence of university students with intellectual disability who are fully integrated versus those who studied in adapted enrichment courses. *PLoS ONE*, 13(4), e0193351. doi:10.1371/journal.pone.0193351.

Loveall, S.J., Conners, F.A., Tungate, A.S., Hahn, L.J., and Osso, TD. (2017). A cross-sectional analysis of executive function in Down syndrome from 2 to 35 years. *Journal of Intellectual Disabilities Research, 61(9)*, 877–887. doi:10.1111/jir.12396.

Martin, A., Quintin, E.-M., Hall, S. S., and Reiss, A. L. (2016). The role of executive function in independent living skills in female adolescents and young adults with fragile X syndrome. *American Journal on Intellectual and Developmental Disabilities*, 121, 448–460. doi:10.1352/1944-7558-121.5.448.

Martin, A., Quintin, E. M., Hall, S. S., and Reiss, A. L. (2016). The role of executive function in independent living skills in female adolescents and young adults with fragile x syndrome. *American Journal on Intellectual and Developmental Disabilities*, 121(5), 448–460. doi:10.1352/1944-7558-121.5.448

Miller, E. M. (1994). Intelligence and brain myelination: a hypothesis. *Personality and Individual Differences*, 17(6), 803–832. doi:10.1016/0191–8869(94)90049–90043.

Moffitt, T. E., Arseneault, L., Belsky, D., Dickson, N., Hancox, R. J., et al. (2011). A gradient of childhood self-control predicts health, wealth, and public safety. *Proceedings of the National Academy of Sciences of the United States of America*, 108, 2693–2698. doi:10.1073/pnas.1010076108.

Naglieri, J. A., Das, J. P., and Goldstein, S. (2014). *Cognitive Assessment System*, Second Edition. Austin, TX: PRO-ED.

Nation, K., and Snowling, M.J. (1998). Individual differences in contextual facilitation: Evidence from dyslexia and poor reading comprehension. *Child Development*, 69, 996–1011. doi:10.2307/1132359.

Neisser, U., Boodoo, G., Bouchard, T. J., Boykin, W. A., and Brody, N., Ceci, S. J., Halpern, D. F., Loehlin, J. C., Perloff, R., Sternberg, R. J., and Urbina, S. (1996). Intelligence: knowns and unknowns. *American Psychologist*, 51(2), 77–101. doi:10.1037/0003–0066X.51.2.77.

Nigg J. T. (2000) On inhibition/disinhibition in developmental psychopathology: views from cognitive and personality psychology and a working inhibition taxonomy. *Psychological Bulletin*, 126, 220–246. doi:10.1037/0033–2909.126.2.220.

Numminem, H., Service, E., and Ruoppila, I. (2002). Working memory, Intelligence and Knowledge base in adult persons with intellectual disability. *Research in Developmental Disabilities*, 23, 105–118. doi:10.1016/s0891–4222 (02)00089–00086.

Orsolini, M., Toma, C., and De Nigris, B. (2009) Treating arithmetical text problem-solving in a child with intellectual disability: an observative study. *The Open Rehabilitation Journal*, 2, 58–72. doi:10.2174/1874943700902010064.

Orsolini, M., Melogno, S., Scalisi, T. G., Latini, N., Caira, S., Martini, A., and Federico, F. (2019). Training verbal working memory in children with mild intellectual disabilities: Effects on problem-solving. *Psicología Educativa*, 25 (1), 1–11. doi:10.5093/psed2018a12.

Palix, J., Giuliani, F., Sierro, G., Brandner, C., and Favrod, J. (2020). Temporal regularity of cerebral activity at rest correlates with slowness of reaction times in intellectual disability. *Clinical Neurophysiology*, 131(8), 1859–1865. doi:10.1016/j.clinph.2020.04.174.

Prado J., Chadha, A., and Booth, J.R. (2011). The brain network for deductive reasoning: a quantitative meta-analysis of 28 neuroimaging studies. *Journal of Cognitive Neuroscience*, 23(11), 3483–3497. doi:10.1162/jocn_a_00063.

Raven, J. C., Court, J. H., and Raven, J. (1992). *Raven's Coloured Progressive Matrices*. Oxford: Oxford Psychologist Press.

Sherif, G., Cornish, K., Wilding, J., Driver, J., and Karmiloff-Smith, A. (2004). Visual search in typically developing toddlers and toddlers with Fragile X or Williams syndrome. *Developmental Science*, 7, 116–130. doi:10.1111/j.1467–7687.2004.00327.x.

Schalock, R. L., Luckasson, R. A., Bradley, V., Buntinx, W. H. E., Lachapelle, Y., Shogren, K. A., Snell, M. E., Tassé, M. J., Thompson, J. R., Verdugo, M. A., and Wehmeyer, M. L. (2012). *Intellectual disability: Definition, classification, and System of Supports (11e) – User's Guide*. Washington, DC: American Association on Intellectual and Developmental Disabilities.

Schmitt, L.M., Shaffer, R.C., Hessl, D., and Erickson, C. (2019). Executive function in fragile x syndrome: a systematic review. *Brain Sciences*, 9(1), 15. doi:10.3390/brainsci9010015.

Schuchardt, K., Gebhardt, M., and Maehler, C. (2010). Working memory functions in children with different degrees of intellectual disability. *Journal of Intellectual Disability Research*, 54, 346–353. doi:10.1111/j.1365–2788.2010.01265.x.

Spearman, C. (1923). *The Nature of "Intelligence" and the Principles of Cognition*. London: Macmillan.

Spearman, C. E. (1927). *The Abilities of Man: Their Nature and Measurement*. London: Macmillan.

Sternberg, R. J. (2004). Culture and intelligence. *American Psychologist*, 59(5), 325–338. doi:10.1037/0003-066X.59.5.325

Sternberg, R. J. (2018). Successful intelligence in theory, research, and practice. In R. J. Sternberg (ed.), *The Nature of Human Intelligence* (pp. 308–321). New York: Cambridge University Press.

Sternberg, R. J. (2021). *Adaptive Intelligence*. Cambridge: Cambridge University Press.

Sternberg, R. J. (Ed.) (2020). *Human Intelligence: An Introduction*. New York: Cambridge University Press.

Swanson, H. L. (1999). What develops in working memory? A life span perspective. *Developmental Psychology*, 35(4), 986–1000. doi:10.1037//0012–1649.35.4.986.

Swanson, H. L. (2011). Intellectual growth in children as a function of domain specific and domain general working memory subgroups. *Intelligence*, 39(6), 481–492. doi:10.1016/j.intell.2011.10.001.

Thomas M. S., Annaz D., Ansari D., Scerif G., Jarrold C., and Karmiloff-Smith, A. (2009). Using developmental trajectories to understand developmental disorders. *Journal of Speech, Language and Hearing Research*. 52(2), 336–358. doi:10.1044/1092-4388(2009/07-0144).

Tourva, A., Spanoudis, G., and Demetriou, A. (2016). Cognitive correlates of developing intelligence: The contribution of working memory, processing speed and attention. *Intelligence*, 54, 136–146. doi:10.1016/j.intell.2015.12.001.

Tracey, D., Morin, A.J.S., Pekrun, R., Arens, A.K., Murayama, K., Lichtenfeld, S., Frenzel, A.C., Goetz, T., and Maïano, C. (2020). Mathematics motivation in students with low cognitive ability: a longitudinal study of motivation and relations with effort, self-regulation, and grades. *American Journal of Intellectual and Developmental Disabilities*, 125(2), 125–147. doi:10.1352/1944-7558-125.2.125.

van der Maas, H. L. J., Kan, K.-J., Marsman, M., and Stevenson, C. E. (2017). Network models for cognitive development and intelligence. *Journal of Intelligence*, 5(2), 16. doi:10.3390/jintelligence5020016.

Van der Molen, M. J., Van Luit, J. E. H., Jongmans, M. J., and Van der Molen M. W. (2009). Memory profiles in children with mild intellectual disabilities: strengths and weaknesses. *Research in Developmental Disabilities*, 30, 1237–1247. doi:10.1016/j.ridd.2009.04.005.

Vernon, P. A., and Mori, M. (1992). Intelligence, reaction times, and peripheral nerve conduction velocity. *Intelligence*, 16, 273–288. doi:10.1016/0160–2896(92)90010-O.

Vigneau, F., Caissie, A. F., and Bors, D. A. (2006). Eye movement analysis demonstrates strategic influences on intelligence. *Intelligence*, 34, 261–272. doi:10.1016/j.intell.2005.11.003.

Wechsler, D. (1940). Non-intellective factors in general intelligence. *Psychological Bulletin*, 37, 444–445. doi:10.1037/h0060613.

Wendelken, C. (2016). Fronto-parietal network reconfiguration supports the development of reasoning ability. *Cerebral Cortex*, 26, 2178–2190. doi:10.1093/cercor/bhv050.

Wilhelm, O., and Engle, R. W. (2005). Intelligence: A Diva and a Workhorse. In O. Wilhelm and R. W. Engle (Eds.), *Handbook of Understanding and Measuring Intelligence* (pp. 1–9). Sage Publications, Inc.

Zigler, E. (1986). Intelligence: a developmental approach. In R. J. Sternberg, & D. K. Detterman (Eds.), *What is Intelligence?* (pp. 149–152). Norwood, NJ: Ablex Publishing.

Chapter 3

Assessments of children with developmental delays and intellectual disability

Margherita Orsolini, Sara Conforti, and Sergio Melogno

This chapter presents the characteristics of three types of assessments. The first assessment type is aimed at longitudinally monitoring children's cognitive and socio-emotional development to identify a developmental delay as early as possible. The authors overview the interview with the child's parents, the need for the critical use of questionnaires and developmental scales as well as the importance of observing parent-child interaction.

The second type of assessment aims to provide a correct diagnosis of intellectual disability, using a battery providing IQ indices and questionnaires to evaluate the child's adaptive functioning.

When a first-step evaluation has led to a diagnosis of intellectual disability, there should be a second-step assessment whose aim is to construct a child's cognitive and socio-emotional profile to orient intervention.

The cases of John and Davide (two fictional names) are described to illustrate how a neuropsychological evaluation can help to identify the mechanisms whose impairment contributes to the child's difficulties. Such evaluation needs to be complemented by clinical observations on the child's contextual use of cognitive functions, and the parents' descriptions of the child's emotional reactions, social life, desires, and aspirations.

I A neuro-socio-constructivist view can inform the assessment practices

1.1 The learning processes underlying development

In the time of quick change characterizing the early years, the development of each child takes form with an emerging profile of strengths and weaknesses. A traditional view conceives individual differences in a highly static way: genes determine a child's characteristics and the

DOI: 10.4324/9781003220367-3

potential to learn; the environment then affects how these dispositions will unfold. According to a neuro-constructivist view, however, neither genes nor environment control or plan human development. Children's developmental profiles and individual characteristics emerge from experience-driven learning processes and are constrained by a wide range of interconnected internal and external factors (D'Souza, D'Souza and Karmiloff-Smith, 2017). The learning processes are triggered by the child's active interaction with caregivers and physical objects. For instance, when children start to grasp objects, their manipulation and exploration is the opportunity to gather information on the objects' perceptual and functional features, leading to laying down the bases of semantic categorization of reality. When a child is involved in feeding or bathing routines, his active interaction with the caregiver is the opportunity to explore and perceive the caregiver's facial expressions and voice and learn how to use them to calm discomfort or fear. The active role of the child is, on the other hand, constrained by temperament and the early development of basic cognitive functions, such as visual and auditory attention, movement, and perception. The state of such early functions is a crucial determinant of the learning processes made possible by experience. If a caregiver is pointing to an object and names it, but the child is not ready to focus her attention on the caregiver's finger or gaze, she will not have the opportunity to elaborate on the link between the object and the speech information. Therefore, early learning of words forms and their meaning will be very fragile or even impaired.

Environmental factors and parent-child relationships have a crucial role in motivating and supporting the children's experience. For this reason, the phrase neuro-socio-constructivism seemed to us more appropriate. If the infant is growing up with highly stressed parents, her interactions with them will be less rewarding. The child's looking at the parents' facial expressions will find inconsistent signals of affection and calm, and thus his or her learning about facial expressions and emotions will be unstable. Also learning to regulate the child's own emotions of discomfort and fear will tend to be compromised. Cultural conceptions of infant development also affect parent-child early relationships and caregiving. How parents or caregivers respond to the child's signals, the conceptions of the role of early social stimulation on infant development, the skills that are most valued in a particular culture, and specific educational contexts (family vs early care centres) constrain a child's experience and learning opportunities.

Learning also relies on the brain's micro and macro characteristics allowing it to extract patterns, regularities, and structure from the information gathered through experience. For instance, if the prosody of speech remains the most important language cue eliciting an infant's auditory processing, other important characteristics of language, including phonological regularities, will not be elaborated (D'Souza, D'Souza and Karmiloff-Smith, 2017). Extracting patterns, on the other hand, is not only a question of the brain's characteristics but also of the frequency of gathering specific types of information. If an infant is rarely stimulated to attend speech, her language processing will not benefit from practice, and the acquisition of language regularities and patterns will be impaired.

The highly interactive, interdependent nature of human development makes the assessment enterprise particularly complex. How can a neuro-socio-constructivist view inform the assessment practices aimed at both providing correct diagnoses of intellectual disability and orienting the intervention programs?

1.2 Davide's story

The early development of Davide – who received a diagnosis of intellectual disability at age 9 – was recollected by his mother when the boy was first assessed in our university clinical centre at age 14. Davide's mother remembered that when she was breastfeeding her son and talked to him in pauses, the baby was not keeping his eyes on the mother's face and started to look at whatever stimulus captured his attention for a very short while. Davide's mother was very frustrated by the son's low responsivity, feeling that she was somehow unable to get him emotionally connected to her. Months later, Davide's parents noticed that, unlike other toddlers who could walk, Davide was still crawling. They were concerned and referred these observations to the paediatrician who reassured them claiming that children meet their milestones at different times. When Davide started to attend preschool, his peers communicated with words, but he only produced some gestures. Davide was then the object of recurrent peer refusal and started to show a tendency to social isolation. The child was then referred to a public developmental health care centre and involved in an assessment when he was 3-year-old. It turned out that Davide was delayed in every area of development and he was then involved in a group therapy focused on communication. Three years later, despite the reciprocity and emotional involvement in communication with his parents, Davide's difficulty to eye-gaze in face-to-face verbal communication was interpreted as a sign of autism. He thus received a diagnosis of pervasive developmental disorder at the age of six and was involved in individual therapy focused on communication and speech. In the next two years, it became clear that Davide could use basic social and verbal skills in interaction with parents or other caring adults. Davide received a diagnosis of mild intellectual disability at the age of 9 and was then involved in a therapy focused on academic learning.

1.3 Three main goals of assessment

Davide and his family met assessment practices that did not address the situation with adequate concepts. First, the paediatrician seemed not to be aware that monitoring the acquisition of milestones and ruling out that several developmental areas might be delayed in a child is a prevention child-care practice. Whenever there is a parents' concern about development, questionnaires should be used asking parents to report about their infant's development. In this way, the early manifestations of what could be transient or persistent developmental delays can be observed and a child's development is monitored.

When Davide was first evaluated at age three, the child-parent interaction and affective relationships were not explored. How did the child respond to parents' communication in a play context, or in a family social routine? Were there episodes of joint engagement, between Davide and his mother or father, focused on the same object or action? What types of everyday activities could Davide effectively participate in at home and school? When the child was evaluated at age six, the suspect of autistic spectrum disorder was only based on Davide's difficulty to eye-gaze in verbal communication and did not rely on any formal standardized instrument.

From the first to the last assessment at age nine, the evaluation did not consider the developmental *relationship* between different functions. What types of impaired basic functions seemed to undermine the development of more complex skills? For instance, was Davide's eye-gaze difficulty also the manifestation of impaired attention control? Could visual and auditory attention, along with other basic skills (e.g., auditory short-term memory) support the child's language learning?

We assume in this chapter that assessments should pursue three main aims. The first is to monitor children's development and identify a developmental delay as early as possible because early intervention has an important positive impact on further development in children with developmental delays (see chapter 4). The second goal of assessment is to provide test results and qualitative clinical observations enabling a correct diagnosis, at the child's age in which it becomes possible. A third, more complex finality is to construct a child's cognitive and socio-emotional profile that can orient intervention.

Parents are co-experts in the assessment enterprise (see Fatigante, 2011; McHale and Dickstein, 2019); they should be actively involved in observing the contexts in which their child seems to be more active, motivated to interact, or confident to explore. Starting from the initial interview, parents should perceive that the clinician is interested in receiving their emotional experience with the child and their thoughts on her/his challenges. In the talk addressing the results of the assessment, the clinician should share with parents the Vygotskian view (Vygotsky, 1978) on the scaffolding role that parents can have for the child's learning. Pulling forward the *zone of proximal development* of specific basic functions (e.g., attention) with everyday activities and ways of interacting with the child, can be discussed and negotiated through the clinician-parents talk.

2 Early identification of developmental delays

The Global Burden of Diseases, Injuries, and Risk Factors Study (GBD) provided a comprehensive database of the prevalence of disabilities among children younger than five years in 195 countries and territories from 1990 to 2016 (Global Research on Developmental Disabilities Collaborators, 2018). Focusing on children with intellectual disabilities, their prevalence globally was 2%, with the highest numbers of children with ID observed in South Asia, North Africa, and the Middle East. Prevalence in high-income countries (North America, Central, Western, and Eastern Europe) ranged from 1.4% to 1.5%. Congenital anomalies (39.7%) and neonatal disorders (21%), including preterm birth complications, infections, and birth asphyxia, were the most frequent causes of intellectual disability, whereas idiopathic forms (that is, ID of unknown origin) accounted for 29%. In 2016 about 15 million children younger than 5 years showed an idiopathic form of developmental intellectual disability.

Developmental screening of infants, through parents' reports delivered to paediatricians, should become a basic child-care practice. In this way early detection of developmental delays can be implemented, leading to identifying infants to involve in a follow-up assessment and early stimulating play activities.

2.1 Parents' questionnaires for developmental screening

When a paediatrician visits an infant and asks about the milestones that are typical of each age, rich information can be collected to orient the possible need for further examination steps (Stein and Lukasik, 2009). An informal questioning can occur while the visit proceeds, addressing the main themes typical of the child's chronological age (see Figure 3.1).

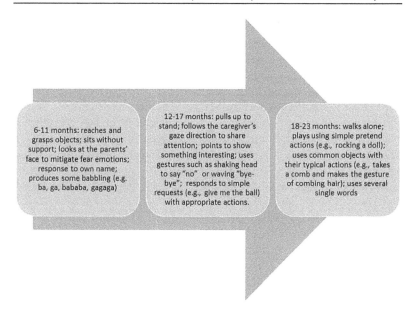

Figure 3.1 The main themes that can be addressed in a childcare visit

There are standardized parents' questionnaires with proven good *sensitivity* and *specificity*. In other words, when compared with more formal expert-administered developmental scales, some questionnaires have been shown to identify both a similar proportion of children performing below age expected level (sensitivity) and a similar proportion of children performing at the expected level (specificity). One of such tools is the Ages and Stages Questionnaire, third edition (ASQ-3), which was published in 2009 and aimed at identifying potential developmental delays in children aged between one month and 5.5 years.

ASQ-3 consists of 21 age-specific questionnaires exploring 5 developmental domains: (a) communication, (b) fine motor, (c) gross motor, (d) problem solving, and (e) personal-social (see Box 3.1 for examples). The questionnaires can be completed by parents in about 15 minutes. It is used in North America but has been also translated and used in several countries in Europe, South America, and Australia (Velikonja et al., 2017). Comparing for the same children the ASQ-3 results and those of well-established tests, such as the Bayley Scales of Infant Development – Third Edition (Albers and Grieve, 2006), the sensitivity values turned out to be high (0.83) (Veldhuizen et al., 2014). Specificity values were also good (0.72) according to a systematic review by

Velikonja et al. (2017). In some studies, the long-term predictive capacity of the ASQ-3 questionnaires has also been evaluated. Charkaluk et al. (2017) analyzed the capacity of the 36-month ASQ questionnaire to predict cognitive delay at the age of 5–6 years in the general population, reporting values of 77% and 68% for sensitivity and specificity respectively. Similarly good values emerged from Schonhaut et al. (2020) who analyzed a sample of 227 children who had attended a pediatric clinic in Chile and had been assessed with both the ASQ-3 (translated to Spanish and adapted for the Chilean population) and the Bailey III, at 8, 18 and 30 months. Evaluating the same children again at 6–8 years of age, with a scale assessing their IQ, the authors found that the ASQ and the Bailey developmental scale showed good sensitivity and specificity. However, for both the ASQ and the Bailey, a longitudinal prediction was high when the children's initial levels were within typical levels (96% of correct prediction) but was very low when children had shown a low level in their early evaluations (14% and 24% of correct prediction for the ASQ and the Bailey respectively). The results of such a study suggest that children showing some delays in early evaluations (before 3 years of age) still have the possibility of adequate cognitive development later in life, particularly when there is an enriched environment (as in the families involved in the study by Schonhaut et al., 2020), or when some intervention has been implemented after the initial assessment. Thus, when a developmental delay emerges from a questionnaire before the age of three, development should be monitored with other types of tools, also exploring the quality of the environment, and particularly of the caregivers-child interactions that are crucial for enhancing the child's experience and learning opportunities.

Box 3.1

Table 3.1 Examples of questions from an ASQ-3 18-month-old questionnaire for the *Communication* domain

Communication			
When your child wants something, does she tell you by *pointing* to it?	Yes	Sometimes	Not yet
When you ask your child to, does he go into another room to find a familiar object? (You might ask, "Where is your ball?" or say, "Bring me your coat", or "Go get your blanket.")	Yes	Sometimes	Not yet
Does your child say eight or more words in addition to "Mama" and "Dada"?	Yes	Sometimes	Not yet

Communication			
Does your child imitate a two-word sentence? For example, when you say a two-word phrase, such as "Mama eat", "Daddy play", "Go home", or "What's this?", does your child say both words back to you? (Mark yes even if her words are difficult to understand.)	Yes	Sometimes	Not yet
Without your showing him, does your child *point* to the correct picture when you say, "Show me the kitty," or ask, "Where is the dog?"	Yes	Sometimes	Not yet
Does your child say two or three words that represent different ideas together, such as "See dog", "Mommy come home", or "Kitty gone"? Please give an example of your child's word combinations:	Yes	Sometimes	Not yet

2.2 Deepening the assessment with developmental scales and other tools

When the parents or the paediatrician have some concerns, and a questionnaire confirmed delays in some of the child's milestones, there is a need for a more in-depth interview with the parents, asking questions about the child's developmental progress, and exploring the cultural differences that may have an impact on it. After such an interview, a standardized *developmental evaluation* can be proposed, using appropriate tools enabling a comprehensive assessment of motor, social, language, and nonverbal skills in infants and toddlers.

We need to be aware of several caution points, considering that each test captures a very partial image of a child's functioning and that the degree of the child's cooperation with the evaluator deeply affects a child's performance. Despite such limits, developmental scales help to evaluate parents' or paediatricians' concerns and take decisions on early psychoeducational interventions.

The *Bayley Scales of Infant and Toddler Development (III edition)* is considered the gold standard to assess infants and young children from 1 to 42 months of age. The third edition has an increased focus on the toddler years and evaluates cognition, expressive and receptive language, fine and gross motor skills, social-emotional aspects, and adaptive behaviour. In each area, the test allows a comparison of the child's responses with a normative sample of same-aged typical developing peers or with a clinical normative sample of children at risk for developmental delay.

The Bayley Scales are an excellent tool for evaluating children with special needs and their eligibility for services (Bayley, 2006).

The *Mullen Scales of Early Learning (Mullen, 1995*) allows an evaluation of cognitive functioning in children from birth through to 68 months of age. Concepts on neurodevelopment and sensory learning, an emphasis on separate and distinct scales of learning over a single global measure, have inspired the test construction. Each scale has interactive tasks that ask the child to perform some action. For instance, the gross motor scale includes standing, walking, and running; the visual reception scale includes matching, sorting, and nesting cups; the fine motor scale includes stacking blocks, drawing, and stringing beads; the receptive language scale includes recognizing body parts and following commands; and the expressive language scale includes answering questions and completing analogies. Separate standard scores for each scale allow to identify the child's strengths and use them to enhance weaker areas.

The *Mullen Scales of Early Learning* have been adapted for use in low resource countries and set in South Africa (Bornman et al., 2018). For an in-depth evaluation of the child's emerging communicative and language development, parents can be given the standardized MacArthur-Bates Communicative Development Inventory (CDI, Fenson et al., 2007). Such a tool asks parents to identify in a large list of gestures, actions, and words, those that their child can produce and /or understand. Using the CDI with the parents of 1,447 children, Bavin et al. (2008) found that gestures and actions with objects at 12 months predicted larger vocabularies at 24 months. Morin-Lessard et al. (2021) explored the communicative and language development of 1,992 children at 12 months and then again at 24 months, using the CDI – Words and Sentences (Fenson et al., 2007) to assess children's productive vocabulary (i.e., the words that are often or sometimes produced by the child to communicate.) When the same children reached the age of five, a third questionnaire was given to their mother (CCC-2; Bishop, 2003) to assess communicative development. Controlling for the influence of biological (e.g., the child's birth weight) and environmental factors (e.g., the mother's level of instruction) that affect language development, the study of Morin-Lessard et al. (2021) found that both gestures and symbolic actions at 12 months predicted the breadth of productive vocabulary at 24 months, which in turn predicted better communicative skills at age 5.

Thus, as far as children showing delays in language development are concerned, it can make a big difference if an 18-month-old child can use gestures and symbolic actions to express and communicate a relatively high number of meanings. In such a case, we can predict that vocabulary will increase in the following six or twelve months.

2.3 Evaluating gestures in children with Down syndrome

As summarized in Box 3.2, language is one of the greatest challenges for children with DS. An adequate assessment should explore the question of which, among various basic skills in a child with DS, might enhance the development of language. To answer such a question we have to complement the results of a parent questionnaire, and even those of a developmental scale, with further evaluations and clinical observations.

In this section we ask whether gestures, which are important antecedents and predictors of expressive vocal language development in typical development (see the previous section), might serve such function also for children with an intellectual disability associated with Down Syndrome.

But why can gestures be considered important, and what is their role within the complex processes enhancing language acquisition? Gestures can be considered "bridges" (Bates and Dick, 2002) between language comprehension and production. A child can show with a simple gesture of pointing that she can identify a referent in the communicative context (e.g., pointing in the direction of a doll); gestures can also express the meaning of a situation, as when a child closes his eyes pretending to sleep, or weaves hands looking at the grandma who is going out. As gestures are tools to express meaning, they can be understood by the child's partners, who can, in turn, express some related meaning and keep the communication going on. Thus, gestures allow a child to actively participate in the game of meaning expression and understanding played by partners in a dialogue. As they are actions related to the visual or functional characteristics of the represented entity, gestures also seem to support the linguistic representation of meaning even when children are older (Pettenati et al., 2012).

Zampini et al. (2009) involved twenty 36-month-old Italian children with Down's syndrome in a free play session with their mother to analyze the production of gestures. At the same time, the children's vocabulary size was evaluated by requesting mothers to fill the MacArthur Communicative Development Inventory, in the Italian adaptation (PVB inventory, Caselli and Casadio, 1995). In a follow-up testing after 6 months, the children's lexical development was evaluated again using the PVB inventory. It turned out when the children were first tested at the age of 36 months, that the total number of gestures produced, and the frequency of deictic and conventional gestures (see Box 3.3), were closely related to the children's lexical comprehension (i.e., the number of words children could comprehend, according to the PVB inventory) whereas it was not related to lexical production. In turn, the lexical comprehension at 36 months predicted the level of lexical production in the follow-up testing at 42 months. The trend emerging from Zampini et al.'s study (2009) thus suggests that gestures support meaning representation, and enhance lexical comprehension that in turn longitudinally promotes lexical production. If such interpretation is correct we should expect that interventions focused on gestures can enhance children's expressive vocabulary.

Dimitrova et al. (2016) observed, at the age of 18 months, 23 children with DS interacting with their parents for over a year. The results of such a study showed that the children often used gestures to communicate and that parents often translated their gestures into words. The study shows that children benefited from their parents' input, acquiring more words for the translated gestures than the not translated ones.

Thus children with DS can use gestures at 18 months, an age in which their expressive lexicon may contain a few words if not one. The communication abilities of children with DS are likely to be more ahead of what word production would tell us. As suggested by the results of Zampini et al. (2009) and Dimitrova et al. (2016), gestures contribute to *bridging* the gap between language comprehension and production, especially when parent-child interaction provides contingent verbal labelling of the meanings that the child tended to express with gestural actions.

Going back to the concept of the *zone of proximal development* (Vygotsky, 1978), gestures allow to pull ahead of the child's language zone of proximal development. The value given by parents to the child's gestures, the interactive practice of translating them into verbal labels within child-parent communication, can be illustrated and discussed by the clinicians involved in assessments of children with developmental delays.

Box 3.2 Language development in children with Down syndrome (DS)

DS, the most frequent inherited cause of intellectual disability (ID), is often related to an extra chromosome – or part of a chromosome – on chromosome 21. It may also be caused by a chromosomal translocation or mosaicism (i.e., the coexistence of two or more cell populations with different genetic compositions) on position 21. There is notable individual variability in the level of cognitive and language delay shown by children with DS (see Abbeduto et al., 2016; Pulina et al., 2019). Language comprehension is typically stronger than language production (Caselli et al., 1998; Laws and Bishop, 2003), and expressive vocabulary is often delayed even in comparison with children with other ID conditions and matched for nonverbal cognitive ability (Martin et al., 2013).

Once children acquire their first words, the transition from one to two-word speech is delayed (Iverson, Longobardi, and Caselli, 2003), and constructing sentences remains a particular linguistic challenge (Laws and Bishop, 2003), as grammar abilities are lower than expected from the children's nonverbal cognitive ability (Caselli et al., 2008). A minority of children with DS still do not produce two-word combinations at five years. Chapman et al. (2002) followed a group of 5 to 20-year-old individuals with DS over six years and found that the utterances length continues to improve through the teenage years for most individuals with DS. An increase in expressive language abilities continues indeed until the young adult age.

Box 3.3

Table 3.2 Examples of communicative gestures and symbolic actions from different developmental studies (Bates and Dick, 2002; Fenson et al., 2007; Caselli and Casadio, 1995; Zampini et al. 2009).

Deictic gestures (identify a referent in the environment)	Pointing, showing (holding up an object in the communicative partner's line of sight)
Conventional gestures (express meaning through a culturally shared gestural form)	shaking head to refuse to do something, waving *bye-bye*
Iconic gestures (refer to objects or events by reproducing their physical or functional characteristics)	Close eyes pretending to sleep, partially rotate hands to pretend driving
Symbolic actions	Pour pretend liquid from one container to another

2.4 Observing parent–child shared attention and joint engagement

Adult-child affective communication, in the first six months of life, unfolds through dynamic flows of emotional sharing, in which caregivers and infants respond to each other's signals. The caregiver leads the game of responding to the infants' expression of stress and discomfort, whereas acting to keep warm contact is a highly pleasant game in which both the infant and the caregiver contribute with an active role. Infants' smiles and laughter align the positive emotions expressed by caregivers in episodes of reciprocal emotional attunement (Stern, 1985) that increase the adult-infant social bond. Such experience of emotional sharing is the substrate on which an intentional use of signals starts to emerge around nine months of age (Carpenter et al., 1998). For the first time at this age, the dyadic adult-child emotional interaction can include objects or the situation around. We then observe a caregiver eliciting attention to an external target and the child following her gaze or finger direction to share such focus. Joint attention to the external world, and not only emotional sharing, has thus entered the communicative scene, along with an early understanding of the pointing gesture (see Tomasello, 2018). Towards the end of the first year, toddlers also start to take an active role in eliciting the caregiver's attention and interest in some specific object or situation. In episodes of coordinated visual attention (Bakeman and Adamson, 1984) children alternate looking at the caregiver and the focused target, accompanying such looking with a pointing gesture, or an emphasized object grasping, along with some vocal expression of exhilaration or eagerness. In such communicative acts, which have been named *declarative*s (Bates et al., 1979) for their function of proto-comment on some portion of the context, children show an active understanding of the intentionality underlying human use of signals. The caregiver starts to be used as a recipient of the communication, a person whose attention needs to be elicited and monitored.

In sum, from dyadically structured emotional proto-dialogues emerge triadic forms of communication. Sharing attention towards objects to explore, actions to perform, and sharing interest and surprise towards people and other entities of the external world, are the first forms of referential communication, a type of dialogue that in the preschool years will become *talking about a shared topic*.

As the complex developmental pathways overviewed above drive the acquisition of language and social cognition, the caregiver-child collaborative use of attention and communication should be evaluated when there are concerns for a child's development.

Early Social Communication Scales (ESCS; Mundy et al., 2003), assesses non-verbal communication skills in typically developing children between 18 and 30 months old and children with delay whose estimated language level is within the same age range. The scales evaluate whether a child can use communicative acts such as pointing and eye-gaze to engage in declarative communicative functions to share an interest in objects and events.

The Joint Engagement Rating Inventory (JERI) can evaluate children between 12 and 42 months interacting with a caregiver (Adamson et al., 2012). Considering 5 or 15 minutes sessions of video-recorded observation, the inventory's categories rate the child's activity (with codes such as *she initiated communication*, or *gave attention to the caregiver*), the caregiver's behaviour, the caregiver-child the joint engagement. A challenge of the JERI rating inventory is that examiners who are used to analysing individual skills are instead asked to focus on triadic communication and reciprocal engagement. The category *joint engagement* applies in fact when a child and her caregiver are both actively engaged in some physical or symbolic action and direct attention to the same referent (for at least 3 seconds), which may be an object, event, or action present in the immediate context or evoked through symbols. If the child participates in an action initiated and supported by the caregiver, but the child's attention is only directed at the action and never switches to the caregiver, there is not a *coordinated engagement* but only a *supported engagement* (the action goes on through the caregiver's scaffolding). If a child looks at the caregiver and what she is doing but does not participate in it, there is social attention (a state of *onlooking*) but not engagement.

Episodes of joint engagement depend not only on the child's but also the caregiver's activity and particularly on the scaffolding of shared activities (e.g., the caregiver continually supports and extends the child's actions), a contingent uptake of the child's current focus of attention (e.g., the caregiver continually joins and acts to sustain the child's interest), the fluency and connectedness of the interaction (e.g., there is a balanced interaction that is not dominated by one of the other participants).

Adamson et al. (2012) involved three groups of children who were typically developing (TD) or diagnosed with either autism (AU) or Down syndrome (DS). The sample consisted of 108 children who were longitudinally observed 5 times at approximately 3-month intervals. Observations started when TD children were 18-month-old whereas children with AU and DS were 30-month-old (and showed a similar overall cognitive development as the TD). Several interesting results emerged from this study. The coordinated joint engagement had low scores (corresponding to low frequency) in each group, but the children with AU were significantly lower. The TD and DS children had similar scores of supported and coordinated engagement. Only when the expressive lexicon of children with DS was higher than 50 words, supported and collaborative joint engagement involved symbol use, with scores comparable to those of 18-month-old TD children.

Focusing on the caregiver, scaffolding had a higher score for TD and DS than children with AU. Highlighting symbols (i.e., the caregiver uses words to name the focused game item) had similarly high scores for each group. The caregiver's following on the child's focus and her affective communication also had similarly high scores in the three groups. Focusing on the child, affective communication and responsiveness were similarly high in TD and children with DS, but significantly lower in children with AU. Initiating communication had lower scores for children with DS and AU.

Observing the caregiver-child interaction allows, along with more formal tools, an early distinction between developmental delay and high risk of autism spectrum disorder. Children with DS or developmental delays of different origins (see Adamson et al., 2019) show interaction profiles with notable differences compared to children with AU. Despite a common severe delay in language, they are much more involved in supported joint engagement, display more often affective communication, and are more responsive to the caregiver's attempts to initiate communication. As the experiences of shared attention and joint engagement predict vocabulary acquisition (Adamson et al., 2019; Bottema-Beutel, 2016), careful observations of the caregivers-child interaction, supplemented by inventories that focus on joint attention skills (Mundy et al., 2003), or on the child's repertoire of gestures and words (such as the CDI, Fenson et al., 2007), can tell us whether the language zone of proximal development can be pulled forward by experiences of joint engagements and gesture use.

3 Toward a correct diagnosis of intellectual disability in school-age children

The wide individual variability in children's developmental trajectories makes it difficult to distinguish transient developmental delays from individual profiles in which the developmental course of a broad range of cognitive functions is hindered by neurobiological impairments. Only when we consider a child's developmental history there can be evidence suggesting whether, despite earlier transient phases of global developmental delays, there are higher-order cognitive functions (e.g., reasoning, discourse, and text comprehension) whose developmental level is consistent with the individual's age.

3.1 John's clinical history

John had been adopted by an Italian family when he was 3-year-old and was living in an orphanage in a Latin-American country. He had been involved with one early adoption that failed when the adoptive parents, natives of John's same country, split up. There had been then two fostering families that for different reasons decided to suspend their engagement with the child. John's Italian adoptive parents recalled that in the weeks of their pre-adoption permanence with the child in the orphanage, John could not speak any Spanish word. After he arrived in Italy, John continued to show severe language deficits that continued throughout the preschool years despite his involvement in intense speech therapy (see Box 3.4 for more details). John showed academic learning difficulties and poor emotional regulation when he started to attend primary school. At 9 years of age, he was diagnosed with mild intellectual disability, and then with borderline intellectual functioning, considering his total IQ score. When John's parents asked for our consultation, John was 10-year-old. Our interview practice does not involve the child (who is not present in the first meeting) and asks parents to engage in a broad child's description. We acknowledge that parents are the true experts on their son or daughter and that their detailed observations are very important to help psychologists to understand how the child's development is going on.

After a first reconstruction of the adoptive history, John was described by his father as *beautiful, warm, joyful...he is a child who can relate very well with adults and children. When he meets a new person, initially takes the role of observer but then he can loosen up.* The mother added that John *loves dancing and artistic gymnastics, attends a boy scout group, has a strong sense of duty and respect for the rules.*

The clinician in the interview asked *What topics can you address when you talk with him?* John's mother replied that John was very interested in topical issues and used to listen to the news on tv. *When ISIS organized the attack in Paris, John had discussed it with his mates at school but then asked us a lot of questions and explanations. He is curious and asks about everything.*

When John's parents were asked to address the weak points of their child, they focused on the behaviour at school that was sometimes disruptive. They recalled that one day John destroyed the drawing of a girl who had been praised by the teacher. John's father interpreted the child's disruptive reactions as always related to jealousy or envy and low self-esteem: *whenever he feels he is not good enough he is very reactive. The teachers have now understood him, and prefer not to give him challenging tasks, to avoid his trouble behaviours.* The clinician asked how John behaved at home when received some prohibition. *When he receives our "no", he gets angry and tries to negotiate but his reactions are contained, like all the other children. When you ask him why he behaves in certain ways at school, he says he does not know, and it's true, he is not aware of his motivations.*

After having described John's severe difficulties in academic learning the parents concluded: *we never felt convinced by the diagnoses of intellectual disability, we did not recognize John in it.*

Box 3.4 John's clinical history

John's clinical history was overspread of several diagnoses: immediately after his arrival to Italy, when he was 3-year-old, a developmental neuropsychiatric centre observed a severe communication and language delay, that was interpreted as related to the orphanage experience. John was then involved in speech therapy, which helped his Italian language to improve. The parents observed that the child was very shy and that when his emotional arousal was high, he often produced a hands "flickering". The child was then referred to a new private developmental neuropsychiatric centre and diagnosed with a developmental language impairment associated with an anxiety disorder. It was observed that John's gait was slightly rigid, the visuomotor integration turned out to be rather low, whereas his receptive language was good. John was then involved for two years in speech, psychomotor and affective therapy in the centre. After such therapy, at 6 years and nine months of age, the motor development appeared very good, but a developmental scale suggested a mild cognitive delay. A severe delay in reading, spelling, arithmetic emerged, and the report mentioned an affective "immaturity".

At school, John was helped by a special teacher who, according to Italian law, gives support to the regular class in which children with special educational needs are included. There were episodes at school in which John expressed discomfort with strong reactions such as spitting or kicking. Such episodes started to decrease when John was involved in individual psychotherapy. The child was also involved, after school, in learning activities at home, with a private expert teacher. John continued to show severe academic learning difficulties, and the parents choose a new private clinical psychologist who assessed the child with the KABC-II (Kaufman and Kaufman, 2004). The results showed that only visual processing was in the norm, whereas all the other scores showed a cognitive delay. When the child was 9 years old and his academic learning impairments continued to appear severe, the parents choose a private association of speech therapists and neuropsychologists for a new assessment. This centre used the WISC IV to examine the child's cognitive profile and issued a diagnosis of mild intellectual disability (see Table 3.3). After one year, the diagnosis became that of borderline intellectual functioning, with John's total IQ increasing from 67 to 76.

3.2 What a diagnosis of intellectual disability should consider

When John, after his first year of residence in Italy and involvement in speech therapy continued to show severe language difficulties, his parents were probably very concerned, started to think that the therapies might not be good, and looked for a new clinical centre. This tendency to change health care centres was shown whenever they were told that the child had a cognitive delay. Although such parental reaction is likely to be related to the difficulty to elaborate and accept that the adopted child is different from an idealized image of *all the other children*, there were some aspects of the assessment results that did not help John's parents to develop trust in clinicians. It was clear to the couple that John had notable academic learning difficulties and that his Italian language continued to be immature for his age. But how could an original language impairment become a more general problem of intelligence? How could this alleged problem fit with a child who showed good motor development, was adequately included in the boy scout activities, was curious, and asked for his parents' explanations?

The parents' doubts met, in the mind of our university clinic's psychologists, with more professional concerns. John's adaptive functioning never had been assessed, although, for a correct diagnosis of intellectual disability, an IQ < 70 should co-occur with impaired adaptive functioning in at least two domains. We also expect from a diagnosis of ID that the highest cognitive functions such as reasoning, show delays when evaluated with tests. We argued that persons with ID can infer rules, have the ability to reason, but are highly sensitive to interference from irrelevant cues (see section 2.3. in chapter 2). However, John's performance with the Matrix reasoning was adequate for his age (see Table 3.3). The WISC IV results also showed a notable difference between basic processing skills (see the very low scores of digit span, letter-number sequencing, and coding in Table 3.3) and John's acquisition of semantic and social knowledge, which was only 1 standard deviation below the mean (see the scores of vocabulary and comprehension in Table 3.3). Such an uneven cognitive profile should have been considered to formulate some doubts concerning the diagnosis of ID. The diagnostic label "borderline intellectual functioning" also denotes a condition in which both cognitive and adaptive functioning limit the person's social, academic, or work performance and restrict their full participation in society (see the *Borderline Intellectual Functioning Consensus Group* in Martínez-Leal et al., 2020).

3.3 The core deficits and the strength points shown by a neuropsychological evaluation

A neuropsychological assessment, unlike an evaluation that only deploys a battery to evaluate IQ indices, selects standardized psychometric tests that target specific cognitive functions and help to identify the mechanisms whose impairment contributes to the child's difficulties (see Hüsser et al., 2020).

Table 3.3 John's performance with the WISC IV when he was diagnosed with mild intellectual disability (subtests with scores approaching 2 standard deviations below the child's chronological age norms are in grey)

Index/subtest	IQ(mean=100)/ scaled scores (mean=10)	IC 95%	Percentile rank	Level of performance
Verbal Comprehension	78	72–86	7.2	Below mean
Similarities	5			
Vocabulary	7			
Comprehension	7			
Perceptual Reasoning	85	78–94	15.5	In norm
Block design	10			
Illustrated Concepts	5			
Matrix Reasoning	8			
Working Memory	64	59–77	0.3	Below mean
Digit span	4			
Letter-number sequencing	4			
Processing Speed	71	65–85	2.3	Below mean
Coding	3			
Symbol search	7			
Total IQ	67	62–74	1.3	Below mean
General Abilities Index	79	74–86	5.0	Below mean
Cognitive Proficiency Index	59	54–72	0.36	Below mean

In our university clinic, the evaluation carried out when John was 10 years old aimed to explore the issues as follows. Would an assessment of adaptive functioning and reasoning confirm a profile of *borderline intellectual functioning*? Did John still show a language impairment? As the cognitive profile was not evenly delayed, a severe language impairment, along with delayed development of working memory and executive functions, might have generated strong academic learning difficulties. Delayed development of inhibitory control and working memory was indeed compatible with John's history of institutional rearing and the sequence of abandonments in his first three years of life (see the neurobiological profiles of children with early life adversities in Blasi et al., 2020). An evaluation addressing such issues was complemented by a detailed assessment of John's academic learning.

Table 3.4 The questions addressed by the evaluation carried out when John was 10. The scores approaching two standard deviations below the child's chronological age norms are grey. See the note on the different types of scores.

Cognitive function/test name	Scores	Observations
WAS BORDERLINE INTELLECTUAL FUNCTIONING CONFIRMED?		
Reasoning: The Raven's coloured progressive matrices (Raven et al., 1995)	37	J. appeared very concentrated, selected 3 non-targets in the series B
Inferences: The Alce Oral text comprehension (Bonifacci et al., 2014)	−0.5*	
Adaptive functioning: Vineland adaptive behaviour scales-II (Sparrow et al., 2005)		
Communication	10	
Everyday skills	11,2	John's parents report that the
Socialization	9,11	child dresses by himself, can select weather-appropriate clothes, got the boy scout nurse speciality, and can cure by himself small wounds. However, when he is at home he asks to be cured by his parents. J. is autonomous in taking a shower from 6 years of age. J. has learned to read the watch, both analogical and digital. He started to make some small shopping by himself. He saved money for a whole year to buy LEGO constructions.
DID JOHN STILL SHOW A LANGUAGE IMPAIRMENT?		
Receptive vocabulary: Peabody Picture Vocabulary Test-Revised (Stella et al., 2000-Italian adaptation)	75	
Grammatical comprehension: TROG-2 (Suraniti et., 2009)	2	Systematic errors are produced with relative clauses and subordinate clauses with pronouns such as *the man saw that the boy was looking at him*

Cognitive function/test name	Scores	Observations
Contextual sentence comprehension: Comprehension of instructions (from the Nepsy II, Italian adaptation; Korkman et al. 2007);	3**	J. did not realize that such a task was difficult for him.
Expressive lexicon: Boston naming test (Italian adaptation: Riva et al., 2000)	–3.28*	J. showed notable lexical access difficulties and is not helped by semantic or phonological cues.
Rapid automatized naming (*De Luca et al., 2005*) Correctness in naming figures	–9.56*	J. errors suggest great sensitivity to phonological interference effects.
Speed in naming figures	–2.31*	

Language use in conversation

J. participation in the conversation is appropriate and highly co-regulated, he considers the adult's requests and can elaborate his answers with short sentences. There are concerns, however, both for the narrative function and the structural aspects of his language, still characterized by phonological simplifications, basic nuclear subject-verb-object utterances, very rare use of connectives.

When we asked John to explain to us what he can do with his favourite app, the explanation was rather confused, with little sequential organization. There were clear difficulties in lexical access, with rather words substituted by "that thing" and "in this way", or gestures.

CAN ATTENTION, WORKING MEMORY, AND OTHER EXECUTIVE FUNCTIONS SUPPORT THE CHILD'S LEARNING PROCESSES?

Selective Attention (Di Nuovo, 2000)

Speed in visual selective attention	<25	J. is very focused on giving correct responses but shows a notable executive slowness both in auditory and visual attention
Speed in auditory selective attention	<25	
Speed in a double task involving both visual and auditory selective attention	<25	

Fluent search in the mental lexicon (Bisiacchi et al., 2014)

Phonological fluency	0.02*	
Semantic fluency	–1.25*	J. produces a high number of words for colours but a few for animals and fruits

Semantic flexibility in categorization (Korkman et al. 2007)

Animal sorting	5**	J. produces only 2 correct groupings. He seems to consider a couple of images that share a characteristic, rather than a group of four, as the task requires.

Cognitive function/test name	Scores	Observations
Inhibitory control: Inhibition (Korkman et al. 2007)		
Inhibition contrast score	7**	J. showed the most notable
Switching combined score (correctness and completion time)	7**	difficulties in the naming condition. The inhibition contrast score -which controls for the influence of the naming
Total errors	2**	condition- suggested a mild difficulty. Also the switching combined score -that considers both correctness and completion time- corresponds to performance with no severe difficulties. The total errors made in the inhibition and switching conditions showed, however, that such executive functions are not used fluently.
Impulsivity		
Test of the small frogs *(Marzocchi et al., 2010)*	−1.4*	In this task, the participant advances in a track of small frogs according to a listened sound that consists of a signal-to go. In some cases, such signal is immediately followed by a signal-not-to-go.
Working memory in the verbal domain		
Direct digit span *(Bisiacchi et al., 2014)*	−1.14	
Wordlist repetition (Korkman et al. 2007)	7**	
Backward digit span *(Bisiacchi et al., 2014)*	0.2	
A double task of semantic elaboration and recall: Listening span test (Pazzaglia et al., 2000)	−1.82*	In this double task, J. recalled a few word sequences in the right order and, at the same time, made a high number of errors in saying whether each sentence was true or false.
Narrative memory: Spontaneous recall of a listened story (Korkman et al. 2007)	10**	

Cognitive function/test name	Scores	Observations
Working memory in the visuospatial domain		
Visuospatial sketchpad (*Mammarella et al., 2008*)	0.02*	
A double task of visual recognition and sequential recall of visual positions in a matrix (Desimoni & Scalisi, in preparation)	0.02*	

Note: standard scores* (mean=0), *percentile ranks* (mean=50), IQ scores (mean=100), scaled scores** (mean=10), age level for the adaptive functioning.

Table 3.4 synthesizes the results of John's neuropsychological evaluation in our centre. It was not confirmed that John's difficulties could be encompassed under the umbrella label of *borderline intellectual functioning*. The child's adaptive functioning was adequate in several areas, and higher cognitive skills such as reasoning, inferential skills in oral text comprehension, and working memory in the visuospatial domain, were within normal limits for the child's chronological age. John's core deficit was language, with severe difficulties ranging from slow and unstable lexical access, restricted expressive vocabulary, utterances produced with phonological simplification processes, and immature grammatical constructions. These difficulties in expressive language were associated with a rather restricted receptive lexicon and notable difficulties in receptive grammar. Attention and executive functions, including working memory in the verbal domain, did not allow fluent coordination and control of the cognitive processes. We did not include in Table 3.4 the academic learning results that required several tests, with both quantitative and qualitative observations. John's reading was characterized by a huge number of errors. The free morphemes (e.g., articles, pronouns, connectives) tended to be omitted when John read aloud a text. Both word and non-word reading, along with spelling, turned out to be severely impaired in terms of correctness, with errors that were affected by a word's complex syllabic structures (e.g., *dorso* written DOSO, *dunque* written DUNEQUE), as occurs in younger Italian children with specific language impairment (Orsolini et al., 2001). Text comprehension was severely impaired if John had to read the text by himself but was in the norm for his age when the text was read aloud by the examiner. The arithmetic skills were all impaired, from a semantic representation of numbers to memorization of arithmetic facts and written calculation procedures.

In our university clinical centre, John's diagnosis was of *severe developmental language disorder in co-occurrence with an unspecified developmental learning disorder*. In John's case, the "specificity" of a learning disorder was incompatible with the complex developmental history. The impaired academic learning might have been the developmental outcome of several heterogeneous factors. Among neurobiological factors: a genetic predisposition to academic learning disorders, that is often associated with language impairments; the likely negative effects of early life adversities on brain development. Among cognitive factors: the low support that attention, working memory and other executive functions could provide to the learning processes; the extremely low motivation generated by the emotional refusal that John experienced whenever he was aware of his difficulties at school. All these factors were likely to be involved in undermining John's progress in academic learning, despite the tutorials that he received at home.

Despite the good adaptive functioning and the adequate reasoning and discourse comprehension skills shown by John at the age of our evaluation, his severe language and academic learning impairments were likely to have long-term detrimental effects both for school achievements and socio-emotional well-being. Children like John need to receive intensive support, even if their cognitive profile cannot be framed by diagnoses such as intellectual disability or borderline intellectual functioning.

4 Toward a cognitive and socio-emotional profile of children with intellectual disability

In children with intellectual disability, developmental delays are shown by a broad range of cognitive functions, including the most complex skills such as reasoning, oral and written text comprehension, arithmetical text problem-solving. The degree of such delays, however, show great individual variability, can be mitigated by the learning processes induced by intervention, have an impact on adaptive functioning that can be eased by compensatory strategies and emotional reactions preserving the person's well-being.

When a first step evaluation has led to a diagnosis of intellectual disability, there can be a more complex – second step assessment – whose aim is to construct a child's cognitive and socio-emotional profile. Such assessment can be constrained by a set of issues to explore. What are the core deficits that may have generated cascading effects on the child's development? If we can answer such a question, we can then look for the cognitive skills that are relatively more preserved and may be used to construct compensatory strategies. We can also identify the contexts in which the most complex abilities seem to emerge, along with interpreting the parents' conceptions and/or child's behaviour and emotional reactions that are risk factors hindering cognitive and affective development.

4.1 Gathering different sources of information and qualitative observations

Reconstructing the child's developmental history means not only collecting the case's medical record, and the reports of previous assessments, but also eliciting the parents' and teachers' descriptions of the child's condition. The aim is to compose a puzzle in which different perspectives on the child's behaviour, emotional reactions, contexts of experience, are put together (see an example in chapter 7). How the parents tried to influence and educate the child's personality also should be considered.

The interview with the child's parents can be one of the most fruitful sources of information if it unfolds within a non-judgmental climate, with pauses allowing parents to add details that are not requested by the clinician but somehow spontaneously emerge because they urge to be expressed.

The initial interview with the parents helped us to clarify, in the case of Lorenzo, one important source of the child's emotional dysregulation. Lorenzo was born pre-term in the seventh month and had received a diagnosis of mild intellectual disability when he was 8-year-old. Lorenzo was looked after by the grandmother in his first years. His parents did not follow the child very much, and it was clear that their cultural conception was characterized by a trust in spontaneous development. There was not any sharing of games or physical activity with their son, explicit parental instructions had been rare. Their older son, they said, had needed no special teaching, had been brilliant in learning a lot of things by himself. On the contrary, they said, Lorenzo did not learn at school and was not autonomous at home. The child had shown highly reactive and sometimes aggressive reactions to his parents, which alternated with requests for protection and affection. Had not we collected the parents' narrative on Lorenzo's context of growing, the child's impulsive and angry reactions, might have been interpreted only as a temperamental trait, rather than also as a child's complex adaptation to the low parental affective availability. Understanding some characteristics of Lorenzo's socio-affective context led to an intervention that included not only psychoeducational activities for the child but also observation of parent-child interaction followed by interviews in which the parents' involvement in our intervention with the child was promoted.

When we assess a child, the more formal work with tests and questionnaires can be alternated with pauses for play and conversation. Such informal activities often provide an ecologically valid perspective to collect observations on the child's cognitive style and attitudes. Pretend play can tell us whether the child's participation in interactions is co-regulated in terms of semantic continuity with the topics or actions introduced by the partner. Games with rules (e.g., dominoes) can show how the child applies the rules, respects turn-taking, and engages in the game. Observing conversations can show us thought, storytelling, and reasoning abilities that might not be revealed by a formal test.

We examine in Box 3.5a an excerpt from the second meeting of an assessment stage. Davide (we have described his history in section 1.2 in this chapter) is a 14-year-old boy with a diagnosis of mild intellectual disability, still showing verbal dyspraxia and a phonological disorder. Several reports in his medical record showed that there was neither a known genetic syndrome nor signs of brain dysfunctions.

It was easy, listening to the dialogue reported in Box 3.5a, to recognize how narrating a peer's trouble was a chance for Davide to indirectly reflect and look for an explanation of his own troubles linked to, among other things, articulatory problems (see Fatigante et al., 2015). Kids can behave childishly, despite not having language problems. With such thought, Davide explicitly questioned why certain events happen, and why people behave in certain ways. Such dialogue, collected in a pause between tests, was the first evidence of Davide's reflective attitude.

Other types of important qualitative observations concern the ways a child behaves when a test seems to be particularly difficult. In such types of situations, Valentina used to close her eyes, showing a kind of shameful reaction, as when shy young children meet a new person. Sandro used to laugh, showing a kind of dissociation from his performance and, at the same time, eliciting the partner's benevolent attention. Davide blamed himself (*Because I am stupid*) and used irony (*Have I been good?*) when the task was perceived as very easy. Federico was very keen to interrupt the difficult tasks, Romina used to fall into a deep silence that continued for some minutes, despite the examiner's attempts to maintain a live interaction.

Such observations can help the psychologist to understand how a child is emotionally relating to an emerging awareness of her difficulties, which probably started to occur at school when a spontaneous comparison with her peers proposed the concept of not being capable of learning or doing things well. A child's emotional reactions to challenges can be the evidence of the developmental course that the personality might take if the person will not be helped to integrate her weak sides into a dynamic and flexible psychic unit.

In Davide's case, for instance, his reflective attitude tended sometimes to take the form of a strict analysis of his behaviour, as in the narrative shown in Box 3.5b that was produced in the last assessment session. The observations Davide made on himself showed not only an introspective attitude but also a constant – almost persecutory – questioning of his reactions and behaviours. This tendency to question himself was considered an important point of the therapeutic work with Davide.

Box 3.5a Davide refers to a scout excursion, focusing on the arrival of a new peer (P. is a psychologist involved in the assessment).

D: still I can't understand this… he talks well. But he behaves like a small child!
P: mh!
D: it's not underst… I cannot understand why this one behaves, (.) as a small child. I cannot understand.
P: eh! he will probably have his difficulties.
D: eh… I would have better understood if… I… I would have better understood if this one could not talk, then
P: eh!
D: but I cannot understand, why this has such big problems

Box 3.5b Davide refers to an episode that occurred at school

D: when I speak I always feel a bit ashamed
P: You feel a bit.
D: Yes… because I am worried to say silly things
P: ah!

D: For instance, the other time I wanted to ask a girl mate if she was happy that in these five days...that we could have a long weekend. Do you know the time it took?

P: eh?

D: Saying that sentence took a lot of time. But talking with my support teacher took little time.

P: and why did it take that time with her, what do you think?

D: I do not know if for don't make a bad impression or for shame. Because even with the boys I can't feel good... imagine with girls, the girls here know lots of things. I can't talk with girls... I don't really talk to them.

4.2 Constructing a cognitive and socio-emotional profile from a neuropsychological evaluation

The focus of an in-depth evaluation of children who have been diagnosed with a developmental disability should be interpreting a profile of the child's weaknesses and strengths to address some questions that are important to design intervention. In which domain (i.e., visuospatial or verbal) does a child's learning processes seem to occur more easily? Which, among basic cognitive functions (e.g., attention, short-term memory), show a lower impairment and can support the development of more complex functions? Which, among higher cognitive skills such as reasoning, or oral text comprehension, are less impaired and can support concept formation and knowledge acquisition? Which emotional and contextual conditions seem to promote or hamper the child's active involvement in home and school experiences?

The first-level assessment with a cognitive battery evaluating the child's IQ can show whether there is a homogeneous cognitive delay or, on the contrary, some tasks have higher performances (e.g., significant differences emerge between different indices). A second-step assessment can focus on in-depth analyses of more specific functions, with neuropsychological batteries such as the Nepsy II (Korkman et al., 2007) that can be complemented by other tests targeting specific cognitive mechanisms (e.g., The Comprehensive Assessment Battery for Children – Working Memory, CABC-WM), along with questionnaires addressing the child's symptoms of disattention and impulsivity (e.g., Conners 3rd Edition), the use of executive functions at home and school (the Behavior Rating Inventory of Executive Function, 2nd Edition), the children's emotional states and behaviour (The ASEBA CBCL, Child Behaviour Checklist), and personality (The Big Five Questionnaire for Children, BFQ-C).

Starting with the basic function of attention, it should be carefully evaluated in its different components and domains, measuring both the correctness and speed of the child's performance. The results of the evaluation with attention tests need to be complemented with those of the parents' and teachers' questionnaires on symptoms of disattention and impulsivity and with qualitative observations on how the child uses attention in the clinical context when asked to address motivating tasks.

Analyses of different executive functions such as inhibition, switching, working memory, fluent phonological and semantic search of words in the mental lexicon, can suggest whether learning processes that require an active and strategic cognitive processing can be supported by such functions. It is also important that working memory is evaluated, following the Baddeley (2010) model, in its short-term store (i.e., the articulatory loop and the visual sketchpad), episodic buffer (e.g., with a narrative memory test), and central executive components. Working memory has a central role in complex learning as it allows the simultaneous storage and manipulation of information. To learn a rule, for instance, individuals must recall examples and keep them in a temporary memory store to develop an abstract schema from them (Anderson et al., 1997). In learning something new, before associations are formed between the parts of a new procedure or a new concept, working memory is particularly taxed (Cowan, 2014).

Again, there can be qualitative observations showing how some components of inhibitory control and other executive functions seem to assist the child in ecologically valid contexts. How did the child react when he was asked to quickly finish a game in an assessment break and be involved again in a test? Did the child show perseverative errors in some tasks? Could she easily understand the rules of a game that had been proposed to her?

Language requires a systematic evaluation even in grown-up children for the central contribution that such function has, along with working memory, in comprehending instructions and discourse, and in providing self-instruction that can support the child's acquisition of new procedures and strategies. Tests on learning, episodic, and long-term memory are also important to clarify whether some new information can be learned after little exposure, or is consolidated after a time delay. It is very important also to collect qualitative information on the amount of repetition that is needed before the child manages to learn more interesting stimuli than those proposed by tests. Teaching the rules of a new game, or the sequence of a simple procedure can offer the opportunity to observe the levels of learning generated by one exposure to target stimuli and suggest, along with test results (e.g., immediate memory of a short listened story), whether episodic memory shows delays.

Evaluating emotion recognition, the ability to map the meaning of social scenes into emotional facial expressions, and to infer intentions from characters' actions and discourse, allows analyzing some components of the children's social cognition. Questionnaires detecting behavioural and emotional problems in children and adolescents, tests concerning visual perception, visuomotor integration, motor coordination, and planning, can also be considered if they are useful to analyze developmental characteristics that have never received an in-depth analysis in previous assessments. Eventually, reading, writing, mathematics, text comprehension, and production, need to be properly evaluated when clinicians are asked to design interventions at school in collaboration with school teachers.

The risk of every type of psychometric evaluation is that the outcome is a list of delayed performances that are not interpreted to explain the child's cognitive and adaptive functioning profile. Integrating psychometric results with qualitative observations on the child's use of specific functions in ecologically valid contexts can lead us to a more useful outcome. We have tried, for the case of Davide, to connect in Box 3.6 the results of several neuropsychology tests (see Orsolini et al., 2015) and the hints of qualitative observations to construct a more integrated cognitive profile.

Davide's cognitive profile was shared with his school teachers and suggested broad guidelines. Attention and language, despite their delays, could be anchor functions to empower complex mental processes and metacognitive strategies when Davide was motivated to participate in a specific activity. Self-instructions and anticipating the steps involved in complex actions could be anchor functions to compensate for the difficulties in visuomotor integration and planning. Semantic elaboration and inferential reasoning could be the primary study strategy if visual resources (e.g., pictures and short movies) were used to complement verbal information. Davide's learning of new concepts required working on consolidation through activities involving the child in active retrieval and argumentative thinking. Participating in social situations was facilitated by Davide's eagerness to follow the rules but the objective of developing more flexible behaviours required to work on the child's deep anxiety concerning his social and cognitive capabilities.

Although difficult, clinicians may try asking themselves not only what types of weaknesses and abilities a child has, but also who is the child they have observed. Where are the child's personality and self-construction heading? At the end of our evaluation, it seemed to us that Davide was heading toward a self-image centred on thinking and reasoning abilities. He loved to engage in reflections, evaluate his behaviour, arguing the reasons and motives underlying it. This boy was trying his best to engage the conversational partner in argumentative thinking as if he expected to experience acceptance and well-being only under this condition. Davide's intellectual attitude was shown to the adults he could trust whereas it was rarely expressed with his peers at school. He was ashamed of his poorly fluent speech and preferred to remain silent to prevent peers teasing and criticism. Davide was starting to experience the power of his thinking abilities but was somehow emotionally blocked by a strict self-evaluation, the lack of social life with peers, low confidence in his body.

Box 3.6 A narrative synthesis of Davide's cognitive profile

Davide's selective attention was slow in both the auditory and visual domain, but maintaining attention was very good when he was involved in games, and pretend play. In all such activities, in which Davide was highly motivated, he could attend the same task for a long time. Such good capacity to maintain attention was complemented however by weak selective attention as suggested by the slowness and lack of strategies in tasks requiring a careful visual search.

Davide's language was impaired in the phonological and grammatical components, whereas semantic representation was pretty good, as shown by the receptive vocabulary and the semantic links he spontaneously used when asked to memorize a list of words. However, when elaborating semantic content required a fluent process in which information from different sources had to be coordinated and integrated, Davide was notably impaired. For instance, when he had to judge whether a sentence was true or false and, at the same time, he had to keep the sentence's last word in memory, he could accomplish only the judgment task and was very slow and uncertain in judging even simple sentences. Inhibitory control also showed important delays in several components, including controlling a dominant response, resisting extraneous mental representations, inhibiting perseveration. Such weaknesses, however, did not hinder Davide's verbal thought and reasoning when the meaning was constructed using consolidated long-term memories (e.g., autobiographical memories). Using verbal instructions that challenged his short-term memory span, was made difficult by his working memory impairment, unless instructions were illustrated by images, or were repeated several times. However, when new semantic content was illustrated by meaningful connected images, Davide's reasoning abilities were almost adequate, also when the characters' mental states had to be inferred.

Learning and memory tests showed that Davide needed repeated exposure to stimuli. Such weakness in constructing an episodic memory from a single exposure emerged in the verbal domain when after listening to a very short narrative, that referred to familiar events, Davide could recollect almost nothing. The same weakness emerged from exposure to a simple action procedure (e.g., laying the table) he was asked to reproduce.

5 Conclusions

As synthesised in Table 3.5, we have discussed three main types of assessment in this chapter. Longitudinal monitoring of children's cognitive and socio-emotional development allows us to identify a developmental delay very early, and involve parents in practising ways of interacting and communicating that empower the child's learning processes (see chapter 4). Delays do not suggest *per se* that a young child will later show an intellectual disability. Describing the case of John we realised that a broad range of developmental and academic learning delays, and an IQ < 70 can be an expression of a range of heterogeneous factors, from early life adversities on brain development to difficulties with language, low processing speed and weaknesses of the executive functions' development. Whenever there is a concern for a child's cognitive delay, an evaluation of adaptive functioning is necessary to interpret the broadness of impairment and ground an associated diagnosis of intellectual disability, as reminded in table 3.5.

We proposed that a second-step assessment, not limited to evaluating IQ and adaptive skills, should be focused on orienting interventions by exploring a set of issues. What are the core deficits that may have generated cascading effects on the child's development? Which cognitive skills are relatively more preserved and can be used to construct compensatory strategies? Complementing the results of specific neuropsychological tests with the parents' and teachers' descriptions of the child's condition, and qualitative observations on the child's use of specific functions in ecologically valid contexts can lead us to compose a puzzle in which different perspectives on the child's behaviour, emotional reactions, contexts of experience, are put together.

Table 3.5 Three aims of assessment

Aims	Methods	Main objectives	Professionals
Identification of early delays	Interview with the child's parents Critical use of questionnaires and developmental scales Observing parent-child interaction	Monitoring cognitive and socio-emotional development Identify risk factors and emerging abilities Involve parents and children in early targeted psychoeducational actions	Pediatricians Developmental psychologists Speech Therapists
Diagnostic classification (see section 5.3 in chapter 1)	Interview with the child's parents A battery analyzing IQ indices and questionnaires evaluating the child's adaptive functioning Qualitative observations in the clinical context	Reconstruct the child's developmental history Consider the case's medical record Identify the correct diagnostic category/categories	Child Neuropsychiatrists Psychologists with expertise in developmental psychology and neuropsychology Psychologists with expertise in developmental psychopathology Speech Therapists Occupational therapists
Description of individual characteristics with a cognitive and socio-emotional profile (see section 5.4 in chapter 1)	Neuropsychological assessment Observing how specific neuropsychological functions are used in ecologically valid contexts Observing behaviors and emotional reactions in adult-child interactions in the clinical context Collecting the parents' observations on the child's emotional reactions, social life, desires, and aspirations	Answering some main questions: Are there core deficits that may have generated cascading effects on the child's development? Which basic cognitive functions can be used to compensate the most impaired ones and anchor the stimulation of complex skills? Which complex skills are emerging in some peculiar conditions and contexts? What types of contexts and activities could support learning, promote active involvement in experience, and keep a good fit with the child's preferences and desires?	

References

Abbeduto, L., McDuffie, A., Thurman, A. J., and Kover, S. T. (2016) Language development in individuals with intellectual and developmental disabilities: from phenotypes to treatments. *International Review of Research in Developmental Disabilities*, 50, 71–118. doi:10.1016/bs.irrdd.2016.05.006.

Adamson L. B., Bakeman, R., Deckner, D. F., and Nelson, P. B. (2012). Rating parent-child interactions: joint engagement, communication dynamics, and shared topics in autism, Down syndrome, and typical development. *Journal of Autism and Developmental Disorders*, 42, 2622–2635. doi:10.1007/s10803-012-1520-1.

Adamson, L. B., Bakeman, R., Suma, K., and Robins, D. L. (2019). An expanded view of joint attention: skill, engagement, and language in typical development and autism. *Child Development, 90(1)*, e1-e18. doi:10.1111/cdev.12973.

Albers, C. A., and Grieve, A. J. (2007). Test review: Bayley, N.(2006). Bayley scales of infant and toddler development – third edition. San Antonio, TX: Harcourt Assessment. *Journal of Psychoeducational Assessment*, 25(2), 180–190. doi:org/10.1177/0734282906297199.

Anderson, J. R., Fincham, J. M., and Douglass, S. (1997). The role of examples and rules in the acquisition of a cognitive skill. *Journal of Experimental Psychology: Learning, Memory, and Cognition*, 23, 932–945. doi:org/10.1037/0278–7393.23.4.932.

Baddeley, A. D. (2010). Working memory. *Current Biology*, 20, 136–140. doi:dx.doi.org/10.1016/j.cub.2009.12.014.

Bakeman, R., and Adamson, L. (1984). Coordinating attention to people and objects in mother-infant and peer-infant interactions. *Child Development*, 55(4), 1278–1289.

Bates, E., Benigni, L., Bretherton, I., Camaioni, L., and Volterra, V. (1979). *The Emergence of Symbols*. New York: Academic Press.

Bates, E. and Dick, F., (2002). Language, gesture, and the developing brain. *Developmental Psychobiology*, 40, 293–310. doi:10.1002/dev.10034.

Bavin, E., Prior, M., Reilly, S., Bretherton, L., Williams, J., Eadie, P., … Ukoumunne, O. (2008). The early language in Victoria study: predicting vocabulary at age one and two years from gesture and object use. *Journal of Child Language*, 35, 687–701. doi:org/10.1017/S0305000908008726.

Bayley, N. (2006). *Bayley Scales of Infant and Toddler Development – Third Edition*. San Antonio, TX: Harcourt Assessment.

Bishop, D. V. M. (2003). *Children's Communication Checklist-2 (CCC-2)*. London, UK: Pearson.

Bisiacchi, P. S., Cendron, M., and Gugliotta, M. (2014). *BVN 5–11: Batteria di valutazione neuropsicologica per l'età evolutiva*. Trento, Italy: Edizioni Centro Studi Erickson.

Blasi, V., Pirastru, A., Cabinio, M., Di Tella, S., Laganà, M. M., Giangiacomo, A.,… Baglio, F. (2020). Early life adversities and borderline intellectual functioning negatively impact limbic system connectivity in childhood: a connectomics-based study. *Frontiers Psychiatry*. 11: 497116. doi:10.3389/fpsyt.2020.497116.

Bonifacci, P., Tobia, V., Lami, L., and Snowling, M. J. (2014). *ALCE. Assessment di Lettura e Comprensione in Età Evolutiva* (Assessment of Reading and Comprehension in Developmental Age). Firenze: Hogrefe Editore

Bornman, J., Romski, M., Tonsing, K., Sevcik, R., White, R., Barton-Hulsey, A., and Morwane, R. (2018). Adapting and translating the Mullen Scales of Early Learning for the South African context. *South African Journal of Communication Disorders*, 65(1), 9 pages. doi:10.4102/sajcd.v65i1.571.

Bottema-Beutel, K. (2016). Associations between joint attention and language in autism spectrum disorder and typical development: A systematic review and meta-regression analysis. *Autism Research*, 9, 1021–1035. doi:10.1002/aur.1624.

Carpenter, M., Nagell, K., and Tomasello, M. (1998). Social cognition, joint attention, and communicative competence from 9 to 15 months of age. *Monographs of the Society for Research in Child Development*, 63(4), i–143.

Caselli, M. C. and Casadio, P. (1995). *Il Primo Vocabolario del Bambino*. Milano: Franco Angeli.

Caselli, M.C., Vicari, S., Longobardi, E., Lami, L., Pizzoli, C., and Stella, G. (1998). Gestures and words in early development of children with Down syndrome. *Journal of Speech, Language and Hearing Research*, 41. doi:10.1044/jslhr.4105.1125.

Caselli, M.C., Monaco, L., Trasciani, M., and Vicari, S. (2008). Language in Italian children with Down syndrome and with specific language impairment. *Neuropsychology*, 22, 27e35. doi:10.1037/0894-4105.22.1.27.

Chapman, R. S., Hesketh, L. J., and Kistler, D. J. (2002). Predicting longitudinal change in language production and comprehension in individuals with Down syndrome. *Journal of Speech, Language, and Hearing Research*, 45(5), 902–915. doi:10.1044/1092-4388(2002/073).

Charkaluk, M.-L., Rousseau, J., Calderon, J., Bernard, J.Y., Forhan, A., Heude, B., and Kaminski, M. (2017). Ages and stages questionnaire at 3 years for predicting IQ at 5–6 years. *Pediatrics*, 139 (4) e20162798. doi:10.1542/peds.2016-2798.

Cowan, N. (2014). Working memory underpins cognitive development, learning, and education. *Educational Psychology Review*, 26, 197–223. doi:10.1007/s10648–10013–9246-v.

D'Souza, D., D'Souza, H., and Karmiloff-Smith, A. (2017). Precursors to language development in typically and atypically developing infants and toddlers: the importance of embracing complexity. *Journal of Child Language*, 44, 591–627. doi:10.1017/S030500091700006X.

De Luca, M., Di Filippo, G., Judica, A., Spinelli, D., and Zoccolotti, P. (2005). *Test di denominazione rapida e ricerca visiva di colori, figure e numeri* (Rapid naming and visual search of colours, figures and numbers). Roma: IRCCS Fondazione Santa Lucia.

Desimoni, M. and Scalisi, M.T. (in preparation) *Prova di memoria di lavoro visuospaziale* (Visuospatial working memory test).

Di Nuovo, S. (2001). *Attenzione e concentrazione (con CD)* (Attention and concentration, with CD). Trento, Italy: Erickson.

Dimitrova, N., Özçalışkan, Ş. and Adamson, L.B. (2016). Parents' translations of child gesture facilitate word learning in children with autism, Down syndrome and typical development. *Journal of Autism and Developmental Disorders*, 46, 221–231. doi:10.1007/s10803–10015–2566–2567.

Fatigante, M. (2011). Resoconto e narrazione nei colloqui di consultazione con bambino e genitori. In M. Orsolini (Ed.), *Quando imparare è più difficile* (pp. 273–292). Roma: Carocci.

Fatigante, M., Bafaro, S., and Orsolini, M. (2015) "And you? What do you think then?" Taking care of thought and reasoning in intellectual disability. In M. O'Reilly and J. Lester (Eds.) *Child Mental Health: Discourse and Conversation Studies* (pp. 597–617). London: Palgrave Macmillan Publications.

Fenson, L., Marchman, V., Thal, D., Dale, P., Reznick, S., and Bates, E. (2007). *The MacArthur Communicative Development Inventories: User's guide and technical manual* (2nd ed.). Baltimore, MD: Brookes.

Global Research on Developmental Disabilities Collaborators (2018) Developmental disabilities among children younger than 5 years in 195 countries and territories, 1990–2016: a systematic analysis for the Global Burden of Disease Study. *Lancet Global Health*, 6 (10), e1100-e112. doi:10.1016/S2214-109X(18) 30309-7.

Hüsser, A., Fourdain, S. and Gallagher, A. (2020). Neuropsychologic assessment. In A. Gallagher, C. Bulteau, D. Cohen, and J. L. Michaud (Eds.), *Handbook of Clinical Neurology, Vol. 174, Neurocognitive Development: Disorders and Disabilities* (pp. 239–249). Amsterdam: Elsevier. doi:10.1016/B978–0-444-64148-9.00017-X.

Iverson, J. M., Longobardi, E., and Caselli, M. C. (2003). Relationship between gestures and words in children with Down's syndrome and typically developing children in the early stages of communicative development. *International Journal of Language and Communication Disorders, 38(2)*, 179–197. doi:10.1080/ 1368282031000062891..

Kaplan, E., Goodglass, H., and Weintraub, S. (1983). *Boston Naming Test.* Philadelphia: Lea and Febiger.

Riva D., Nichelli F., and Devoti M. (2000) Developmental aspects of verbal fluency and confrontation naming children. *Brain and Language*, 71, 267–284. doi:10.1006/brln.1999.2166.

Kaufman, A. S., and Kaufman, N. L. (2004). *Kaufman Assessment Battery for Children, Second Edition.* Circle Pines, MN: AGS.

Korkman, M., Kirk, U., and Kemp, S. L. (2007). *NEPSY II. Administrative Manual.* San Antonio, TX: Psychological Corporation (Italian version: Urgesi, C., Campanella, F. and Fabbro, F., NEPSY II: Contributo alla taratura Italiana. Firenze, Italy: Giunti, OS.

Laws, G., and Bishop, D. V. M. (2003). A comparison of language abilities in adolescents with Down syndrome and children with specific language impairment. *Journal of Speech Language Hearing Research*, 46, 1324. doi:10.1044/1092–4388(2003/103).

Laws, G., and Bishop, D. V. M. (2003). A comparison of language abilities in adolescents with Down syndrome and children with specific language impairment. *Journal of Speech, Language and Hearing Research*, 46, 1324. doi:10.1044/1092-4388.

Mammarella, I. C., Toso, C., Pazzaglia, F., and Cornoldi, C. (2008). *BVS-Corsi. Batteria per la valutazione della memoria visiva e spaziale. Con CD-ROM* (Battery for the assessment of visual and spatial memory). Edizioni Erickson.

Martin, G. E., Losh, M., Estigarribia, B., Sideris, J., and Roberts, J. (2013). Longitudinal profiles of expressive vocabulary, syntax and pragmatic language in boys with fragile X syndrome or Down syndrome. *International Journal of Language and Communication Disorders*, 48(4), 432–443. doi:10.1111/1460-6984.12019..

Martínez-Leal, R., Folch, A., Munir, K., Novell, R., and Salvador-Carulla, L. (2020). The Girona declaration on borderline intellectual functioning. *Lancet Psychiatry, 7(3)*, e8. doi:10.1016/S2215-0366(20)30001-8..

Marzocchi, G. M., Re, A. M., and Cornoldi, C. (2010). *BIA. Batteria italiana per l'ADHID per la valutazione dei bambini con deficit di attenzione-iperattività. Con DVD e CD-ROM.* Trento, Italy: Erickson.

McHale, J. P., and Dickstein, S. (2019). The interpersonal context of early childhood development: a systemic approach to infant–family assessment. In R. DelCarmen-Wiggins and A. S. Carter (Eds.), *The Oxford handbook of Infant, Toddler, and Preschool Mental Health Assessment* (pp. 79–96). Oxford University Press.

Morin-Lessard, E., Hentges, R.F., Tough, S.C. and Graham, S.A. (2021). Developmental pathways between infant gestures and symbolic actions, and children's communicative skills at age 5: findings from the all our families pregnancy cohort. *Child Development*, 92, 799–810. doi:10.1111/cdev.13567.

Mullen, E.M. (1995). *Mullen Scales of Early Learning Manual.* Circle Pines, MN: American Guidance Service, Inc.

Mundy, P., Delgado, C., Block, J., Hogan, A. and Seibert, J. (2003). *A Manual for the Abridged Early Social Communication Scales (ESCS).* Available through the University of Miami Psychology Department, Coral Gables; Florida.

Orsolini, M., Melogno, S., Latini, N., Penge, R., and Conforti, S. (2015). Treating verbal working memory in a boy with intellectual disability. *Frontiers in Psychology*, 6, 1091. doi:10.3389/fpsyg.2015.01091

Orsolini, M., Sechi, E., Maronato, C., Corcelli, A., Penge, R. (2001) The nature of phonological delay in children with SLI. International Journal of Language and Communication Disorders. 36(1), 63–90.

Pazzaglia, F., Palladino, P., and De Beni, R. (2000). Presentazione di uno strumento per la valutazione della memoria di lavoro verbale e sua relazione con i disturbi della comprensione. *Psicologia clinica dello sviluppo*, 4(3), 465–486.

Pettenati, P., Sekine, K., Congestrì, E. and Volterra, V.(2012). A Comparative study on representational gestures in Italian and Japanese children. *Journal of Nonverbal Behaviour*, 36, 149–164. doi:10.1007/s10919–10011–0127–0.

Pulina, F., Vianello, R., and Lanfranchi, S. (2019). Chapter three – Cognitive profiles in individuals with Down syndrome. *International Review of Research in Developmental Disabilities*, 56, 67–92. doi:10.1016/bs. irrdd.2019.06.002.

Raven, J. C., Court, J. H., and Raven, J. (1992). *Raven's Coloured Progressive Matrices*. Oxford: Oxford Psychologist Press (Italian normative data: Belacchi, C., Scalisi, T.G., Cannoni, E., and Cornoldi C. Taratura italiana del test Matrici di Raven Forma Colore (CPM-47). Manuale. Firenze, Italy: Giunti Organizzazioni Speciali, 2008).

Reynolds, C. R., and Bigler, E. D. (1994). *Test of Memory and Learning (TOMAL)*. Austin, TX: Pro-Ed. (Italian version: 2003. Test TEMA – Memoria e Apprendimento. Trento: Erikson).

Schonhaut, L., Pérez, M., Armijo, I., and Maturana, A. (2020). Comparison between Ages and Stages Questionnaire and Bayley Scales, to predict cognitive delay in school age. *Early Human Development*, 141, 104933. doi:10.1016/j. earlhumdev.2019.104933.

Sparrow, S. S., Cicchetti, D. V., and Balla, D. A. (2005). *Vineland Adaptive Behavior Scales Vineland-Ii: Survey Forms Manual*. Minneapolis, MN: Pearson. (Italian version Balboni, G., Belacchi, C., Bonichini, S., and Coscarelli, A. (2016). Vineland-II. Vineland Adaptive Behavior Scales Second Edtion-Survey Forms. Adattamento italiano. Manuale).

Stein, M. T. and Lukasik, M. K. (2009). Developmental screening and assessment: infants, toddlers, and pre-schoolers. In W. B. Carey, A. C. Crocker, W. L. Coleman, E. R. Elias, H. M. Feldman (Eds.) *Developmental-Behavioral Pediatrics* (Fourth Edition) (pp. 785–796). Philadelphia: W.B. Saunders.

Stella, G., Pizzoli, C., and Tressoldi, P. (2000). *Peabody Picture Vocabulary Test – Revised (PPVT-r) – Italian adaptation*. Torino: Omega, 2000.

Stern, D. N. (1985). *The Interpersonal World of the Infant: A View from Psychoanalysis and Developmental Psychology*. New York: Basic Books.

Suraniti, S., Ferri, R., and Neri, V. (2009). *Test For Reception of Grammar-TROG-2*. Italian edition. Firenze: Giunti OS.

Tomasello, M. (2018). *Becoming Human: A Theory of Ontogeny*. Cambridge (MA): Belknap Press of Harvard University Press.

Veldhuizen, S., Clinton, J., Rodriguez, C., Wade, T. J., and Cairney, J. (2014). Concurrent validity of the ages and stages questionnaires and Bayley developmental scales in a general population sample. *Academic Pediatrics*, 15, 231–237. doi:10.1016/j.acap.2014.08.002..

Velikonja, T., Edbrooke-Childs, J., Calderon, A., Sleed, M., Brown, A. and, Deighton, J. (2017). The psychometric properties of the Ages and Stages Questionnaires for ages 2–2.5: a systematic review. *Child Care Health Development*. 2017 January43(1):1–17. doi:10.1111/cch.12397.

Vygotsky, L. S. (1978). *Mind in Society: The Development of Higher Psychological Processes*. Cambridge, MA: Harvard University Press.

Zampini, L., and D'Odorico, L. (2009). Communicative gestures and vocabulary development in 36-month-old children with Down's syndrome. *International Journal of Language and Communication Disorders*, 44, 1063–1073. doi:10.1080/13682820802398288.

Chapter 4

Intervention to empower children's learning

Margherita Orsolini and Sergio Melogno

Research on the effects of an enriched environment shows that learning processes can change certain crucial brain characteristics in mice, even in the presence of genetic variations resembling human genetic syndromes (Restivo et al., 2005). Such evidence suggests that experience with enriched environments can also empower children's learning processes and therefore affect brain plasticity. A cognitive stimulation tuned to a child's weaknesses and strengths profile should be interwoven with emotional and social sharing, active engagement induced by novelty and explorative behaviour, and systematic exercise.

The evidence overviewed in the present chapter suggests that intervention focused on early caregiver-child communication and, starting from preschool children, training focused on both general learning mechanisms and metacognitive skills, can produce promising effects. Such training should alternate with an intervention focused on more specific skills, such as motor and practical skills, academic learning, or social behaviours.

1 Parents-child interaction and communication: the main component of an enriched environment

1.1 The characteristics of enriched environments

How can intervention influence developmental trajectories when children's acquisition of human abilities is undermined by the brain's characteristics? There is not yet a conclusive answer to such a question as evidence-based treatments for children with intellectual disabilities are still rare and experimental research on the neurophysiological effects of intervention programs is also scarce. However, clear evidence is provided by research on animal models that brain characteristics can be changed by experience, even in cases when genetic mutations altered a brain's typical

DOI: 10.4324/9781003220367-4

development. In the 1960s, researchers at UC Berkeley showed for the first time that mice brain plasticity could be dramatically affected by an enriched environment leading to higher performance in learning and memory tasks (Rosenzweig et al., 1962). An enriched environment is characterized by socialization, exploration induced by novelty, and exercise. Mice are living in cages equipped with different objects eliciting movement (e.g., plastic tubes, wheels); the objects are regularly changed to maintain novelty; mice live in a group of four-five individuals. When reared in such environments, mice show performances and brain changes that are not displayed by mice living in cages with standard or impoverished conditions. It is not clear precisely which of the components of an enriched environment have the greatest role in inducing brain changes, but it is likely that the synergistic action of all the factors (i.e., exercise, novelty and exploration, sociality) involve the neurotrophic factors promoting synaptic plasticity. Research on the effects of an enriched environment shows that learning processes can change some crucial brain characteristics in mice, such as dendritic arborisation and neurogenesis (Garthe et al., 2016), even in presence of genetic variations resembling human genetic syndromes (Restivo et al., 2005). Such evidence suggests that experience with enriched environments might also empower children's learning processes and therefore affect brain plasticity.

Each component of an enriched environment for mice has extremely more complex implications for human beings. For children, sociality is not only playing with peers but a question of building warm and secure relationships with caregivers, constructing mental representations of others' feelings and intentions, acquiring symbolic means to communicate, and participating in cooperative actions. Exercise cannot concern only movement and should target a wide range of abilities allowing a person to adapt to the environment and reach personal autonomy. Novelty can elicit motivation, exploration, and problem-solving in mice, and at the same time, these same crucial components of cognitive activity are intertwined with higher-level abilities such as reasoning, self-construction and self-esteem in human beings. Thus, intervention objectives obviously must be more complex and more clearly articulated for human beings and the goals of interventions cannot be confined to improving performance in memory and learning tasks. However, the empowerment of learning which is induced by enriched environments can inspire intervention for children with ID. The challenge for parents, therapists, and schoolteachers is to collaborate to implement multidimensional interventions including all the components which characterize enriched environments for human beings. A cognitive stimulation tuned to a child's weaknesses and strengths profile should be interwoven with emotional and social sharing, active engagement induced by novelty and explorative behaviour, and systematic exercise.

There is an important factor that is absent in even the most enriched environments for mice but present in different degrees in the experience of human beings: children grow with caregivers and other adults (teachers, therapists) who attempt to convey skills and knowledge using *cultural learning* (Vygotsky, 1978). Human environment is enriched by indirect teaching/learning processes that are conveyed through interactions and relations, and are mediated by symbolic means, language in primis.

As emphasized by Vygotsky (1978), there is a reciprocal dependency between learning and development. What a child can do and learn without any help is deeply constrained by his or her developmental level and current brain organization. Conversely, the nurturing learning that children experience through supportive social interactions helps advance development, especially when the interaction involves a person who is cognitively and emotionally tuned to the child's expressions and actions.

"One step only in the learning process can mean one hundred steps in development" (Vygotskij, 1934, p.202): the consequences of learning can be deep and change the functional links between different cognitive processes, as when a child starts to read not only to recognize and name written words but also to understand the meaning of what has been read.

Following Vygotskij's teachings, we propose the metaphor that learning is *wider* than a single brain. It uses the brain circuits of different people (e.g., caregivers, teachers, therapists, and the child), to transmit cultural tools (e.g., mnemonic devices, maps representing space, symbols representing meaning) linking a child to the intelligent creations of entire generations of other human beings. Using cultural tools – language in the first place – contributes in unique ways to learning, enhances children's participation in daily routines and social life, and the construction of the individual personality and identity.

1.2 The effects of sensitivity and responsiveness in parent-child interaction

In this section we consider an important characteristic of enriched environments: the caregiver-child relationship and communication. Starting from the research on mother-child attachment bonds (see Ainsworth et al., 1978), the quality of responsiveness in parent-child interaction has been related to a secure attachment. Infants who have received prompt, warm, and sensitive responses to their signals of distress and who have been accepted as unique individuals, show a relationship with their mothers characterized by trust and emotional connection.

Sensitivity to the infant's emotional cues and a tendency to maintain a positive, lively mother-child interaction, play an important role in children's social and emotional development. In a study on a sample of 1,215 mother-child couples (NICHD, 1999), two groups – distinguished by the presence or absence of clinical signs of maternal depression – were compared at different points of the child's age (1, 6, 15, 24, and 36 months). Measures of maternal sensitivity were gathered by videotaping and then coding mother-child free-play. Child behaviour was also analysed in free play with their mothers and evaluated – when children were 36 months – in terms of social competence, presence of disruptive behaviours, social cooperation, and cognitive and language development. The results of this study show that maternal sensitivity during free play with their child varied as a function of whether a woman reported elevated symptoms of depression consistently over the three years of the study. Family income turned out to affect the expressions of sensitivity, with depressed lower-income women showing a tendency to have the lowest sensitivity. Maternal sensitivity was an extremely strong predictor of children's development, over and above the presence of the mother's depressive symptoms. Higher maternal sensitivity was related to children's fewer disruptive behaviours and higher social cooperation at 36 months of age.

Studies grounded on a sociocultural framework have targeted not only mothers' sensitivity but also the responsiveness shown by the contiguity and contingency of the caregivers' uptake of the child's actions. For instance, when 14-month-old children were observed exploring an object (Tamis-LeMonda et al., 2013), responsiveness was shown by mothers who produced a temporally contiguous reciprocal action and a semantically contingent verbal response (e.g., pointing or touching, and simultaneously naming the object that the child was exploring). Even if the children's explorative behaviours were not intentionally communicative, the tendency of mothers from different cultural and ethnic backgrounds (Tamis-LeMonda et al., 2013) was to maintain and respond to the child's focus of attention by producing a contingent reciprocal action and verbal response. Several studies show that such type of caregivers' responsive behaviour is associated with children's language skills, cognitive development, and social competence (Landry et al., 2008; Lugo-Gil and Tamis-LeMonda, 2008; Tamis-LeMonda et al., 2004).

Among the most important developmental effects of parents' responsiveness are those concerning the children's attention. Infants' attention was observed at 9 months of age in two play conditions with the same unfamiliar adult (Miller et al., 2009): in the *responsive condition* the adult interacted following the infant's attentional focus; in the "intrusive" condition the adult-guided the infant's attention toward some new target. It emerged that infants had longer durations of sustained attention when interacting in the responsive condition. Similar results emerged in a study in which caregivers interacted with their 13–16 month-old infants either maintaining (responsive condition) or shifting to a new target (intrusive condition) the infant's attention. It was observed that children displayed sustained attention for longer intervals and were more engaged when the caregiver interacted in the responsive condition (Miller and Gros-Louis, 2013).

Why might it be so important that children have longer times of attention directed toward a socially shared focus? We considered in chapter 3 (section 2.4) that when children respond to joint attention, they can cooperate with caregivers on a shared action. The adult can thus complement what the child is already doing by proposing a simple acknowledgement (e.g., touching the same object), a verbal label (e.g., eh… *that's a truck*), or a description (e.g., *what a big truck*). The contingency between the child's action and the caregiver's language input facilitates language learning (Tamis-LeMonda et al., 2014). The child's sustained attention and emotional involvement provide those neurophysiological energies that support a deeper processing and memory encoding of the new information passed along by the caregiver. Sustained attention associated with emotional involvement generates the enhancement of neural activity and learning (Striano et al., 2006; see also Dehaene, 2021) within shared attention episodes.

In sum, as illustrated by Figure 4.1, sensitivity in caregiver-child interaction enhances social motivation, results in a sense of self-efficacy

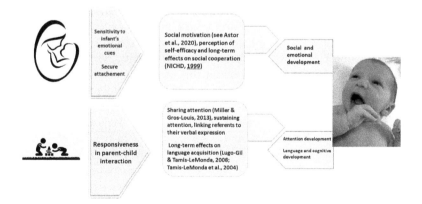

Figure 4.1 The reciprocal influence between the outcome of caregivers-child interaction and the child's developmental profile

(i.e., the child experiences that her expressions and actions lead to advantageous consequences), and has long-term effects on social cooperation. Responsiveness in parent-child interaction motivates sharing attention, and make children link, in a temporally short window, the objects and actions that are perceptually salient for them with the caregiver's symbolic means. Referents of the caregivers' words can be identified easier by children within shared attention episodes (Tamis-LeMonda et al., 2014). Thus social motivation and sharing attention operate as longitudinal facilitators of *cultural learning* (Vygotsky, 1978).

As suggested in Figure 4.1, there is a dynamical reciprocal influence between the outcome of caregivers-child interaction and the child's developmental profile (see Masek et al., 2021). For instance, temperamental characteristics such as a child's low emotional regulation affect social cooperation. In the same way, the child's cognitive characteristics (e.g., her short-term memory) influence language acquisition. On the other hand, the child's socio-emotional and language developmental levels will be enhanced by the learning experience involved with the caregivers-child interaction.

1.3 Coaching parents to increase responsiveness in parent-child interaction

In the Universal Declaration of Human Rights, childhood is entitled to special care and assistance, and the family – as the natural environment for the growth and well-being of children – is considered to be the target of *the necessary protection and assistance so that it can fully assume its responsibilities within the community.* This principle is particularly important for children with developmental disabilities. If society recognizes the need for special care for children who are at risk of developmental disabilities, intervention should start from the family to foster the early interactions and bond relationships between a child and her/his parents.

Parents of children showing risk factors challenging their cognitive and social development can benefit from intervention programs aiming to increase parents' responsiveness. One of such programs is Responsive Teaching (RT) (Mahoney and MacDonald, 2007; Mahoney and Nam, 2011) which coaches parents and other caregivers to use responsiveness strategies in interactions with young children. The idea is not to transform parents into therapists, but to make-the-most-of everyday routines and home play situations to support the functional processes that promote learning and development. Functional processes such as social play, intentional communication, empathy, are the main objectives that parents are invited, week after week, to address by practising responsive strategies.

Unlike intervention delivered by specialised figures such as physical or speech therapists, RT aims to encourage children to engage in doing things they already know by increasing active involved participation in home routines, play, and other contexts of everyday life. For instance, as social play is concerned, parents are coached to engage in balanced, give-and-take activities in which their child contributes to the activity as much as they do. First, parents can encourage children to play more frequently and for longer periods and use responsive strategies to motivate the child to initiate or continue what she finds interesting. The concept proposed to parents is that the more children practice even their repetitive play behaviours within social play, the more they can propose some new information that gradually can become incorporated into the child's play action.

Parents are instructed to respond to whatever play activity their children initiate. Children should be the ones who make choices about what toys and objects to play with, and how to play (see the strategy *expect my child to interact* among the responsive strategies in Box 4.1). Parents' imitation of a child's action with some variation can work as an indirect suggestion leading the child to learn alternative ways of doing similar things. Parents can also provide guidance and suggestions related to what the child is looking at, or what she intended to communicate. Box 4.1 shows some of the specific responsive strategies parents are instructed to use in an initial phase to promote social play, and the issues discussed between parents and an expert to promote *initiation* in the child's social play.

Box 4.1 Coaching parents to promote their child's social play (from Mahoney and Perales, 2019; page 65)

Level 1 Strategies

1   Use mirroring and parallel play to join the activity
2   Act as a playful partner
3   Imitate actions and communications
4   Take one turn and wait
5   Play face to face games without toys
6   Expect my child to interact

Level 2 Strategies

1   Follow my child's lead
2   Communicate without asking questions

> **Discussion topics: Level 1–2 Initiation**
> - Children begin or change activities on their own
> - Parents promote children's active learning by following and supporting rather than leading their activity
> - Children's initiations occur across a variety of situations, such as starting a new game, changing activity with the same toy, asking for help to solve problems

Parents of children with developmental delays are encouraged to accept their child's play behaviours that may appear regressive, such as putting objects in the mouth. Such actions do not mean that the child does not have the physical ability to use objects in more functional ways but that the objects are not conceptualised yet for their functional characteristics (something to comb hair, or feed a doll, etc.). Parents are invited to consider that any activity is an opportunity for learning if the child is actively engaged. Even low-level play activities provide the important experience of initiating actions, implementing them within a social, emotionally warm context. The learning opportunities offered by such an informal context complement the more specialized experiences the child can have when involved in speech or physical therapy. Parents are also advised to choose toys that their child can manipulate or handle autonomously, otherwise, they will be forced to give help and the child will not have a chance to initiate a play activity.

After this short overview of what is, in our opinion, a very well designed curriculum to promote children's experience and learning processes through responsive strategies, we consider the evidence stemming from studies that have tested early intervention programs promoting parent-child communication and interaction.

1.4 Early intervention programs involving parents of children with developmental delays or intellectual disabilities: evidence on the effects

Karaaslan and Mahoney (2015) investigated two groups of 17 Turkish children (age range 2–6 years) with intellectual disabilities (in both groups, the majority had Down syndrome, a small subgroup had been diagnosed with autism). Children of the control group only received two days a week of early intervention at their local special rehabilitation centre. Children of the experimental group, beside continuing their usual intervention at the local special rehabilitation centre, participated in four months of biweekly mother-child home sessions in which the mother interacted with the child trying to apply the responsive strategies she had been taught in an instruction phase. Children of both groups were pre- and post-tested with a developmental scale, a rating scale that assessed the parents' interactive style, and one scale that rated the child's inter- active engagement (persistence, social cooperation, joint attention, and initiation). The parent-child interaction in the experimental sessions was also analysed to identify the mother's use of strategies. The results of this study show that there was a significant change in the mothers' use of responsive strategies in the experimental group, and there were large statistically significant impacts of the experimental intervention on the children's performance on the developmental scale. Interestingly, the children's developmental advances in the post-test were not directly related to the changes in the mothers' use of responsive strategies, as they were mediated by the changes in the children's interactive engage- ment. The mothers' changes in responsiveness were related to children's changes in *interactive engagement* behaviours (such as persistence, shared attention, initiation). This latter factor had the greatest weight in explaining the pre- and post-test changes in children's language and cognitive development. The results of this study replicated those reported in previous research work (Karaaslan and Mahoney, 2013).

Brown and Woods (2015) analyzed the effects of a parent-implemented intervention targeting parent-child communication. They involved 9 tod- dlers (age range 12–28 months) with Down syndrome, autism spectrum disorder, and developmental delays (three children for each condition) and their caregivers who were coached using the KTTP, a program combining the use of responsive strategies (contingent uptakes of the child's focus, imitating the child's action) and behavioural procedures such as responding to the child by selecting and teaching specific language targets appropriate to the child's language level. Table 4.1 provides examples of the commu- nication strategies parents were coached to use. Each family identified the home routines (e.g., play, early literacy, chores) in which to practice the intervention strategies and were coached also observing an expert who used the target communication strategies with the child. In each intervention session, there were four people: an expert, one parent and the child, and a research assistant who video recorded. Each weekly session lasted about one hour and the intervention included 24 sessions. The study used multi- ple-baseline single-case studies, in which each child's communication expressions were observed at different times before the intervention, within several intervention sessions, and in a post-intervention maintenance phase (after 1 and 3 months by the end of the intervention). The child's commu- nication was coded in terms of expressive components: gestures, vocalizations, single words, two words, multiple words utterances. The coding system was based on an observative measure with normative data to compare each child with chronological age norms. Before the intervention, the large majority (7 out of 9 children) showed severe communication delays (more than 2 standard deviations below the age mean), whereas two cases had a mild delay (1 standard deviation below the mean). After the end of the intervention, in the maintenance phase, only two children continued to show severe communication delays, and the large majority showed either an age-appropriate communicative level or a mild delay. All nine children increased at least one step toward the appropriate age level in communication (e.g., from no communication to one signed word, or from single-word to two-word utterances). A statistical analysis suited to single-case studies showed that the parents' measures of responsive and teaching strategies were closely associated with the measures of the children's communication. The children's pre-post intervention progression in communication was statistically significant for all the cases. A survey given in the maintenance phase of the study suggested that parents considered themselves to be effective in supporting their children's communication and that they continue to use the strategies in daily routines and activities.

Despite the limited number of cases involved, this study used a rigorous single-case method that showed the feasibility of an early intervention in which parents collaborate with an expert, participate in the selection of the learning target appropriate for their child and choose the home routines to engage in enhanced communication with their child. Brown and Wood's (2015) study extended to a younger group of children, the findings emerging from a previous study using a similar intervention program with a larger sample of preschool children with Down syndrome (Kaiser and Roberts, 2013).

1.5 Early intervention programs in low- and middle-income countries

In several low- and middle-income countries (LMIC) early intervention involving children with developmental delays is implemented through community-based rehabilitation in which non-professionals are trained to provide educational activities to children in their homes. The Portage project is one of those home-based early interventions whose manuals and curricula have been adapted for LMICs (Shin et al., 2009). The Portage program has been translated into several languages and used to train parents in countries where there are no early intervention centres. It targets both basic functions, such as gross motor skills (e.g., locomotion, balance, coordination) and academic learning (e.g., early literacy

Table 4.1 Examples of the communication intervention strategies (Brown and Wood, 2015)

Responsive Strategies	Examples
Mirroring: Imitating the child's actions and mapping a word or phrase to the action	The child raises her arms and the parent does the same saying *up*
Expansions: Responding to the child's utterance/gesture/sign with an expanded form of communication	The child points to a cookie out of reach and says *uh* the parent says *cookie* The child says *ball* and the parent replies *bounce ball*
Teaching strategy	
Prompting The child makes a request and the parent, after proposing without success an open question or a two-choice question, gives a prompt targeting a slightly higher form of communication	The child seemed to ask for a soap The parent says: *what do you want?* The child does not answer and the parent after a few seconds says: *do you want brush or soap?* The child does not answer and the parent gives a prompt: *says soap*

and math). A preliminary study involving 30 preschool-aged children with intellectual disabilities in Vietnam (Shin et al., 2009) evaluated the effectiveness of the Portage project delivered for 12 months by special education teachers through home visits. In this first study, the children's initial adaptive functioning was moderate or severe and the intervention had a large effect in the domain of daily living skills (e.g., being able to eat, or wash independently) that had been targeted with a special focus. A further study (Shin and Duc, 2017) involved 4-year-old children who had mild delays in adaptive functioning and were trained by students through weekly home visits for 6 months. Students came from the Psychology or Pedagogy departments and had received 3 months of weekly training on the Portage program. The students worked on improving children's academic and socialization skills, and the intervention yielded significant improvement in the areas of socialization, communication, motor skills, as shown by the different pre- post-test gains in the experimental and control group.

The World Health Organization has included guidelines for sensitive and responsive caregiving in a program developed to improve the care of young children in LMIC (Eschel et al., 2006; WHO, 2012). The *Caregiver Skills Training* programme addresses children aged 2 to 9 years of age with heterogeneous developmental difficulties. Using a family-centred approach designed to be delivered by non-specialists (nurses, community-based workers or peer caregivers) in Pakistan, the programme trains the care-givers on how to use every day play and home activities and routines as opportunities for learning and development (Salomone et al., 2019). There are group sessions aimed at teaching parents some basic strategies to facilitate children's development. The training is complemented by three individual home visits allowing the program to be tailored to each child's developmental level and the family's priorities. Home visits include one-to-one coaching that provides the caregiver with individua-lized feedback oriented to develop competencies suiting the child's needs. The program's teaching is implemented within the family con-text, by transforming everyday activities and routines (e.g. meals, bath time) into learning opportunities that target the child's active engage-ment and initiative and work with a specified structure. Pilot testing of such programs both in high and medium-low income settings is still underway.

Early intervention programs are particularly important to address the social inequality that tends to be associated with ID. As shown by Emerson (2003), families who are caring for children with ID are at higher risk of socio-economic disadvantage, and socio-economic depri-vation tends to be associated with poorer psychological outcomes for mothers in general, including those of children with ID. Thus children with ID who are growing up in a family with socio-economic disadvantage are more likely to interact with mothers suffering the psychological consequences of low and unstable socioeconomic conditions.

1.6 Lifelong support to parents of children with intellectual disabilities

Selma Fraiberg, a social worker and brilliant psychoanalyst practised a new way of fostering children's early development through her "kitchen-table therapy" taking place within families' homes and with therapists who facilitated loving relationships between parents and children. Observing the interactions between blind infants and their mothers, Fraiberg noticed that most children showed a consistent delay in the first appearance of a smile in response to a mother's stimulation. The mothers seemed not particularly involved with eliciting their child's emotional responses as they were somehow blocked. The absence of all the signals that are normally con-veyed by vision elicited in the mothers the sensation of being left out of their blind infant. *How will he/she know me?* This was one of the first questions mothers were asking. Fraiberg's pioneering work was focused on helping mothers to find alternative ways to experience children, find pleasure in interacting with them, using the hints and interpretations that therapists drew from their observation of the target child and knowledge of human development (Fraiberg, 1971).

Similarly to what may occur to parents of blind children, mothers and fathers of developmentally delayed children may have experienced that their intuitive ways of adapting to the child's affective and communicative needs did not work. *How can we elicit her gaze and smile? How can we involve this child in playing?* Interacting with infants who tend to be slightly passive, have limited attention abilities, or produce signals that are not immediately interpretable, may block the dynamic and reciprocally rewarding interaction that is foundational to children's development.

An intention to teach and exploit every occasion to somehow induce the child to reach a more advanced developmental level may lead some caregivers towards a directive rather than a responsive style of communication. Findings for directiveness and intrusiveness emerging from developmental research are mixed, however, with some studies showing that parents of children with Down syndrome or developmental delays use more directiveness and intrusiveness compared to parents of typically developing children matched for mental or chronological age, while other studies did not find differences between the two groups of parents (see the review of Daunhauer et al., 2017).

Families of children with intellectual disabilities experience several stressors that put at risk their socio-emotional well-being. There may be a parents' challenge, as daily routines are burdened by the child's care responsibilities, and participation in social events is often hindered by the parents' perceived acceptability of their child's behaviour. Such factors lead to a perception of social isolation and a need for support. There are also child challenges, such as strong difficulties with academic learning, the anger reactions with which the child can react to her perceived social isolation, the disruptive behaviours that may emerge at school.

Involving parents of children with intellectual or other types of disability in positive parenting programs can increase the family's wellbeing and have a positive impact on the child's behaviour problems. Stepping Stones Triple P-Positive Parenting Program (SSTP; Sanders et al., 2004) is based on the social learning theory of Bandura and combines teaching strategies to improve parent-child communication, prevent children's emotional and behavioural problems and treat specific difficulties. The basic objectives are creating a warm, nurturing environment, adopting an assertive style to teach social rules, observing the context of problem behaviours, adapting to the child's developmental level, supporting the child's participation in social life (see Ruane and Carr, 2019). Level 4 of the SSTP program targets a wide range of clinically significant children's behaviour problems, and learning difficulties, involving parents in coaching a wide range of skills for managing challenging behaviours. An evaluation of several studies investigating the outcomes of such programs when parents of children with disabilities were involved (Ruane and Carr, 2019), showed a range of significant treatment effects (with a medium or large effect size): a reduction of the children's behaviour problems, improvement in the parental style, increase of the parents' perception of parenting self-efficacy. Positive parenting training seems to also improve the perceived well-being of mothers of children with ID (Ashori et al., 2019).

The SSTP program, similarly to other intervention programs, has a licensed publisher or supplier organization that merchandises practitioner and parent resources, along with professional and technical support. Although programs such as SSTP have been effectively adapted to culturally diverse contexts (Sanders et al., 2021), their high costs make open access programs (such as the *Parenting for Lifelong Health* of the World Health Organization) more useful to pursue wider dissemination of positive parenting.

1.7 Sharing the objectives of intervention with parents

The case of Lorenzo, an 8-year-old child with a diagnosis of mild intellectual disability, has been briefly introduced in chapter 3 (see section 4.1). After the initial interview, we had hypothesized that the parents' claims of the low autonomy shown by the child, and Lorenzo's angry behaviours with his parents, were signs of rather inconsistent parental caring and impoverished parent-child communication. At the end of our assessment, we proposed to Lorenzo's parents that observing their play interaction with the child could be important to share the intervention objectives. Lorenzo's mother decided to be involved in four sessions that were carried out in our university clinic, in a room in which there were playdough, colours and sheets for drawing, picture books. In the first session, Lorenzo's mother alternated spending time looking at picture books by herself and asking the child what he was doing. Lorenzo's answers were very short, with no attempt to involve the mother in his actions. Discussing later what had been observed in that session, Lorenzo's mother claimed that being present with Lorenzo while he was doing something on his own was their typical way of being together. The psychologist acknowledged that such a way of being together might induce Lorenzo to be autonomous but doubted that could be functional to enhance his emotional and cognitive development. Some guidelines to engage in responsive communication with Lorenzo were proposed, and in the second session, Lorenzo and his mother participated in a parallel play in which they had the argument that is reported in Box 4.2. Discussing with Lorenzo's mother the week following that session, the psychologist acknowledged that an important mother-child dialogue had occurred, in which the child had shown good reasoning abilities. Lorenzo's mother was eventually asked to share thoughts on the child's anger. What might have triggered Lorenzo's angry reaction in that session? The answer was that Lorenzo was very often angry with her mother and that he simply did not want to do what she asked (i.e., going to the swimming pool). It was suggested that Lorenzo might have been disappointed that his justification (i.e., better not go to the swimming pool if you have a cough) had not been considered by his mother, as if it was an unimportant thought. The psychologist proposed that explaining motives and reasons underlying what to do or what not to do is a reciprocal contribution that can create trust and mutual understanding in parent-child discourse. She also proposed a metaphor: Lorenzo and his mother were as two fiancés who had been reciprocally disappointed for some reason. Being insecure about the other's love made their communication sometimes harsh, or distant, and hindered the pleasure of being together. Showing interest in Lorenzo's thoughts, looking very often at the child, collaborating in play actions, were the objectives proposed for the next mother-child sessions. A week after such a discussion, Lorenzo's mother narrated that for the first time, entering the house with Lorenzo, she allowed the child to open the door with the key. *I thought he was able to do it, and in fact, I was surprised to have waited so much to allow him to do this.* Sharing with us the idea that the child had to be considered for his thinking abilities, may have induced Lorenzo's mother to a deeper reflection on Lorenzo's skills. The key episode, and the way it had been narrated, also suggested to the psychologist a more symbolic interpretation: *this mother allowed her child to open her heart.*

In designing an intervention, we agreed to focus on two main medium-term objectives: enhancing Lorenzo's expressive and receptive vocabulary and improving arithmetic skills that were much behind an age expected level. There were activities both for home and clinic intervention. At home, Lorenzo's parents were asked to involve the child in playing card games with numbers and interacting with picture books that were read aloud by his parents. In the clinic, we used social pretend play, conversation, reading comprehension activities to enhance language, and several types of games to stimulate arithmetic concepts. After two months of intervention, Lorenzo's father came to visit us without an appointment. He was visibly moved and wanted to thank us because going back home in the last few days he had found Lorenzo playing with his mother with much fun. *Lorenzo learned to play with whatever object he can use at home. He may transform toothpicks into soldiers, books in houses. He is very creative and talks a lot. His anger seems to be disappeared.*

Box 4.2

Table 4.2 Lorenzo (LO:) and his mother (MO:) are using play dough sitting at each other's side. Lorenzo had been ill and did not go to school in the last few days. A video camera is recording their interaction.

MO: You do know that you will be back at school tomorrow, don't you?	Modelling from play dough
LO: But not in the swimming pool, right?	Lorenzo stops his action with playdough and looks at the mother
Mo: Yes, with your brother.	
LO: To the swimming pool? Have I to go there?	Looking to her mother
MO: You will not be forced, but you did not go last Friday.	Looking to Lorenzo
LO: But I have a cough!	Screaming and looking to the mother
MO: Ehhh, until tomorrow ... will you still have a cough?	Modelling from play dough
LO: Oh, If I have a cough I do not go, right?	Screaming and looking to the mother
MO: All right, do whatever you like.	Modelling from play dough
LO: Mom but you...	Screaming
MO: (interrupting Lorenzo) Why are you screaming, mommy?	Looking to the child and leaning towards him
LO: Because, are you stupid? In the swimming pool with a cough?	Screaming and looking to the mother
MO: But you do not have a cough as Friday	Modelling from play dough
LO: But what?	Screaming and looking to the mother Lorenzo slams playdough on the table and turns away from his mother
MO: (4 seconds) Listen, we'll think about it later, right?	Modelling from play dough
LO: We'll think about it later...	Turning his head to look to the mother
MO: We will think about it. Are you getting tired? Mm?... Are you angry? You do not like going to the swimming pool anymore?	Modelling from play dough
LO: I have a cough now	Turning his head to look to the mother and almost crying

MO: Then you don't have to go, but just get it over with now, ok?	Modelling from play dough
(…)	
LO: I cannot go to the swimming pool with a cough	Looking to the mother
MO: I do not care, we will think about it tomorrow, be good now	Modelling from play dough

Discussing and sharing the targets of intervention with parents requires also negotiating concepts on the source of children's learning errors and often rigid behaviour. As errors are concerned, some parents of children with intellectual disabilities may tend to interpret them as generated by low intelligence, related to the child's global developmental delay. When more specific concepts are proposed concerning the child's errors (e.g., attention, inhibitory control, working memory, literal interpretation of meanings), a pathway to move development ahead can be considered with a more positive attitude. For instance, parents can share how to facilitate attention by preparing a setting that is not full of distracting stimuli, how to increase times of sustained attention by stimulating curiosity and emotional involvement, and to improve children's elaboration of instructions by keeping low the working memory load (e.g., using short sentences, illustrating them also with gestures to improve short-term memorization, using a clear schematic sequence of what to say). Children's peculiar ways of consolidating memories of school concepts or complex procedures are also particularly important to discuss. There is a need to share that when the child's episodic memory has an important deficit, as shown by Davide (see Box 3.6 in chapter 3), one single learning experience does not allow the child to construct an even sketched memory representation. Parents and special teachers should share how to help children in such cases without adopting the strategy of inducing the child to learn everything by rote. A productive strategy is enriching the multimodal elaboration of the new concept or procedure to learn, starting with initial materials that ask the child to activate concepts or actions close to the new target. After such phase, there can be some teaching supported by visual, written or multimedia information, and then a shared construction of a conceptual map. Eventually, new contexts can be proposed in which the acquired concept/procedure should be retrieved, used, and applied. This teaching process can lead to effectively acquiring new knowledge in children with intellectual disabilities, but the pace of such learning is slow and there is a need to drastically reduce the number of new concepts and procedures to learn within each time unit (e.g., one week). Thus, we should share with parents that their children can acquire the strategies to elaborate, memorize, and retrieve concepts, but do need more time compared to typically developing children. More time means less acquired concepts, and this may be difficult to accept for the parents.

As rigid behaviours are concerned, we can hypothesize with parents about the schematic beliefs and expectations on which they tend to rely. For instance, Davide's parents had told the boy not to accept offers of giving car rides from strangers, *people who you do not know very well.* Thus, after a pizza with his classmates, Davide did not accept the offer of a car ride from one of his schoolteachers. He explained to the parents that he did not know that teacher very well. In such a case Davide's rigid behaviour relied on a somehow literal interpretation of the parents' sentence. We shared with Davide's parents that when a new rule is proposed, several examples should illustrate it.

We will be discussing a questionnaire facilitating the sharing of the intervention objectives with parents in chapter 7.

2 Different and complementary approaches for intervention

2.1 How can learning be empowered?

Starting with a view of what learning is, neuroscientists and developmental psychologists agree that one basic function of learning is allowing human beings to predict the world around them, identify/recognize what can be useful for survival, enable the achievement of an individuals' life goals. Language, for instance, begins to take form by *seizing* brain areas when infants hear the mother's voice. Repeated experience of hearing such a voice can predict something familiar, that will calm the infant's fear and unease. The tone and prosody of the mother's voice will be coded by the brain, recognized, and preferred over many other voices. A few months later, not only the prosodic but also the phonological characteristics of the human voices will be coded, and perceived, allowing an initial recognition of familiar syllables and words.

Coding the characteristics of sounds, faces, movement, objects, and places is a basic – mainly unintentional – learning process involving brain areas to build connection nets allowing individuals to predict/recognize different types of input. Through such coding, which partly depends on innate brain circuitry and partly relies on the frequency of exposure to specific inputs, the children's minds can build internal maps simulating real-world characteristics. Semantic concepts, for instance, correspond in the brain to multimodal maps relying on the convergence of visual, auditory, somatosensory, kinesthetic, emotional experiences with the exemplars of a specific category (Damasio, 1989; Simmons et al., 2008). Thus, when a child hears the word /cat/ she can simultaneously recollect the visual form of a small-tailed body, the tactile experience of stroking the fur, the noise he makes and so on. Initially, categories are strictly tuned to a child's experience with a single exemplar, but as experiences with other exemplars accumulate, the category becomes more abstract and relationships with similarly structured categories emerge.

As far as children with ID are concerned, it is not clear whether impoverished detection of input characteristics is involved in delayed development of motor, language, and perceptual skills. Thus, if we aim to enhance learning, it may be the case that higher-level functions, such as attention and strategic exploration of objects, images, sounds, need to compensate for a basic level of perceptual coding that may be partly impoverished.

The second type of basic learning mechanism is attention (see Dehaene, 2021; Tomasello, 2018). As children develop, their attention will be more often intentional than automatically triggered by stimuli. Intentional attention allows a child a deeper exploration of the interesting aspects of reality. Shifting attention from the child's point of view to that of another person supports the integration of different sources of information and opens the way to social learning (Mundy and Newell, 2007). When a child imitates the gesture shown by a physical therapist, when she infers from the other people's faces that what has just been done is warmly approved, when she collaborates with someone else at resolving a game, shared attention is the learning mechanism enabling such experiences to generate new abilities. Social and emotional learning relies on eye contact and shared reciprocal attention.

Attention, along with inhibitory control, is one main deficit for children and even adults with ID (Cornish et al., 2013; Bexkens et al., 2014). We concluded in chapter 2 that the visual attention of persons with ID seems to be more often automatically triggered by some irrelevant stimulus. Empowering attention in intervention can thus have positive cascade effects on children's cognitive and social development.

The third type of basic learning mechanism is active engagement, as emphasized by the experiments on enriched environments (see section 1.1 in this chapter). Motivation is an energetic component that interacts with attention in sustaining deep processing. There are several experiments showing that when human beings are in positive moods, they are more likely to activate semantically related concepts (e.g., cat-bone) from memory, use categories and inferences to globally organize a task content, whereas more stimulus-specific processing occurs when they are in a negative mood (see Clore and Huntsinger, 2007). Thus, enjoying the activity is an energetic component that enhances deep processing and makes learning more likely. Such learning component, which is largely deployed in the early intervention program overviewed in a previous section (see section 1.3), should be seriously considered also in intervention programs for older children that are often more inspired by an academic type of teaching than by a sportive format. On the contrary, a playful and challenging workout is a better format to facilitate active engagement in intervention. A secure child-therapist or child-educator relationship, and sensitive responsive interaction in intervention activities, are also important conditions promoting active engagement in children with ID (see chapter 6 on this issue).

Along with coding, attention, and active engagement, we need to consider three functions that offer fundamental support to learning. The first is language, whose primary function of communication must be complemented by a regulative function.

We draw on Vygotsky (1978) assuming that language is a cultural tool facilitating the executive organization of problem-solving actions: Even a simple thinking-aloud strategy can increase reasoning in problem-solving tasks (Fox and Charness, 2010). Thus, although language development is commonly delayed in children with ID, enhancing a functional use of language to regulate actions and organize problem-solving is a fundamental goal of the intervention. Supportive verbal communication will allow caregivers and therapists to *mediate* those metacognitive components (e.g., planning, monitoring, organising sequence of steps in a procedure to apply) that are likely to be weak in a child with ID (see Akhutina, 1997).

The second crucial support to learning comes from inhibitory control, an executive function that we have considered in chapter 2 (see Box 2.2), for its involvement in supporting control of impulsivity, delay of gratification, and resistance to activating an already acquired response in favour of a new one. Inhibitory control, which is important both for social learning and for a child's flexible refinement/change of already acquired concepts and procedures, tends to be impaired in several children with ID (Bexkens et al., 2014) even though the extent of the delay, compared to chronological age controls, seems to be highly variable.

Further important support to learning comes from working memory, a complex function in which attentional resources are used to keep information in a short-term memory buffer and, simultaneously, coordinate its elaboration. We considered in section 1.2 that shared attention is the learning mechanism supporting the link between a symbolic form expressed by a caregiver (e.g., the sound of a new word in saying *here's your pizza*) and the entity to which that new form refers (e.g., the round and good smelling stuff on the plate). However, for a child to understand and learn a new word, working memory is also involved. A new word sound structure must be kept active in phonological short-term memory whereas, at the same time, the attention is focused on the context to infer the new word's meaning.

Working memory is not only a mechanism that supports language learning, but also a mechanism of wider application, which enhances thinking and reasoning. In every new task and social situation in which we need to choose and coordinate mental operations and, at the same time, keep new information active in memory, working memory is involved. This occurs in several situations, such as when we receive instructions for new procedures or games, when someone explains a new concept or rule, when we try to understand a text, or analyse the visual characteristics of objects and use them to construct something.

2.2 Cognitive empowerment for children with intellectual disabilities

The first question clinicians, parents, and therapists address is whether intervention should tap specific skills or a general empowerment of learning, targeting the mechanisms and supports overviewed in the previous section. For instance, should we teach some important adaptive but specific practical skills (e.g., putting on a shirt, turning on the tablet and selecting a favourite game), or should we stimulate attention, language, and working memory to promote the general empowerment of learning skills? We propose that an intervention should balance with adequate dosage the training of specific adaptive and academic learning skills along with the empowerment of general learning mechanisms.

Considering the results of the studies overviewed in Box 4.3, two main points emerge. Children with ID who were involved in intensive but short training (e.g., about 5–6 weeks), can improve selective attention skills, and working memory, in both the visual and verbal domains. When we ask whether such improvements show general beneficial effects and transfer to practical, academic learning or reasoning skills, evidence is still rare (but see some limited evidence in Box 4.3). However, to observe a training's generalization effects, longer periods of intervention are probably needed. Moreover, including metacognitive strategies along with exercises on attention or working memory, could be more likely to produce generalization effects, as shown by studies involving children with typical development or with attention and hyperactivity disorders (Capodieci et al., 2019; Pozuelos et al., 2019).

Maintenant et al. (2021) involved 7 to 12-year-old children with mild ID to categorize images by analyzing abstract semantic relationships. Children in the experimental group received metacognitive training which encouraged them to analyze, explain, and compare conceptual relationships, whereas children in the control group received direct explicit instruction about how to categorize images. It turned out that children receiving metacognitive training showed a much higher performance than the controls in the conceptual post-intervention test showing that they had constructed conceptual strategies.

In a single case study, we explored metacognitive training targeting arithmetical text problem solving (Orsolini et al., 2009). The training was proposed to an 8-year-old child who had been diagnosed with mild ID in a public health centre. Focusing on problems with a multiplicative structure, the child was guided to represent explicitly the situation involved in the text, as in the example below.

Lu. is reading aloud the text problem: *A squirrel has two bracelets on each paw. How many bracelets does the squirrel have in total?*

1 Therapist: wait, you can take some time to think, what should you consider?
2 Lu.: think of the bracelets...
3 Therapist: of the bracelets...where does he have them?
4 Lu.: on his paw...
5 Therapist: but he does not have just one paw. Because here it says...
6 Lu.: two bracelets...
7 Therapist: on each paw... each! ...let's pretend that I am a squirrel now. So I have one paw (knocking on the table with a hand closed as if it was a paw)...then?
8 Lu.: one more...
9 Therapist: (showing the other hand) ...then?
10 Lu.: you have two bracelets...
11 Therapist: do I have only two little paws?
12 Lu.: yes
13 Therapist: oh my God, and how can I walk if I have only two paws? I also need two more for eating my nuts...

14 Lu.: FOUR
15 Therapist: four, ok… so we remembered that there are four paws
16 Lu.: four times…two

Continuing the training, the therapist used hints and showed a new symbolic action (e.g., drawing a schematic model of the situation involved in the text) to be used as a strategy. Such a guide was accompanied by the request of explaining *what we have done and why* and alternated with the request to think and anticipate how to address a new text problem. Using language to regulate attention, describing shared procedures, anticipating hypotheses, along with practising graphic representations, eventually stimulated the child to invent a simple new calculation procedure. Thus, a child with an intellectual disability can not only learn to deploy metacognitive strategies that have been explicitly taught by a teacher (Jitendra et al, 2002) but also develop an internal cognitive construction, leading from implicit to a more explicit representation of conceptual or procedural knowledge (Karmiloff-Smith, 1992).

Using the metacognitive approach developed by Feuerstein (Feuerstein et al., 1979; 2002), Lifshitz et al. (2005) explored the conceptual skills of 48 adolescent and adult persons with mild and moderate ID involving them in a *dynamic assessment* (i.e., an assessment including a teaching phase). The results of such a study showed that analogical reasoning can remarkably improve in persons with ID even after a brief metacognitive teaching. Engevik et al. (2016) also show that abstract reasoning can be stimulated in some children with Down syndrome through metacognitive dialogic activity with a school teacher. The belief that individuals with mild and moderate ID cannot go beyond a concrete level of reasoning should be dismissed.

Some of Feuerstein's mediation learning strategies are indeed particularly important to promote a child's metacognitive self-regulation (Feuerstein et al., 2002; see also Tzuriel, 2013). The first strategy, *intentionality and reciprocity*, is the condition for starting an intervention: the child should be asked to share and make explicit an intention of being involved in training. When we proposed to 14-year-old Davide to come to our clinic once a week to be involved in exercises and games training attention, he refused because, as he said, he was full of engagements between school tasks and scout activities. We then asked him if he might come two or three times and afterwards decide. He accepted, and at the second session decided that the types of exercises proposed to him could be useful. Chiara, a 10-year-old child with mild ID and symptoms of ADHD, had explicitly accepted to be involved in training, but then very often, when she perceived a task was challenging for her, used to interrupt the activities and sit under the table for rather long intervals. We then proposed a contract to Chiara in which we committed to proposing both useful and playful activities but leaving it for her to decide the game to play in the breaks. Chiara committed to participating in our workouts and to explaining what her needs are rather than abruptly interrupting the activities. When she asked why she should sign a contract, we said that in this way we were both sure: we could trust her and she could trust us. She signed saying in a low voice that we should have had more trust in her. Since then, the intervention went on with Chiara showing engagement and several improvements.

A second mediation strategy is called by Feuerstein *Mediation of transcendence:* the mediator, being a caregiver or therapist, teaches strategies, rules, and procedures. She also involves the child in thinking of other situations to which a suggested strategy could be usefully applied. Davide learned, for instance, to verbally describe complex images, to explore a visual input systematically (e.g., from left to right, from top to bottom). We were surprised when after some sessions with us he arrived saying that was happy to have been wrong in getting to the metro. He then explained that at some point he looked to the train's signboard where all the stops are written, and realized he had taken the train heading in the wrong direction. *But instead of calling mommy on the phone, I got off and took the train in the other direction.* We thus realized that the intervention was working, Davide was using new strategies and felt he could rely on himself. Such episode also showed that our *mediation of feelings of competence,* another important Feuerstein principle, started to be interiorized by Davide.

Mediating the control of behaviour is the core of Feuerstein's and other Vygotskians' approaches (see also Akhutina, 1997; Tzuriel, 2013). The idea is that boosting task persistence, prompting a new procedure and teaching a problem-solving strategy, are interpersonal actions that will be internalized by children to become self-encouragement, self-instructions, and internal language. Such outcomes, however, should not be taken for granted when children with ID are involved. If a mediator teaches too much and does not manage to actively engage the child, if the activity does not promote a child's deep elaboration, learning will be limited. If a close trusting relationship does not develop between the mediator and the child, self-esteem will not be truly promoted, and learning cannot induce those generalization effects improving a child's everyday behaviour.

Integrating the main Feuerstein principles with neuropsychologically inspired activities which target attention and executive functions, we documented in a multiple case study that there were training effects empowering working memory and improving reasoning skills (Orsolini et al., 2019). Taking care of the child's emotional experience with the training activities, and starting the session with a conversation that promotes narrative thinking also characterize our program (see Orsolini, 2019). In one of such initial conversations Rosa, a 13-year-old girl who had been diagnosed in a public health centre with moderate intellectual disability, shared important thoughts on herself.

(…)

1   Therapist: wait, does this happen to you at school?
2   Rosa: yes… I often find… find myself in a corner alone
3   Therapist: Uhm…
4   Rosa: you get it?
5   Therapist: mh…mh
6   Rosa: I find myself in a corner alone but… do you know the group?
7   Therapist: yes
8   Rosa: that one makes…girls at school make a group, send messages, everything… and they leave me alone.

(…)

1   Therapist: but you have a friend at school…with whom you are a bit more…
2   Rosa: yes
3   Therapist: but… you both would like to be part of the group.
4   Rosa: we want to be together with the other classmates.
5   Therapist: right
6   Rosa: but they leave us alone and we feel very bad about it.

(…)

1   Rosa: everything… and they make me feel weaker, weak, weak.
2   Therapist: do you feel this way when such things happen, do you feel weak?
3   Rosa:yes, when I'm alone… alone … that I do not have somebody to talk with. do you know?

(…)

1   Therapist: and did you tell them that you feel bad when they leave you alone?

2   Rosa: I always tell them… but for them… it's as if I would not exist
3   Therapist: mh…mh
4   Rosa: it's as if … as a transparent paper… do you know that transparent paper that put… when you draw something?
5   Therapist: yes
6   Rosa: they are…like that… they throw the paper they have wrong… they crumple it and throw me
7   Therapist: you feel this way… you feel thrown away.

When children with ID feel that their thoughts are valued and find the cognitive and emotional resources facilitating the organization of narrative thinking, therapists are allowed to look out in their interior world. We then realize that most children with ID, as shown by Rosa's brilliant metaphor, feel like *children of a lesser God*. Even in schools that, as occurs in Italy, are fully inclusive, peers tend to isolate those who are perceived as different, not ready to interact as expected by the other children, and whose ideas are sometimes difficult to understand.

The reduced experience of social life and informal peer interaction emerges clearly in a study (Solish et al., 2010) in which parents were asked to complete a questionnaire about their child's participation in social, recreational, and leisure activities. Comparing the participation of children with typical development, autism, and intellectual disability between the ages of 5 and 17 years, it turns out that social and recreational activities with peers were significantly higher in children with typical development and no significant differences emerged between children with autism and children with ID. Social participation is a very important component of intervention that must be considered to promote well-being and a sense of belonging in children with ID.

Box 4.3 Training attention and working memory: effects for children with ID

As concerns attention, Kirk et al. (2016) involved a heterogeneous sample of children with ID or other developmental disabilities (e.g., Autism spectrum disorder) in a training program using computerised exercises on selective attention (locating a target fish among other distractors), sustained attention (keeping attention on a moving coin until it stops moving), attention control (a target elephant in the centre of a row facies right or left whereas the other elephants in the row face its same direction or a different one), and response inhibition (press the screen when an elephant appears but do not press it when a lion appears). The training lasted 20 minutes once a day at the child's home, 5 times a week for 5 weeks under the supervision of a parent. Children in a control group (similar for age, IQ, adaptive behaviour, autism symptoms) participated at a computerised training with a completely different task but with the same dosage as the experimental group. Only children involved in the experimental training showed immediate and follow-up (after 3 months) improvements in selective attention skills. However, the training did not stimulate other attention components and parent-rated attention difficulties did not differ in the experimental and control groups.

Focusing on working memory training studies, Moalli et al. (2004) explored the effects of training that stimulated metacognitive concepts on memory and specific mnemonic strategies with verbal and visuospatial tasks. Improvements from pre- to post-treatment in verbal short-term memory and visuospatial WM occurred in children with Down syndrome (DS) when they were compared to a control group.

Van der Molen et al. (2010), involved participants with mild-to-borderline intellectual disabilities with a computerized visual WM complex dual-task while a control group was trained with a simpler single task. Results showed that only children trained with dual tasks improved their visual WM at follow-up testing. The authors found transfer effects on arithmetic and story recall at follow-up, but no transfer effects on performance with Raven's matrices. Söderqvist et al. (2012) analyzed the effects of a training procedure combining WM and non-verbal reasoning (NVR) tasks. The results showed that improved performance in verbal or visual working memory at post-testing occurred only in children who were making progress in the training phase.

Bennett et al. (2013) involved children with Down syndrome (DS) aged seven to twelve years with computerized training consisting of visuospatial simple and complex span tasks. Comparing the pre- and post-testing changes in children of the intervention group or the waiting list showed significant improvements in visuospatial WM. Parents' ratings of behaviour showed that after training there was a highly significant reduction in difficulty with attention shifting behaviours for children in the intervention group. Danielsson et al. (2015) in a meta-analytic review concluded that only mixed WM training, with both verbal and visuospatial components, showed significant training effects in studies involving children with ID.

Hessl et al. (2019) involved 100 children and adolescents with Fragile X syndrome (FXS) in a computerized training of WM (Cogmed) for about 25 caregiver-supported sessions over 5–6 weeks. The pre/post/follow-up (3 months of no training from the end of intervention) measures of WM, the child's distractibility and cognitive flexibility, as well as parent- and teacher-reported attention and executive functions showed significant improvements, with many changes maintained at follow-up. Although this study lacks a true control group, the extent of the children's improvements, and comparison with other studies in which a control group was used, suggest that the post-training and follow-up changes of children with FXS cannot have been generated by placebo effects or familiarity with the assessment tests.

Most studies involving children with ID used computerized training of visual or visuospatial WM (see Pulina et al., 2015; Lanfranchi et al., 2017). Such training seems to generate remarkable enhancements in visual and spatial working memory. Enhancement of verbal working memory in children with ID is rarer but documented (Söderqvist et al. 2012; Costa et al., 2015; Orsolini et al., 2015; Lanfranchi et al., 2017). Transfer effects of the training to academic learning, everyday functioning or reasoning are also rare (but see Van der Molen et al. 2010; Bennett et al. 2013; Orsolini et al., 2019).

2.3 Promoting social life of children and adolescents with ID

Learning social, practical, and conceptual skills can decrease the mismatch between the social demands of the environment and the behaviour of preteens and adolescents with ID. Autonomy in using public transportation, self-care skills, and being able to use money, are examples of practical skills that have an important impact on social life. Conversational and pragmatic skills, such as story-telling, jokes, and evaluations of videogames or movies, also facilitate peer interactions among adolescents.

A method explored in some studies (see the review of Carter and Hughes, 2005) to promote social interaction has been involving school peers in delivering social skills. Behaviour analytic techniques such as modelling, prompting, corrective feedback, and reinforcement have been taught to students who volunteered to teach schoolmates with ID how to initiate conversation. Using picture booklets or short movies, participants with ID can learn how to self-instruct themselves on asking a question, wait for a response, or elaborate on a response. Teaching how to use social video games seems also to spontaneously enrich social initiation skills with peers while using the trained computer activity (Carter and Hughes, 2005).

An intervention involving two pre-adolescents with mild ID, Davide and Federico, combined different settings. In a laboratory at school, each of the two boys with ID participated in a different small group of peers who volunteered to meet once a week for discussing themes they had selected as interesting. The discussion was completely free, nobody was evaluated for his ideas, and listening to each other's opinions was promoted. The groups were guided by a trainee psychologist who was also involved, on another day, in training Davide's and Federico's social skills in our university clinic. Using behaviour analytic techniques, Davide and Federico practised some basic social interaction skills (e.g., how to start a conversation, how to make a compliment, how to respond when someone teases you). In the second hour of our clinic session, the two boys dedicated some time to addressing the topic that had been planned for the next discussion at school. In this way, the two adolescents could have arguments to bring to the discussion with school peers.

Figures 4.2.a and 4.2.b plot the mean raw occurrence of different behaviours observed in several sessions pre-, during, and post-intervention, coded when the two boys were involved in the school recreation time. Interestingly, the most frequent occurrence before the intervention was imitating the antisocial behaviours produced by some classmates, such as threatening gestures, being spiteful, and offending. In the post-intervention observations, the three most frequent behaviours both for Davide and Federico were greeting, thanking, and intervening in conversation.

The two small groups of peers in which Davide and Federico participated have had the opportunity to experience a new side of their mates with ID. They had discovered that a boy who used to remain silent all the time in class, showed annoying behaviours or talked only to answer a teacher's question, could participate in a discussion, express his thoughts, and have ideas. These guys could be considered and respected, despite their language difficulties (which were present both in Davide and Federico). In turn, knowing that there was no evaluation, no comparation, perceiving that other students considered their point of view, led Davide and Federico to engage in the discussions and dare start a conversation even in a different context (the recreation time). A virtuous circle seemed to be promoted by this intervention, suggesting to us how important it is for typically developing children to discover the abilities, humanity, and feelings of their peers with ID or other types of atypical development. Even in the Italian inclusive school system, students who receive the support of a special teacher – no matter if within the same classroom as the other students – are soon labelled as different, looked like someone who is probably sick and is not normal. However, even minimal changes in the school context reveal to typically developing peers how their school mates with ID can be: persons with their unique characteristics, personality, abilities, people who are able to join a group, start a conversation, communicate their thoughts.

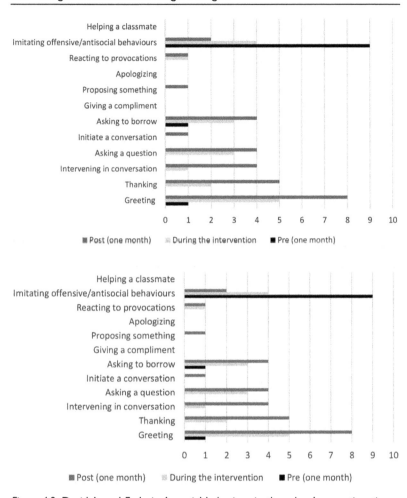

Figure 4.2 Davide's and Federico's social behaviors in the school recreation time

3 Conclusions

Research on intervention for children with intellectual disabilities is still in an early stage. Larger samples of subgroups of children with ID are needed, grouping individuals for their strengths and weaknesses profiles to identify the training conditions that are more suited to the neuropsychological characteristics of specific subgroups. On the other hand, there is also a need for a single case – clinically-focused – intervention studies, to follow the children's changes from a longitudinal perspective, and build a large repertoire of case histories that can document with quali-tative methods the intertwined dynamical influence of relational, socio-affective, and cognitive dimensions of intervention.

The evidence that we have overviewed in such a chapter suggests that intervention focused on early caregiver-child communication and, start-ing from preschool children, training focused on both general learning mechanisms and metacognitive skills, can produce promising effects. Such training should alternate with an intervention focused on more specific skills, being the motor and practical skills, academic learning, or social behaviours.

The most promising type of intervention, however, has still to come: it is made of places and contexts in which preteens and adolescents, each with their developmental peculiarities, are free to interact, play, organize their time, find resources to ask for help for their school tasks, or engage in sports. In such a place, there are some therapists and parents who col-laborate to facilitate the emergence of intention, desire, trust. Adults who can wait and retain from giving directives, and rather support the person's process of thinking and decision, the group interaction, the children's reciprocal help. Therapists are informed of the different neuropsychologi-cal developmental trajectories, of how cultural differences can affect such trajectories but, above all, are involved in observing what seems to work for individuals and groups and sharing such observations with parents. Parents are not overwhelmed by the fragility of their child, because a whole community decided to become a community of caring, in which each child with some fragility can live and find a place to be, to use the name of a promising community-led intervention in Reggio Emilia.

References

Ainsworth, M. D. S., Blehar, M. C., Waters, E., and Wall, S. (1978) *Patterns of Attachment: A Psychological Study of the Strange Situation*. Hillsdale, NJ, USA: Erlbaum.

Akhutina, T.V. (1997). The remediation of executive functions in children with cognitive disorders: the Vygotsky-Luria neuropsychological approach. *Journal of Intellectual Disability Research*, 41 (2), 144–151. doi:10.1111/j.1365-2788.1997.tb00691.x..

Ashori, M., Norouzi, G., and Jalil-Abkenar, S. S. (2019). The effect of positive parenting program on mental health in mothers of children with intellectual disability. *Journal of Intellectual Disability*, 23 (3), 385–396. doi:10.1177/1744629518824899.

Bennett, S. J., Holmes, J., and Buckley, S. (2013). Computerized memory training leads to sustained improvement in visuospatial short-term memory skills in children with Down syndrome. *American Journal of Intellectual and Developmental Disability*, 118, 179–192. doi:10.1352/1944-7558-118.3.179.

Bexkens, A., Ruzzano, L., Collot D' Escury-Koenigs, A. M., Van der Molen, M. W., and Huizenga, H.M. (2014). Inhibition deficits in individuals with intellectual disability: a meta-regression analysis. *Journal of Intellectual Disabilities Research, 58 (1)*, 3–16. doi:10.1111/jir.12068..

Brown, J. A., and Woods, J. J. (2015). Effects of a triadic parent-implemented home-based communication intervention for toddlers. *Journal of Early Intervention*, 37 (1), 44–68. doi:10.1177/1053815115589350.

Capodieci, A., Re, A. M., Fracca, A., Borella, E., and Carretti, B. (2019). The efficacy of a training that combines activities on working memory and meta-cognition: transfer and maintenance effects in children with ADHD and typical development. *Journal of Clinical and Experimental Neuropsychology*, 41 (10),1074–1087. doi:10.1080/13803395.2019.1651827.

Carter, E. W., and Hughes, C. (2005). Increasing social interaction among adolescents with intellectual disabilities and their general education peers: effective interventions. *Research and Practice for Persons with Severe Disabilities*, 30, 179–193.

Clore, G. L., and Huntsinger, J. R. (2007). How emotions inform judgment and regulate thought. *Trends in Cognitive Science*, 11 (9), 393–399. doi:10.1016/j.tics.2007.08.005.

Cornish, K., Cole, V., Longhi, E., Karmiloff-Smith, A., and Scerif, G. (2013). Mapping developmental trajectories of attention and working memory in Fragile X syndrome: developmental freeze or developmental change? *Development and Psychopathology*, 25, 365–376. doi:10.1017/S0954579412001113.

Costa, H. M., Purser, H. R. M., and Passolunghi, M. C. (2015). Improving working memory abilities in individuals with Down syndrome: a treatment case study. *Frontiers in Psychology*, 6, 1331. doi:10.3389/fpsyg.2015.01331.

Damasio, A.R. (1989). Time-locked multiregional retroactivation: a systems-level proposal for the neural substrates of recall and recognition. *Cognition*, 33, 25–62. doi:10.1016/0010–0277(89)90005-x.

Danielsson, H., Zottarel, V., Palmqvist, L., and Lanfranchi, S. (2015). The effectiveness of working memory training with individuals with intellectual disabilities – a meta-analytic review. *Frontiers in Psychology*, 6, 1230. doi:10.3389/fpsyg.2015.01230

Daunhauer, L.A., Schworer, E., and Howshar, M. (2017) Chapter one – parenting matters: parent–child interactions in down syndrome and recommendations for future research. *International Review of Research in Developmental Disabilities*, 53, 1–43, doi:10.1016/bs.irrdd.2017.08.003.

Dehaene, S. (2021). *How We Learn. The New Science of Education and the Brain*. London: Penguin Press.

Emerson, E. (2003). Mothers of children and adolescents with intellectual disability: social and economic situation, mental health status, and the self-assessed social and psychological impact of the child's difficulties. *Journal of Intellectual Disability Research*, 47(Part 4/5), 385–399. doi:10.1046/j.1365-2788.2003.00498.x.

Engevik, L. I., Kari-Anne, B. Næss, K.-A. B., and Hagtvet, B. E. (2016). Cognitive stimulation of pupils with Down syndrome: A study of inferential talk during book-sharing. *Research in Developmental Disabilities*, 55, 287–300, doi:10.1016/j.ridd.2016.05.004.

Eshel, N., Daelmans, B., de Mello, M. C., and Martines, J. (2006) Responsive parenting: interventions and outcomes. *Bulletin of the World Health Organization*, 84 (12), 991–998. doi:10.2471/blt.06.030163.

Feuerstein, R., Feuerstein, R. S., Falik, L. H., and Rand, Y. (2002). *The Dynamic Assessment of Cognitive Modifiability: The Learning Propensity Assessment Device, Theory, instruments, and techniques.* Jerusalem: ICELP Press.

Feuerstein, R., Rand, Y., Hoffman, M. B., and Miller, R. (1979). Cognitive modifiability in retarded adolescents: Effects of instrumental enrichment. *American Journal of Mental Deficiency*, 83 (6), 539–550. PMID:443268.

Fox, M. C., and Charness, N. (2010) How to gain eleven IQ points in ten minutes: thinking aloud improves Raven's Matrices performance in older adults. *Neuropsychology, Development, and Cognition.* Section B, Aging, Neuropsychology and Cognition. 17(2), 191–204. doi:10.1080/13825580903042668.

Fraiberg, S. (1971). Intervention in infancy: a program for blind infants. *Journal of American Academy of Child Psychiatry*, 10 (3), 381–405. doi:10.1016/s0002-7138(09)61746-5.

Garthe A., Roeder I., Kempermann G. (2016) Mice in an enriched environment learn more flexibly because of adult hippocampal neurogenesis. *Hippocampus*, 26, 261–271. doi:10.1002/hipo.22520.

Hessl, D., Schweitzer, J. B., Nguyen, D. V., McLennan, Y. A., Johnston, C., Shickman, R., and Chen, Y. (2019). Cognitive training for children and adolescents with Fragile X syndrome: a randomized controlled trial of Cogmed. *Journal of Neurodevelopmental Disorders*, 11, Article 4. doi:10.1186/s11689-11019-9264-9262.

Jitendra, A. K., DiPipi, C. M., and Perron-Jones, N. (2002). An exploratory study of word problem-solving instruction for middle school students with learning disabilities: an emphasis on conceptual and procedural understanding. *The Journal of Special Education*, 36, 23–38. doi:10.1177/00224669020360010301.

Kaiser, A. P., and Roberts, M. Y. (2013). Parent-implemented enhanced milieu teaching with preschool children with intellectual disabilities. *Journal of Speech, Language, and Hearing Research*, 56, 295–309. doi:10.1044/1092-4388(2012/11-0231.

Karaaslan, O., and Mahoney, G. (2013). Effectiveness of responsive teaching with children with Down syndrome. *Intellectual and Developmental Disabilities*, 51 (6), 458–469. doi:10.1352/1934-9556-51.6.458.

Karaaslan, O., and Mahoney, G. (2015). Mediational analyses of the effects of responsive teaching on the developmental functioning of preschool children with disabilities. *Journal of Early Intervention*, 37 (4) 286–299. doi:10.1177/1053815115617294..

Karmiloff-Smith A. (1992). *Beyond Modularity.* Cambridge, MA: The MIT Press.

Kirk, H. E., Gray, K. M., Ellis, K., Taffe, J., and Cornish, K. M. (2016) Computerised attention training for children with intellectual and developmental disabilities: a randomised controlled trial. *Journal of Child Psychology and Psychiatry*, 57 (12), 1380–1389. doi:10.1111/jcpp.12615.

Landry, S. H., Smith, K. E., Swank, P. R., and Guttentag, C. (2008). A responsive parenting intervention: the optimal timing across early childhood for impacting maternal behaviors and child outcomes. *Developmental Psychology*, 44 (5),1335–1353. doi:10.1037/a0013030.

Lanfranchi, S., Pulina, F., Carretti, B., and Mammarella, I. C. (2017). Training spatial-simultaneous working memory in individuals with Down syndrome. *Research in Developmental Disabilities*, 64, 118–129. doi:10.1016/j.ridd.2017.03.012

Lifshitz, H., Tzuriel, D., and Weiss, I. (2005). Effects of training in conceptual versus perceptual analogies among adolescents and adults with intellectual disability. *Journal of Cognitive Education and Psychology*, 5 (2), 144–170. doi:10.1891/194589505787382504.

Lugo-Gil, J. and Tamis-LeMonda, C. S. (2008). Family resources and parenting quality: Links to children's cognitive development across the first 3 years. *Child Development*, 79 (4),1065–1085. doi:10.1111/j.1467-8624.2008.01176.x.

Mahoney, G., and MacDonald, J. (2007). *Autism and Developmental Delays in Young Children: The Responsive Teaching Curriculum for Parents and Professionals*. Austin, TX: PRO-ED.

Mahoney, G., and Nam, S. (2011). Chapter three – The parenting model of developmental intervention. In R.M. Hodapp (Ed.), *International Review of Research in Developmental Disabilities*, 41, 73–125. doi:10.1016/B978-0-12-386495-6.00003-5

Mahoney, G., and Perales, F. (2019). *Responsive Teaching. Relationship-based developmental Intervention*. https://www.lulu.com/spotlight/Responsiveteaching/.

Maintenant, C., Nanty, I., and Pivry, S. (2021). Flexibilité catégorielle chez des enfants scolarisés en ULIS: les effets d'un étayage métacognitif. *Pratiques Psychologiques*, 27 (2), 93–106, doi:10.1016/j.prps.2020.09.004.

Masek, L. R., McMillan, B. T. M., Paterson, S. J., Tamis-LeMonda, C.S., Golinkoff, R. M., and Hirsh Pasek, K. (2021). Where language meets attention: how contingent interactions promote learning. *Developmental Review*, 60, doi:10.1016/j.dr.2021.100961.

Miller, J. L., and Gros-Louis, J. (2013). Socially guided attention influences infants' communicative behavior. *Infant Behavior and Development*, 36 (4), 627–634. doi:10.1016/j.infbeh.2013.06.010.

Miller, J. L., Ables, E. M., King, A. P., and West, M. J. (2009). Different patterns of contingent stimulation differentially affect attention span in prelinguistic infants. *Infant Behavior and Development*, 32 (3), 254–261. doi:10.1016/j.infbeh.2009.02.003.

Moalli, E., Rota Negroni, S., and Vianello, R. (2004). Conoscenze sulla memoria e prestazioni di memoria in ragazzi con sindrome di Down: effetti di due diversi training di breve durata. *Giornale Italiano delle Disabilità*, 3, 23–40.

Mundy, P., and Newell, L. (2007). Attention, joint attention and social cognition. *Current Directions in Psychological Science*, 16, 269–274. doi:10.1111/j.1467-8721.2007.00518.x.

NICHD Early Child Care Research Network. (1999). Chronicity of maternal depressive symptoms, maternal sensitivity, and child functioning at 36 months. *Developmental Psychology*, 35, 1297–1310. doi:10.1037/0012-1649.35.5.1297.

Orsolini, M. (Ed.) (2019). *Pensando si impara* (Thinking you learn). Milano: Franco Angeli.

Orsolini, M., Melogno, S., Latini, N., Penge, R., and Conforti, S. (2015). Treating verbal working memory in a boy with intellectual disability. *Frontiers in Psychology*, 6, 1091. doi:10.3389/fpsyg.2015.01091.

Orsolini, M., Melogno, S., Scalisi, T. G., Latini, N., Caira, S., Martini, A., and Federico, F. (2019). Training verbal working memory in children with mild intellectual disabilities: Effects on problem-solving. *Psicología Educativa*, 25 (1), 1–11. doi:10.5093/psed2018a12.

Orsolini, M., Toma, C. and De Nigris, B. (2009). Treating arithmetical text problem solving in a child with intellectual disability: an observative study. *The Open Rehabilitation Journal*, 2, 58–72. doi:10.2174/1874943700902010064.

Pozuelos, J. P., Combita, L. M., Abundis, A., Paz-Alonso, P. M., Conejero, Á., Guerra, S., and Rueda, M. R. (2019). Metacognitive scaffolding boosts cognitive and neural benefits following executive attention training in children. *Developmental Science*, 22 (2), e12756. doi:10.1111/desc.12756.

Pulina, F., Carretti, B., Lanfranchi, S., and Mammarella, I. C. (2015). Improving spatial-simultaneous working memory in Down syndrome: effect of a training program led by parents instead of an expert. *Frontiers in Psychology*, 6, 1265. doi:10.3389/fpsyg.2015.01265.

Restivo, L., Ferrari, F., Passino, E., Sgobio, C., Bock, J., Oostra, B.A., Bagni, C. and Ammassari-Teule, M. (2005). An enriched environment promotes behavioural and morphological recovery in a mouse model for the fragile X syndrome. *Proceedings of the National Academy of Sciences of the United States of America*, 102 (32), 11557–11562. doi:10.1073/pnas.0504984102.

Rosenzweig, M. R., Krech, D., Bennett, E. L., and Diamond, M. C. (1962). Effects of environmental complexity and training on brain chemistry and anatomy: a replication and extension. *Journal of Comparative Physiological and Psychology*, 55, 429–437. doi:10.1037/h0041137.

Ruane, A., and Carr, A. (2019). Systematic review and meta-analysis of stepping stones triple p for parents of children with disabilities. *Family Process*, 58 (1), 232–246. doi:10.1111/famp.12352.

Salomone, E., Pacione, L., Shire, S., Brown, F. L., Reichow, B., and Servili, C. (2019). Development of the who caregiver skills training program for developmental disorders or delays. *Frontiers in Psychiatry*, 10, 769. doi:10.3389/fpsyt.2019.00769.

Sanders, M. R., Mazzucchelli, T. G., and Studman, L. J. (2004). Stepping Stones Triple P: The theoretical basis and development of an evidence-based positive parenting program for families with a child who has a disability. *Journal of Intellectual and Developmental Disability*, 29, 265–283. doi:10.1080/13668250412331285127.

Sanders, M.R., Divan, G., Singhal, M., Turner, K.M.T., Velleman, R., Michelson, D., and Patel, V. (2021) Scaling up parenting interventions is critical for attaining the sustainable development goals. *Child Psychiatry and Human Development*, May 4, 1–12. doi:10.1007/s10578-021-01171-0.

Shin J. Y., and Nguyen, S. D. (2017). The effects of a home-based intervention conducted by college students for young children with developmental delays in vietnam. *International Journal of Developmental Disabilities*, 63 (2), 110–123. doi:10.1080/20473869.2016.1144316.

Shin, J. Y., Nhan, N. V., Lee, S.-B., Crittenden, K. S., Flory, M. and Hong, H. T. D. (2009). The effects of a home-based intervention for young children with intellectual disabilities in Vietnam. *Journal of Intellectual Disability Research*, 53 (4), 339–352. doi:10.1111/j.1365-2788.2008.01151.x.

Simmons, W. K., Hamann, S. B., Harenski, C. L., Hu, X. P., and Barsalou, L. W. (2008). fMRI evidence for word association and situated simulation in conceptual processing. *Journal of Physiology – Paris*, 102, 106–119. doi:10.1016/j.jphysparis.2008.03.014.

Söderqvist, S., Nutley, S. B., Ottersen, J., Grill, K. M., and Klingberg, T. (2012). Computerized training of non-verbal reasoning and working memory in children with intellectual disability. *Frontiers of Human Neuroscience*, 6:271. doi:10.3389/fnhum.2012.00271.

Solish, A., Perry, A., and Minnes, P. (2010). Participation of children with and without disabilities in social, recreational and leisure activities. *Journal of Applied Research in Intellectual Disabilities*, 23 (3), 226–236. doi:10.1111/j.1468-3148.2009.00525.x.

Striano, T., Chen, X., Cleveland, A., and Bradshaw, S. (2006). Joint attention social cues influence infant learning. *European Journal of Developmental Psychology*, 3(3), 289–299. doi:10.1080/17405620600879779.

Tamis-LeMonda, C. S., Kuchirko, Y., and Song, L. (2014). Why is infant language learning facilitated by parental responsiveness? *Current Directions in Psychological Science*, 23(2), 121–126. doi:10.1177/0963721414522813.

Tamis-LeMonda, C. S., Shannon, J. D., Cabrera, N. J. and Lamb, M. E. (2004). Fathers and mothers at play with their 2 and 3-year-olds: contributions to language and cognitive development. *Child Development*, 75 (6), 1806–1820. doi:10.1111/j.1467-8624.2004.00818.x..

Tamis-LeMonda, C. S., Kuchirko, Y. and Tafuro, L. (2013) From action to interaction: infant object exploration and mothers' contingent responsiveness. *IEEE Transactions On Autonomous Mental Development*, 5 (3), 202–209, doi:10.1109/TAMD.2013.2269905.

Tomasello, M. (2018). *Becoming Human: A Theory of Ontogeny*. Cambridge (MA): Belknap Press of Harvard University Press. doi:10.4159/9780674988651.

Tzuriel, D. (2013). Mediated learning experience strategies and cognitive modifiability. *Journal of Cognitive Education and Psychology*, 13, 59–80. doi:10.1891/1945-8959.12.1.59.

Van der Molen, M. J., Van Luit, J. E. H., Van der Molen, M. W., Klugkist, I., and Jongmans, M. J. (2010). Effectiveness of a computerised working memory training in adolescents with mild to borderline intellectual disabilities. *Journal of Intellectual Disability Research*, 54, 433–447. doi:10.1111/j.1365-2788.2010. 01285.x.

Vygotskij, L. S. (1934). *Myšlenie i reč*. (Italian translation Pensiero e linguaggio, edited by L. Mecacci, Roma-Bari: Laterza, 1990).

Vygotsky, L. S. (1978). *Mind in Society: The Development of Higher Psychological Processes*Cambridge, Mass.: Harvard University Press.

World Health Organization. (2012). *Care for Child Development: Improving the Care of Young Children*. World Health Organization. https://apps.who.int/iris/handle/10665/75149.

Chapter 5

Attachment and intellectual disability

Promoting secure attachment in relationships

Furio Lambruschi, Ciro Ruggerini, and Melvin Piro

This chapter offers a conceptual framework within which to integrate attachment theory into clinical practice with people with intellectual disabilities (ID), and explores a more detailed consideration of affective and relational variables in the possible evolution of conditions of ID. How much attachment relationships are central to every aspect of our lives is discussed. Although attachment difficulties have now been definitively linked to a wide range of clinical outcomes in children and adults, many professional caregivers continue to be uncertain about how to work in an attachment-informed manner with people who have ID.

This chapter, taking into account the special attachment needs of people who have ID, emphasizes the dynamic interplay between neurobiological vulnerability and parenting, and illustrates how work with patients, families, and organizations providing care and treatment services can be usefully integrated with attachment theory. In particular, it describes the factors, tools and techniques to consider during the assessment, the case formulation, and the intervention process. Key evidence-based interventions are also reviewed, and an interesting work proposal on challenging behaviors is presented, together with the description of a complex clinical case.

I The conceptual framework

This chapter is based on the well-established conceptual framework of developmental psychopathology and attachment theory (Bowbly, 1969-1982, 1973, 1980). The inception of developmental psychopathology occurred in the 1970s starting from different areas of research: developmental psychology, cognitive psychology, child psychiatry, clinical psychology, and ethology (Cicchetti, 1984). Sroufe and Rutter (1984) defined it as a discipline that focuses on development and its deviations, investigating the origin and evolution of individual patterns of

DOI: 10.4324/9781003220367-5

maladaptive behavior, in relation to the most significant changes that occur along different stages of the life cycle. If we consider the degree of adaptation and social integration of an individual in the various stages of his or her lifespan, this can be considered to be the momentary and transient result of a process characterized by the dynamic interaction of negative risk factors on the one hand, and protective factors on the other. Depending on which of the two is more prevalent, the subject may appear as vulnerable, non-integrated, with manifestations of maladjustment of various kinds, or as a resilient subject, relatively not vulnerable, and possessing a substantial degree of integration and social adaptation.

1.1 Risk factors of psychopathology

DeKlyen and Greenberg (2008) propose an interesting model (see Figure 5.1) that highlights four general risk domains: (1) child-internal characteristics, such as biological vulnerability, neurocognitive functions, and temperament; (2) quality of primary attachment relationships; (3) parental educational style and socialization strategies; and (4) critical life events, family life stress and trauma, family organizational resources,

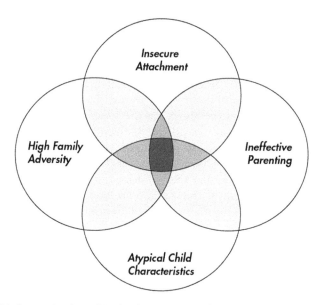

Figure 5.1 Factors implicated in the determination of child psychopathology: possible overlapping of the various risk areas. Source: DeKlyen and Greenberg (2008).

and extended social networks. It is unlikely that only one of these risk domains (e.g., atypical temperament or a chaotic family environment) will determine a mental disorder. Moving toward the center of the model, where more areas of risk overlap, the likelihood of negative outcomes will increase. For example, even a severely insecure attachment to the primary attachment figure, if isolated, is not a definitive factor of psychopathology; however, if it is associated with other risk factors, it may then give rise to a developmental pathway with possible externalizing psychopathological outcomes, i.e., behavioral type, or internalizing psychopathological outcomes, i.e., emotional type.

It is worth noting that, among all of the factors, the one related to objective family adversity (e.g., poverty, job loss, transfers, accidents, bereavement, etc.) is paradoxically the least significant in predicting possible psychopathological outcomes. It actually conditions the development of the subject only through the quality of the other variables involved, and is filtered and modulated by the quality of parenting in its dual function of education and affection. At first glance, the ability to establish rules and the protective ability to convey affectivity could appear to be distinct constructs. Yet, clinical experience and research data demonstrate that these two components are closely related, suggesting that it is impossible to educate without loving and to love without educating (Lambruschi and Muratori, 2013). Some results of longitudinal and correlational studies assist to better understand how providing affection and setting rules are interrelated: insecure attachment and, to a greater extent, disorganized attachment, are predictive of and/or associated with the development of various behavioral problems (Barone and Lionetti, 2012). In other words, the emotional regulation strategies that the child develops in the affective relationship with his or her parent(s) also influence the degree of adherence to educational rules on a behavioral and social level. Sensitivity and discipline (or *sensitive discipline*) are confirmed as focal components of parenting. Indeed, each is connected to the other, and they contribute to the development of a harmonious organization of the child's Self, interacting with his or her temperament and with his or her skills and resources with which he or she faces the world.

1.2 The dynamic interplay between neurobiological vulnerability and parenting

The most recent literature that simultaneously examines individual and environmental factors converges on the following hypothesis: having a "difficult" temperament or a particular neurobiological vulnerability is not the variable that necessarily determines the quality of development in a negative way, but rather acts in interaction with the environment by increasing the permeability of the child to influences of his or her relational context (Lionetti et al., 2014). Children with neurobiological vulnerability and difficult temperament, e.g., highly responsive to environmental stimulation, have the best behavioral developmental outcomes when placed in positive growth environments, and more maladaptive outcomes, in terms of oppositional behaviors and failure to adhere to rules, when growing up in relational risk contexts. In other words, they are more permeable to contextual influences, e.g., the quality of maternal and paternal care, irrespective of whether such contextual influences are beneficial or deleterious. Therefore, the affective quality of care interacts with the quality of development on pro-social, moral, and educational levels, and more broadly with the quality of social adaptation (Ramchandani et al., 2010).

Even intellectual disability can be analyzed using this model, considering its aspects of vulnerability on the genetic and neurobiological level in dynamic interaction with all of the other risk or protective domains, in order to determine his or her possible evolutionary trajectories, in terms of adaptation or potential psychopathological implications. This conceptual perspective has been applied to the understanding of the condition of people with intellectual disabilities (ID) only very recently, but already provides implications of great clinical relevance, as highlighted, for example, in the thorough work of Fletcher et al. (2016).

1.3 The relationships between attachment and cognitive functions

It is necessary, in our opinion, to consider two levels of mutual interaction between attachment and cognitive functions. On the one hand, the most recent developments in evolutionary and relational neurobiology suggest that the quality of attachment constitutes one of the main "architects" of brain development, influencing a subject's ability to use his or her mind and shaping the structuring and integration of his or her memory systems (Schore, 2003; Hill, 2015). Only a secure attachment allows for the development of flexible thinking and more pronounced cognitive and metacognitive skills (Arnott and Meins, 2007).

Insecure attachment, on the other hand, which substantially influences the processes of emotional and behavioral regulation, leads to acting in a poorly regulated, impulsive manner, as if one were constantly facing a threat. Here, we find the so-called *challenging behaviors* frequently related to the condition of intellectual disability which, as will be discussed later, through an appropriate functional analysis, can be better understood in light of the history of attachment. In this perspective, in fact, the symptoms have a clear interpersonal meaning as *means aimed at maintaining the state of relationship with the caregiver* (Lambruschi, 2014).

2 Attachment and self-organization

The Self could be described as the active emergence of a sense of uniqueness and personal individuality, and unity and continuity over time, i.e., the feeling of having specific and personal attributes that differentiate us from any other individual, and consistent with each other and permanent over time. These characteristics can only emerge within relationships, such as those of attachment, endowed with similar ones: uniqueness, exclusivity, unity, and constancy, which show that this constitutes a strict interdependence between attachment and Self. Each of us will be able to build a defined perception of ourselves only by recognizing ourselves in the mirror, represented by the consciousness that our attachment figures have of us.

2.1 Children's self-organization and attachment

Interdependence between attachment and Self applies to every child, irrespective of the genetic heritage, and neurobiological and temperamental structure, with which he or she comes into the world. The attachment system is biologically programmed to be activated in situations of perceived vulnerability and, in all children, including those with ID, searches for protection and comfort. Obviously, in a child with more or less marked intellectual vulnerability, we should expect particular modalities in his or her perception, evaluation and understanding of danger, in his or her recognition of his or her feelings of vulnerability, and in his or her non-verbal and verbal expression/communication towards attachment figures. Reciprocally, in his or her attachment figures, we should anticipate greater difficulties in the processes of attunement with the child in terms of sensitivity and/or responsiveness.

Patricia Crittenden's *Dynamic Maturational Model (DMM)* of attachment (Crittenden and Landini, 2012) allows, in our view, a rich differentiation of the interpersonal patterns that are determined in the transition from preschool, to school age, adolescence, and adulthood (see Figure 5.2.).

These configurations are arranged in a complex circular pattern along a continuum that represents increasing integrative deficits (and thus increasingly poor self-reflective and metacognitive skills): on the one hand, a set of type C configurations (termed *anxious resistant* in early

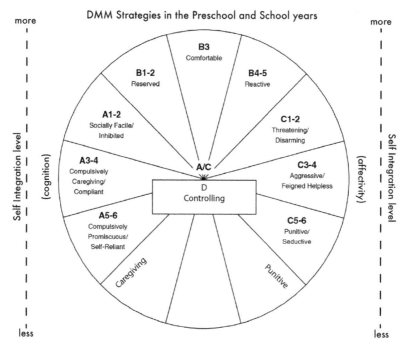

Figure 5.2 Attachment patterns in preschool and school age according to the Dynamic Maturational Model of Attachment (DMM) Source: Lambruschi (2014).

childhood and *coercive* in later stages) that deviate from safety by a greater extent of unpredictability; on the other hand, a set of type A configurations (*avoidant* in early childhood and *defensive* in later stages) that deviate from safety by a greater extent of distancing from affect. The model therefore assists us to elucidate attachment patterns not in categorical, but rather, in dimensional terms. It also enables us to observe and conceive of the different attachment configurations as they are structured in early childhood and evolve over time, not only as specific interactive patterns observable on the behavioral level, but also: a) as specific *strategies of protection from danger*: "high index" defensive and coercive patterns (in the lower part of the circle in the figure) represent the strategies that children attempt to structure within the most dangerous and self-threatening developmental contexts; b) and more importantly, as specific *ways of regulating emotional states* on a long continuum that ranges from styles of autonomous, internal and rigid regulation, to styles characterized by a constant and sometimes dramatic tendency to amplify emotional states by using them instrumentally to burden the relationship with the significant other.

2.2 Attachment and emotional regulation

Indeed, each of us learns to recognize, differentiate, name, express, and then regulate emotional states and related behavioral dispositions within primary attachment bonds. Secure attachment is the condition that promotes the most accurate knowledge of a broader range of emotional states, along with strategies for their harmonic regulation. Specific developmental contexts characterized by different forms of insecurity lead, however, to specific forms of emotional dysregulation. Primary affective experiences characterized by a constant lack of sensitivity and affective responsiveness of the caregiver (A model) lead functionally to structure *a deactivating style* of emotional regulation: a tendentially autonomous and internal regulation of affects and emotional states that avoids the internal recognition and/or external expression of the same as much as possible. Experiencing, instead, unpredictability and discontinuity of maternal affective response (C models) lead to a *hyperactivating style,* i.e., an abnormal amplification of all of the typical signals of the attachment behavioral system, with strong neurophysiological, emotional and behavioral activation, sometimes expressed in dramatic form. In other words, in certain affective learning contexts, losing emotional control is functional to maintaining the state of the relationship with the caregiver (paradoxically making the relationship more predictable and controllable). In more complex relational situations, in which the context of caregiving is characterized by high levels of danger and threat to the Self (high index coercive or defensive models), deficits in the regulation of affects become even more conspicuous, with strong conflicts and unpredictability in the emotional repertoire of the child.

From this perspective, then, insecure attachment, with its various possibilities of emotional dysregulation, can serve as an important basis for the development of various forms of critical behavior in contexts of cognitive vulnerability. We can imagine that the whole life path of a person with ID (including the care and clinical path), with its developmental steps and criticalities, are somehow influenced by the quality of the affective context him or her. A *secure* state of mind will allow caregivers to recognize, process, and resolve the critical emotions related to the countless challenges determined by the condition of disability of the child in a more balanced and functional manner, starting from communication of the diagnosis. In contrast, insecure mental states will more likely lead to exacerbation and dysregulated expression of these emotions, with possible psychopathological manifestations, as well as attitudes of poor cooperation and adherence to treatment proposals.

In this perspective, the *symptoms* that may emerge in each phase of the life cycle should be viewed in terms of their affective meaning. Psychic health and pathology should be sought in the vicissitudes of affective ties, and in the possibility of preserving the continuity and coherence of one's own self-organizing processes over time. Those signs that, on a descriptive level, we define as child behavioral and emotional "disorders", take on a precise affective meaning if we consider them within his or her attachment bonds.

When specific life events put the usual relational configurations with parents in crisis, symptoms can emerge in order to manage and regulate the perceived state of emotional/affective dysregulation. Accurate knowledge and differentiation of one's own emotional experience, built within sensitive and secure attachment bonds, constitutes the fundamental basis for developing an adequate ability to regulate the same emotional states, and therefore a sufficient degree of psychological well-being. Indeed, it could be stated that where there is a symptom, there is a particular emotional area that is poorly recognized and articulated in the patient, and therefore subject to experiential avoidance. Consequently, symptoms could then be seen as "sketchy metaphors" of such areas of experience that are not adequately processed (Liotti, 2001).

3 Attachment and the pathway to intellectual disability support

3.1 Guidelines to incorporate attachment in clinical practice

An important document of the *British Psychology Society* (2017), with the title *Incorporating Attachment Theory into Practice: Clinical Practice Guideline for Clinical Psychologists working with People who have Intellectual Disabilities,* acknowledges this new orientation that aims to integrate attachment theory into clinical practice with people with ID. It suggests that affective and relational variables should be taken into greater account in the possible evolution of ID conditions. The guidelines recall how much attachment relationships are central to all aspects of our lives, and attachment difficulties have now been linked to a wide range of problematic clinical outcomes in both children and adults. Many clinicians and professional caregivers, however, continue to be uncertain about how to work in an attachment-informed way with people who have ID.

The purpose of the guidelines is therefore to provide information about the attachment needs of people with ID, and is aimed at psychologists working in health and social care services. The document includes an overview of attachment theory, taking the special needs of people who have ID into consideration, and identifies factors to consider during assessment, case formulation, and intervention. Additional considerations are included for specific areas of work, e.g., challenging behaviors, persons with dementia, persons diagnosed with autism spectrum disorder (ASD), persons with multiple ID, parents who have ID, persons diagnosed with personality disorders, and supervision and self-care by psychologists. Intellectual disability does not necessarily preclude the development of secure attachment relationships, although an ID may represent a challenge in this regard, increasing the likelihood of interruption of healthcare and safety-promoting behaviors. Children with ID could be less able to manage emotional stressors on their own, especially when attachment figures are less readily available.

By *case formulation*, we mean a shared effort between the subject, caregivers, and psychologists to summarize his or her difficulties, explain why they may occur, and make understandable sense of them. Professionals should construct their hypotheses collaboratively, as provisional and subject to change based on new information, avoid labeling or stigmatization, and respect the dynamic nature of attachment relationships.

3.2 Reactions to the diagnosis of intellectual disability

As noted in chapter 1, there is a first moment in which the individual and his or her family have to deal with the assessment of specialists and with a diagnosis, with all the difficulties that this may entail. In the field of ID, professionals often use concepts that are not very easy to understand; whereas, confrontation should lead to a shared understanding of the data, which is a basic element in establishing a good working alliance. The important emotional implications that such sharing entails must also be carefully considered. Parents and caregivers face important challenges when caring for an individual with ID. In spite of their best intentions and efforts to protect and care for them, the disability or health condition tends to persist painfully over time. This can lead to emotional distress and difficult coordination in attachment and care systems from the earliest moments of communication of the diagnosis.

The relationship between parents and their child begins as soon as they find out that they are expecting. Parents-to-be begin to picture their baby, its appearance, and its personality traits. Early diagnostic assessments, while offering the prospective parent the opportunity to begin to bond with his or her developing child, also allows for early diagnosis of fetal health issues. This experience can have a profound impact on the mother-to-be, putting her at risk of experiencing a variety of critical emotional states, such as anxiety, depression, and symptoms of post-traumatic stress disorder (PTSD) (Horsch et al., 2013). As a consequence, these mothers will require consistent emotional and social support. The challenge for these parents will be trying to meet their child's needs in addition to managing their feelings of loss, fatigue, and sometimes guilt from thinking that they "caused" the disability or were unable to prevent it and thus protect their child.

Many parents experience shock, distrust, and sadness when they learn that their child has a disability or chronic health problem (Bowlby, 1980). This condition has been described as grieving for the "healthy" or "perfect" child. Hornby (1994) and Holder (2000) report how some parents manage to resolve grief related to their child's disabling condition within a reasonable time, while others continue to experience difficulties for many years. Marvin and Pianta (1996) proposed attachment theory as a useful framework within which to understand this grieving process associated with having a child with a disability. In this regard, they proposed the *Reaction to Diagnosis Interview* (RDI), an instrument that is easily applicable to parents of children with ID. The parent is asked to recall the moment when he or she was told about his or her child's condition, what reflections he or she made, what he or she thought about the nature and possible evolution of the disease, and whether his or her thoughts have changed since then. Both the verbal responses of the parents and their non-verbal communication (e.g., facial expressions, emotional expressions, crying, etc.) are considered as evaluation indicators. At the conclusion of the interview, the collected data are organized within two categories: resolved and unresolved. The first dimension indicates subjects who show themselves able to cope with the pathological diagnosis, accepting the risks and negativity in an attitude of consistency and acceptance that may include the possibility of recovery and healing. Moreover, the expectations of the subject appear realistic, and the attitude towards the child is responsive and simultaneously not limiting his or her freedom. In other words, the needs of the child are acknowledged, and those of the whole family are maintained, in a perspective of adaptation that facilitates balance and well-being of the nucleus despite the disease. In contrast, the interviews of unresolved subjects are characterized by unrealistic expectations, search for an alternative diagnosis, denial, and despair. Negative emotions paralyze, hindering the grief process, which is the emotional context of the whole family, which cannot evolve in an adaptive dimension.

Barnett et al. (2003) highlight that parents who continue grieving for the healthy child they had desired are unable to revise their expectations in light of evidence of their child's disability. Parents' difficulty or inability to develop an internal representation of their child's actual abilities in lieu of their hoped-for abilities may impede or prevent their ability to care sensitively, and thus develop a secure attachment with their child (Atkinson et al., 1999). Pianta and Marvin (1992) also suggest that the parents' unresolved mental state may give rise to coping strategies that negatively affect the relationship with the child, as well as cognitive distortions that may prevent parents' sensitive and balanced response to their child's signals of need. Resolution of this type of grief, however, is regarded as an ongoing process, and it is possible that parents may also experience states of crisis at multiple points in their child's life, particularly during transitional phases (Wilker et al., 1981).

Some researchers have postulated that parents must go through several stages of grieving the loss of the "healthy" or "perfect" child that they expected before they are able to adjust to their child's disability (Bicknell, 1983). Such staged models assume that parents' feelings of grief will eventually be processed and replaced by acceptance of their child and resolution of their loss if the outcome is positive. Other researchers have critiqued these models by proposing that resolution is an ongoing developmental process related to life transitions (Bruce et al., 1994). Korff-Sausse (1999) suggests that resolution is a cyclical process that is influenced by developmental transitions, such as going to school, adolescence, and leaving home, further asserting that it is unrealistic to expect families to fully resolve their grief, and instead they may continue to relive grief at key and transitional times in the family life cycle. Each family will respond differently to the discovery that their child has an intellectual disability (ID) based on the basic self-organization of their members (with particular regard to parental figures), but also depending on their cultural beliefs about disability, ethnicity, religious tenets, socioeconomic status, and broader societal attitudes toward disability (Miltiades and Pruchno, 2002). Although most extant literature has focused on the experience of mothers, important differences may also exist in the reactions of fathers and other family members that remain unexplored.

3.3 Assessment procedures and tools

From many years, cognitive clinical models with a constructivist and evolutionary orientation have integrated the "bowlbyan lesson" within the classical cognitive-behavioral model (Guidano and Liotti, 1983; Guidano, 1987, 1991; Liotti, 1994; Bara, 2006; Lambruschi, 2014). Within this perspective, the classic tools of functional and historical symptom analysis are used in a relational manner to conduct in-depth investigations of the functional value that the symptoms possess within the quality of attachment bonds. These key elements of the assessment can be integrated with data based on direct observation of the attachment relationship, conducted through observational tools derived from the Dynamic Maturational Model of Attachment (DMM). Such an assessment allows one to move from a *descriptive* diagnosis (based on the classic nosographic categories: DSM-5, ICD-10) to an *explanatory* one aimed at formulating a reasonable hypothesis on the mental state of caregivers, on the organization of the patient's Self (critical emotional areas and operational models of the Self in the relationship with the other), on his or her interpersonal functioning, on the possible mechanisms of clinical decompensation, and on the possible meaning of the symptom as a means to maintain the state of relationship with caregivers in that particular phase of affective imbalance felt in the significant bonds (Lambruschi, 2014).

Similarly, at the therapeutic level, in addition to the classic procedures of cognitive-behavioral intervention, psychotherapeutic modalities are integrated that are aimed, in childhood, to improve the quality of attachment and support parenting, and in adulthood, to the exploration and acquisition of greater awareness of the organization of personal meanings that guide their experience of Self, the world, and their interpersonal style.

Concerning observation of attachment patterns, Crittenden (2005) indicates that a good measure of attachment must be recordable, refer to more than one memory system, be standardized so that assessments are comparable, and be validated by a strong research evidence base. For people with ID, this has not yet been fully achieved. However, it is worth noting that the conceptual framework constituted by the DMM and the instruments based on it (*Infant CARE-Index, Toddler CARE-Index, Preschool Assessment of Attachment, School Age Assessment of Attachment, Adult Attachment Interview* DMM oriented) offer, for different developmental stages, powerful observation criteria as an interpretative and integrative grid of the patient's dyadic behavior.

All of our usual assessment techniques possess well-established reliability in evaluating attachment in children and adults with typical development. It may not be so easy, however, to adapt them to people with ID. First, it may not be possible for people with ID to draw fully on more than one memory system due to cognitive limitations, and this is also a problem with measures that have been developed to date. Indeed, existing measures rely on the ability to recall and reflect on childhood experiences, which may be affected by autobiographical memory functioning. The ability to mentally place oneself in the past, future, or counterfactual situations, analyze thoughts, and reflect on current adult relationships may be significantly impaired in people with ID.

Second, although there is some evidence that the same types of attachment observed in the typical development population are found in people with mild ID (Larson et al., 2011), it cannot be assumed that attachment dynamics and behavior are comparable across the range of people with ID. For instance, Cicchetti and Serafica (1981) found that children with Down Syndrome exhibited similar attachment behavior to typically developing children, but important differences in affective response existed, which was significantly slower and affected the caregiver's ability to process and respond to attachment behavior. In addition, many existing assessments of adult attachment make explicit or implicit assumptions about adult life and the experience of romantic relationships (Hazan and Shaver, 1987) that may not be applicable to persons with ID.

When using interviews with people who have moderate ID, there is a documented tendency for acquiescence and suggestibility on the part of the interviewee, especially when using closed-ended questions (yes/no), and this compromises the use and integrity of many forms of questionnaire-based interviews and assessments. This problem is further compounded by memory impairment, especially in immediate and delayed recall, and poor performance in narrative recall assessments (Beail, 2002).

In order to overcome these challenges, some attempts have been made to develop measures of attachment assessment aimed specifically at people with ID. We indicate, by way of example, only a few:

• The *Self-report Assessment of Attachment Security* (SRAAS) (Smith and McCarthy, 1996) was designed to assess the current attachment experiences of individuals with ID by observing the seeking of comfort from a significant other in the face of a range of negative emotions (e.g., unhappiness, worry, fear, etc.) that are related to attachment security.

• The *Adult Attachment Projective Picture System* (AAP) (George and West, 2001) assesses attachment through the use of pictures, rather than relying on autobiographical memories of childhood experiences or assessments of current relationships, both of which can be problematic for people with ID. The AAP involves telling a story for each of seven stimulus images, six of which depict attachment-related scenes, such as images of loss and separation, with an additional neutral image.

• The *Secure Base Safe Haven Observation* (SBSHO) (De Schipper and Schuengel, 2006) was developed from the *Attachment Q Sort (AQS)*

(Waters, 1995) by taking 20 specific observational items related to secure attachment behaviors, and then constructing additional items to reflect the attachment behavior exhibited by children and adolescents with ID in stressful situations, e.g., "He looks at me when something exciting or dangerous is happening", "I am able to comfort him by paying attention and talking to him", "When other people make him uncomfortable, he seeks contact with me", and "When he enters the group, he greets me immediately".

- The *Manchester Attachment Scale – Third Party* (MAST) (Penketh et al., 2014) is also based on the AQS to identify a consensus of secure attachment in people with ID. The considered items provide an assessment tool that is easy to use, quick, and requires minimal training.

- Finally, the *Quality of Early Relationship Rating Scale* (QuERRS), which can also be used with adults, is a 20-item rating scale that assists clinicians to engage in psychological therapy with individuals with mild to moderate ID who are able to report about their family of origin and current relationships.

4 Clinical intervention

In children, we can assume that internal working models of the Self-with-others are still in a plastic stage of development. Therefore, we should aim for a clear centrality and relevance of attachment figures of children with ID in the various stages of the psychotherapeutic process, focusing on their mental state and the promotion of higher levels of sensitivity and affective responsiveness towards the child (Lambruschi, 2014; Lambruschi and Lionetti, 2015).

4.1 Interventions through parenting support

As the person with ID grows older, when the organization of the self and social skills assume more defined and autonomous characteristics, individual therapeutic interventions will become more usable. To be effective, however, such interventions must always be carefully "tailored" to his or her identity and interpersonal structure.

In preschool and early school age, a variety of parenting support interventions are gaining increasing prominence (Lambruschi and Lionetti, 2015), beginning with classic individual or group cognitive-behavioral and psychoeducational interventions, referred to as *parent training* (PT). The effectiveness of different PT programs is now recognized and supported by rigorous empirical studies and extensive meta-analyses (Kaminski et al., 2008) in clinical settings as diverse as autism

(McConachie and Diggle, 2007), anxiety disorders (Cartwright-Hatton et al., 2011), and externalizing disorders (Scott, 2010).

In addition to these classic treatments for parents, innovative *evidence-based* and *attachment-based* interventions are being developed. They integrate psychoeducational and behavioral support with more specific work on the mental state of the parent in terms of promoting sensitivity and responsiveness to the affective signals of the child. This is accomplished through a joint review with the parent of videotaped clips of significant moments of interaction with the child, within a therapeutic context that is empathic and non-judgmental, aimed primarily at stimulating the ability to mentalize and explore the mind and heart of the child (e.g., thoughts, emotions, feelings, intentions, etc.).

Among the best known and currently deployed, we can mention the VIPP *(Video-feedback Intervention to Promote Positive Parenting)* family protocols: VIPP-SD, *Video-feedback Intervention to Promote Positive Parenting and Sensitive Discipline* (Barone et al., 2018; Juffer et al., 2008, 2014); VIPP-AUTI for parents of children with autism (Poslawsky et al, 2014); an adaptation of the VIPP for parents with ID (Hodes et al., 2014); VIPP-V for children who are parents of children with visual or visual and intellectual disabilities (Hodes et al, 2014; Platje et al., 2018); COS, *Circle of Security* (Powell et al., 2016); and *Connect* (Moretti et al., 2018). These interventions appear to be promising in changing attachment behaviors in caregivers and patients, but require further empirical validation for people with ID.

How do video-feedback techniques work? First, they act on the parents' ability to reorient themselves perceptually to their child, to their child's body, and are often "scotomized" in situations of disability and insecurity in the attachment bond. Subsequently, they attempt to promote the ability to explore the interior of the child him or herself: the parenting variables most involved are those related to the ability of insightfulness (Oppenheim and Koren-Karie, 2002) or *mind-mindedness* (Meins, 1997, Meins et al., 2003), i.e., of mentalizing the child in the third person, represented as a "mental agent". Such an orientation to the child's mind by the parent explains the child's ability to understand the minds of others, and to develop an adequate ability to distinguish between appearance and reality, and between different views of reality, i.e., to develop more pronounced metacognitive skills (Main, 1991; Fonagy et al., 2002; Allen and Fonagy, 2008; Arnott, 2008).

Secondly, the video allows one to see "again and again", i.e., to examine the behavior of the child and the parent in depth to better understand their mutual influences. It works on real and specific situations that directly concern them on the interactive level (e.g., the moment of lunch, of dressing or undressing, of washing, and of the management of daily routines, all of which are often so critical for children with ID). The video enables one to carefully identify the facial expressions, postural and gestural aspects of the child with ID, and represents a training ground for the parent who wants to interpret what drives and moves his or her child in a genuine and attentive way, putting "subtitles" to the meaning of his or her actions ("speaking for the child", giving voice to the child).

Furthermore, in terms of clinical interventions on adults, attachment theory has been incorporated into a number of theoretical and clinical models that have long shown a wide flexibility of application, and therefore potential calibration to the cognitive and relational skills of the person with ID (see Guidano and Liotti (1983), Guidano (1987, 1991), Liotti (2005, 2001), see also Cognitive Analytic Therapy (Ryle, 1990), Schema Therapy (Young, 1990), or some forms of brief psychodynamic psychotherapy, for which there is preliminary evidence of effectiveness). Working with subjects with ID, of course, will constitute privileged access to, and processing of, their internal experience through the procedural and experiential affective/emotional dimension, rather than through verbal semantic codes.

4.2 Working with challenging behaviors as an example of integrated intervention

In the behavioral tradition, focused largely on classical reinforcement procedures (based on the operant paradigm), the needs for attachment and maintenance of strong emotional bonds with significant others have not received sufficient consideration. However, symptomatic change, such as a reduction in the risk or frequency of challenging behaviors in ID, may vary with improvement in relationship quality (Skelly et al., 2014). Although attachment theory, which is heavily grounded in empirical work, arose and developed independently of social learning theories, ABA (*Applied Behavior Analysis*), and the broader tradition of behaviorism, some interesting developments and empirical evidence are emerging to support integration of these approaches (De Schipper and Schuengel, 2010).

Skelly (2016) proposes a promising model for working with challenging behaviors within a framework based on attachment theory, in addition to the classic behaviorist model. It is a model that also pays attention to caregivers of patients with ID, with a focus on how the child's attachment behavior affects the caregiving task. Emotionally connecting to a patient's ID condition can cause distress to caregivers, professionals, and family members who may perceive the diagnosis as discriminatory or prejudicial. Therefore, it is important to converge on a developmental model and assessment that normalizes behavior, such as the *Vineland Adaptive Behavior Scale (VABS)* (Sparrow et al., 2005). Whichever method is used to explain the actual state of the patient's abilities, however, the explanation should be returned empathically and with the express intent of identifying what is realistic to expect in terms of new learning, seeking a balance between the acquisition of new skills and dependence on assistance.

It is essential, as previously mentioned, in working with people with ID and challenging behaviors, to be able to view these acts as possessing individual and interpersonal meaning. Such meaning is usually not explicitly available, but must be searched together with the patient him or herself and those who care for him or her. Similarly, it will be crucial to move from technical language, marked more by the "management" or "planning of strategies" of the patient and his or her behaviors, to one that is based more on attachment, and on the understanding of the affective value of his or her behaviors and on reflection. Self-reflectiveness and the ability to empathically mentalize the person with ID, exploring his or her emotions, thoughts, intentions, goals, etc., becomes a critical aspect of the intervention, rather than responding with therapeutic actions to the actions of the individual that is being cared for. This proposed intervention can be summarized in the following points.

4.3 The main dimensions of working with challenging behaviors

Assessment: Behavior, Safety-Insecurity, and Emotions. Alongside the functional analysis of challenging behaviors, the construction of *explanatory* hypotheses for them by professionals is of equal importance. A key part of the assessment process is to introduce the idea that emotional safety is central to psychological well-being.

Developing a joint hypothesis. Based on this principle, a joint hypothesis should be developed by all who are involved in working with the challenging behavior. A hypothesis that may or may not be expressed in technical language, in any case, should be consistent with functional analysis and informed by those principles of care that engender emotional safety. The use of punishment (e.g., time-out, response cost, punishment, etc.) or emotional withdrawal by professionals should be discouraged, and challenging behaviors considered on the basis of an explanatory hypothesis compatible with both the principles of operant conditioning and the principles of attachment theory.

Understanding emotions and resisting ejection. Inevitably, working with people who have histories of traumatic relationships can also lead professionals to experience deep negative feelings, which can result in dysfunctional coping strategies based on their own attachment patterns. All of this, at the most critical times, can also lead to a conscious or unconscious desire to "get rid" of the patient, and this often underlies what is known as the *multiple placement phenomenon*, in which the people who would least need to start over in their closest relationships are forced into this situation. Therefore, it is imperative to consider attachment styles, emotional competencies, support networks, and the care of professional caregivers and family members. Constant attention to the mental state of caregivers and their subsequent reactions, aiming for maximum self-reflectiveness and awareness, therefore becomes a central part of the intervention.

Team meetings. Staff team meetings constitute a key pillar of the intervention. The primary focus is to consider how the patient's relationship with the caregiver is progressing in terms of physical and emotional safety, mutual satisfaction, and sufficient enjoyment/stimulation.

Emotional Containment. Containment, in caregiving contexts, can mean a physical act (e.g., a hug) or a psychological act (showing empathy), through the use of one's own emotional capacities, to reduce the other's distress. Physical care itself, to be effective, must always involve empathy, unconditional consideration, and genuineness toward the other. Containment should be understood as any intentional act of care that involves effectively understanding a person's sign of distress, keeping it in mind without retaliating or switching off from it, attempting to understand what need is being signaled, and responding to it as calmly and effectively as possible.

Retaining Empathy. It may seem obvious that caregivers should remain compassionate and empathic toward the people that they care for; however, it may be helpful to acknowledge that this is difficult even under the best of circumstances. Processing painful emotions is a fundamental part of the caregiving role. To this end, it is necessary to keep in mind that behavior problems are highly informative, fulfill an underlying human need, and are not necessarily inevitable. Moreover, the loss of empathy that sometimes occurs, often at the time of greatest concern for the safety of the patient or others, may occur unevenly, depending on the personalities of caregivers and their attachment histories.

Continuous Commitment. The stability and predictability of a relationship is central to an intervention based on attachment principles. It is essential that psychological services provide a "secure base" for the person with ID, remain available, and develop long-term relationships with caregivers. In addition, monitoring should be done at regular but relatively distant times, and eventually in subsequent discharge and follow-up. Only by recognizing that the person's challenging behavior is aimed at fulfilling an underlying need and that his or her emotional safety is tied to the possibility to contain this behavior within current caregiving relationships, will it be possible to face all of the risks involved in treating and managing these complex patients.

5 The intervention with Veronica

5.1 Veronica's history

Charitas is a residence for people with intellectual disabilities and extensive support needs (Ruggerini et al, 2021). It was founded in Modena (Italy) in 1942. People with ID and extensive support needs constitute a highly heterogeneous group, generally characterized by severe limitations in intellectual functioning and adaptive behavior. People in this group might also experience motor disorders, sensory deficits, severe communication problems, and other physical or mental conditions. This group also includes people who do not share the mentioned characteristics, but present severe challenging behaviors that significantly constrain their functioning to the extent that they require extensive or generalized support in their daily life (Esteban et al., 2021).

Veronica belongs to the latter subgroup. She entered Charitas in 2014, when she was 23 years old, after numerous admissions to diagnosis and treatment wards since the age of 16 and after the failure of several "territorial" proposals. Veronica lived with her mother, her mother's partner, and a half-brother. She was admitted to a psychiatric setting where it was decided that she would be admitted to Charitas. The presentation that the reference psychiatrists made of Veronica essentially concerns her behavior, described as follows: "Veronica has a low threshold of irritability for which she enacts explosive acts, but not repetitive behaviors, as are the stereotypes for autistic people: contained in her room, for example, she does not continually bang her head against the wall, but she may punch or kick the wall". Veronica is able to imagine her future in her family, but only with the support of an educator and/or assistant; she has her own "work project"; she sleeps in a room with her friend; and she asked her psychiatrist to suspend the Depot psychopharmacological therapy because "after the injection, she feels groggy".

Veronica was taken care of by Child Neuropsychiatry Services from the age of two years and at the age of 18 years by the Mental Health Center of Territorial Competence. Over time, she has received many categorical diagnoses, some of which are related to neurodevelopmental disorders: *Mild Cognitive Retardation* (school age), *Moderate Mental Retardation* (2014), *Middle Grade Phrenasthenia* (2015), *Mild Intellectual Disability/ Limited Intellectual Level* (2016); and others to the co-morbidity of a mental disorder: *Impulse Control Difficulty* and *Oppositional/Provocative Behavior* (school-aged); *Psychosis* (adolescent-aged); *Passive-Aggressive Personality Disorder* (after 18 years old); *Borderline Personality Disorder* (after 18 years old); *Anxiety Disorder; and Somatoform Disorder.*

In her clinical pathway, Veronica received three assessments aimed to evaluate the kind of ID. Specifically, in a first evaluation, the Wechsler Test (a multi-componential test) was used; in a recent evaluation, the Raven Matrices Test (a test that analyzes only one component of cognitive functioning) was used; and in an intermediate evaluation, the Vineland Scale (which measures adaptive functioning) was used. The three methods led to different results that did not overlap, and were probably induced in the context different expectations. The most reliable categorical diagnosis for Veronica, compatible with the data of scientific knowledge and with the data of her history (in the years 2014–2020), is the one that takes into account her positive evolution in the face of the modification of a set of contextual factors. It does not seem possible, therefore, to confirm the categorical diagnoses of psychosis and personality disorder.

5.2 Interpreting Veronica's interpersonal style

In Veronica's biography, there is a key episode: a sexual abuse carried out by her mother's partner and denounced by Veronica herself when she was an adolescent. This was an abuse that occurred in a context that a clinical report defines as an "important socio-cultural disadvantage". As is well known, even more important than abuse, in terms of psycho-pathological effects, is whether or not it is experienced in a context of protection and security by one's primary attachment figures. In Veronica's case, unfortunately, her mother, when she learned of her partner's abuse, painfully ended up choosing her partner over her. This suggests the basic characteristics of the attachment bond with the mother, the sense of invalidation of her own experience, together with deep feelings of abandonment potentially experienced by Veronica.

In Veronica's story, there is also an indication of her desire to be able to live in her family, with her mother, despite her mother's explicit refusal to do so. This key desire is obviously expressed by Veronica on a behavioral level. In one of the many reports accompanying Veronica's admission to Charitas, the following is written: "… the reasons for the aggressive episodes would seem to be almost always attributable to the lack of acceptance of the impossibility of returning to her mother's house." Often, in these relational contexts, there is a more or less explicit ambivalence ("I love you, but I can't keep you") that keeps intense feelings of abandonment alive, together with constant and often dramatic, albeit indirect, ways of signaling by the child.

All of the observations of Veronica's interpersonal style found in her clinical history, up to the behavioral observations in the current context, refer to internal operating models of resistant anxiety type in early childhood and then of active coercive type (in the language of the DMM): hyperactive emotional/affective regulation style, difficulty in negotiating needs, difficulty in exploration processes, and tendency to burden the state of relationship with the other through modes that oscillate between anger (used as an anxiolytic) and instrumentally passive attitudes. Strategies focused on managing deep feelings of vulnerability in the relationship with a world perceived as unpredictable and dangerous. Obviously, the intellectual deficit can make such perceptions of unpredictability and poor sense of mastery of their environment even more intense.

In the 2016 evaluation, a formulation of the critical event, in the light of attachment theory, was proposed (but also shared and emotionally processed within the care team). The critical event may have allowed Veronica to directly confront how unpredictable, insecure, and unprotective her attachment bonds are. Her protesting and aggressive behaviors possess, precisely, a tacit meaning of an active coercive type, forcing the context to reorient itself to her need for predictability and a "secure base".

5.3 The actions that were the most effective

Veronica has a modest cognitive deficit. This suggests her high capacity for (non-academic) learning when exposed to appropriate situations. It should be noted that Veronica aspires to a visible and stable social role. The issue, still open, in her personal history is that of the ties with her family (mother and brother). The psychopharmacological therapy was regulated through periodic meetings with healthcare service psychiatrists, who also received contributions from specialist consultants of Charitas. A consensus existed on the advisability of an initial simplification of the therapy, but there were unequivocal evaluations afterwards. The answer to Veronica's issue has important ethical implications: is her issue, given the diagnosis of ID, *a priori* unreliable? Can it constitute the basis of a therapeutic alliance? Veronica's issue, carefully examined by the treating specialists, highlights the particularity of the therapeutic relationship in the residential context and, once again, the ease with which it could be evaded with a simplified solution, depriving her of any capacity for self-determination.

Veronica, in the examined time frame, had good clinical development, but what type of action was most effective for her?

Contrasting the "sick role": In the first months of stay in the residence, Veronica presented as a person who is totally dependent on her reference operator, and who has made the negative aspects of her biography the essential elements of the identity with which she presents herself in relationships. In the period October/November 2014, in order to overcome this problem, a strategy was elaborated that divided management and pedagogical support from the relational "psychological" part (to note the importance in these organizations of the Self, introducing boundaries, cognitive order, defined roles, etc.). In January 2015, it is noted that the weekly intervention yielded good results. Specifically, the operators confirm that Veronica has reduced the frequency with which she proposes the telling of her story and, if she does propose it, they manage to postpone it with ease.

Encourage self-narrative in periodic meetings: Starting in January 2016, Veronica participates in weekly meetings with educators on the same day at the same time with the goal of talking about herself. Each meeting is summarized by Veronica and her educators in a paragraph of a text entitled "My Story". The text is surprising for its wealth of information, accuracy of temporal order, and reference to episodes that were significant for Veronica in her school and family life. In the text, we notice that, after approximately two years, a greater number of terms that define emotional states (e.g., anger), and this occurs after Veronica's participation in a group activity dedicated to the description of emotional states. The educators maintain a relationship based on listening and sharing, and consciously avoid application of psychotherapy techniques. It should be noted that the sexual violence committed by the stepfather is rarely in the foreground. Veronica describes how, feeling at ease, she talked about it with one of her educators on a particular occasion.

Reconstruction of a relationship perceived as more authentic, less ambiguous, and therefore sufficiently "safe" with the family of origin: Veronica, together with her educators, slowly approaches her family once her stepfather has moved away. The approach is supported by the physical and emotional closeness of the educators, and is articulated in different times and modalities. In this context, the death of the mother represented a particularly critical event. The mother died on a Saturday, at which time all of the operators gathered at Charitas to inform her, ready to welcome any kind of reaction, which at the moment was not there. Subsequently, she cried for days uninterruptedly. She exhibited no aggressive reaction, but wanted to know all of the details of her mother's passing. This was a very hard period, marked by great suffering, which with time and work changed her perspective on herself and others. She has had her brother and grandmother with whom she is very close, but the death of her mother changed her way of seeing her future life. Specifically, it made her more adult, and constituted the key moment of her growth. The educators accompanied her for a long time in the memory and reconstruction of the figure of her mother. Currently, visits to the family, composed of the grandmother and her brother, are an ordinary event driven by desire or suggested by an anniversary. As for her father, Veronica had known him when she was a child, and then she no longer remembered him, but she always asked about him. For a certain period of time, the operators protected her, perhaps excessively, with the objective of isolating her from further suffering. Then, an operator, in a purely random manner, found the phone number and Facebook contact information of her father, found him, and one day they met. They saw each other a few times, immediately after the mother's death, and then called each other fairly regularly. Veronica thus managed to better understand the father figure, and resolved the emotions connected to it.

Allowing the acquisition of a social role inside and outside Charitas: Since her admission to Charitas, the educators have "bracketed" her diagnoses and her challenging behaviors, highlighted her abilities in daily life, and sought a positive and active role for her. The goal was to facilitate an experience of meaning that is appropriate to her abilities. As an apprentice, Veronica has made her own path: she took care of some of her classmates when she belonged to the "Napoleon Group"; she collaborated with the operators in keeping the vacation home tidy; and she had a paid role within the "Charitas Wardrobe". In this research, the educators literally invented a new service for her within Charitas: a snack bar that she could manage for the residents and staff. The educators have also diligently attempted to establish the same opportunity outside of the residence.

Solidity of response to challenging behaviors: In the first few years of her stay at Charitas, Veronica had problem behaviors that greatly alarmed the residence staff, including aggressive fighting, burning a cart in a toilet facility, and direct requests made for help to 911. Sometimes, these behaviors led to hospitalization in a psychiatric setting and other times did not. The actions of the operators were guided by the reflexivity allowed by a constantly mentalizing attitude towards Veronica, and supported by the reading of the meaning of the problem behaviors in light of attachment theory, keeping in mind the perception of vulnerability and unpredictability, and the feelings of abandonment underlying the coercive behaviors enacted. For this reason, the response was always both restraining and empathic (sensitive discipline), as if to reaffirm the solidity of the "secure base" residence and the interpersonal bonds established.

Veronica's last hospitalization was two years ago. Her psychopharmacological therapy has not been weighed down in terms of dosages, but rather, has been lightened: the *clinical* outcome is therefore good. Veronica maintains her own activity in the Charitas wardrobe department; she participates in an agricultural activity outside of Charitas; and she has even participated in a sailing activity. The *functional* outcome is therefore once again favorable. The *personal* outcome is probably the most difficult metric to determine: what is Veronica's greatest desire or priority? One of them is certainly to return to her family as a "safe" place, something that currently takes place with the support of educators. For now, this aspiration seems to be, at least partially, satisfied, but there are still other common aspirations (e.g., work, emotional relationships, friendships, etc.) towards which to continue to strive.

References

Allen J. G. and Fonagy P. (2008). *La mentalizzazione: psicopatologia e trattamento*. Bologna: Il Mulino.

Arnott, B. and Meins E. (2007). Links among antenatal attachment representations, postnatal mind-mindedness, and infant attachment security: a preliminary study of mothers and fathers. *Bulletin of the Menninger Clinic*, 71(2), 132–149. https://doi.org/10.1521/bumc.2007.71.2.132.

Arnott, B. (2008). Continuity in mind-mindedness from pregnancy to the first year of life. *Infant and Behavioral Development*, 31(4), 647–654. https://doi.org/10.1016/j.infbeh.2008.07.001.

Atkinson, L., Chisolm, V. C., Scott, B., Goldberg, S., Vaughn, B. E., and Blackwell, J. (1999). Maternal sensitivity, child functional level and attachment in Down syndrome. *Monographs of the Society for Research in Child Development*, 64(3): 45–66. https://doi.org/10.1111/1540-5834.00033.

Barnett, D., Clements, M., Kaplan-Estrin, M., and Fialka, J. (2003). Building new dreams: supporting parents' adaptation to their child with special needs. *Infants and Young Children*, 16(3), 184–200.

Bara, B. G. (Ed.) (2006). *Nuovo manuale di psicoterapia cognitiva*. Torino: Bollati Boringhieri.

Barone, L., Barone, V., Dellagiulia, A., and Lionetti, F. (2018). Testing an attachment-based parenting intervention VIPP-FC/A in adoptive families with post-institutionalized children: do maternal sensitivity and genetic markers count? *Frontiers in Psychology*, 19(9), 156. https://doi.org/10.3389/fpsyg.2018.00156.

Barone, L. and Lionetti F. (2012). Attachment and social competence: a study using MCAST in low-risk Italian preschoolers. *Attachment and Human Development*, 14(4), 391–403.

Beail, N. (2002). Interrogative suggestibility, memory and intellectual disability. *Journal of Applied Research in Intellectual Disabilities*, 15(2), 129–137. https://doi.org/10.1046/j.1468-3148.2002.00108.x.

Bicknell, J. (1983). The psychopathology of handicap. *British Journal of Medical Psychology*, 56(2), 167–178. https://doi.org/10.1111/j.2044-8341.1983.tb01544.x.

Bowlby, J. (1969-1982). *Attachment and Loss: Vol. 1. Attachment*. New York: Basic Books.

Bowlby, J. (1973). *Attachment and Loss: Vol. 2. Separation: Anxiety and Anger*. New York: Basic Books.

Bowlby, J. (1980). *Attachment and Loss. Vol. 3: Loss, Sadness and Depression*. New York: Basic Books.

British Psychology Society (2017). *Incorporating Attachment Theory into Practice: Clinical Practice Guideline for Clinical Psychologists working with People who have Intellectual Disabilities*.

Bruce, E. J., Schultz, C. L., Smyrnios, K. X., and Schultz, N. C. (1994). Grieving related to development: a preliminary comparison of three age cohorts of parents with children with intellectual disability. *British Journal of Medical Psychology*, 67(1): 37–52. https://doi.org/10.1111/j.2044-8341.1994.tb01769.x.

Cartwright-Hatton, S., McNally, D., Field, A. P., Rust, S., Laskey, B., Dixon, C., Gallagher, B., Harrington, R., Miller, C., Pemberton, K., Symes, W., White C., Woodham, A. (2011). A new parenting-based group intervention for young anxious children: results of a randomized controlled trial. *Journal of the American Academy of Child and Adolescent Psychiatry*, 50(3), 242–251. https://doi.org/10.1016/j.jaac.2010.12.015.

Cicchetti, D. (1984). The emergence of developmental psychopathology. *Child Development*, 55(1), 1–7.

Cicchetti, D., and Serafica, F. C. (1981). Interplay among behavioral systems: illustrations from the study of attachment, affiliation, and wariness in young children with Down's syndrome. *Developmental Psychology*, 17(1), 36–49. https://doi.org/10.1037/0012-1649.17.1.36.

Crittenden, P. M. (2005). Teoria dell'attaccamento, psicopatologia e psicoterapia: L'approccio dinamico maturativo. *Psicoterapia*, 30, 171–182. http://www.patcrittenden.com/include/docs/attachment_theory_2005.pdf.

Crittenden, P. M., and Landini A. (2011). *Assessing Adult Attachment: A Dynamic-Maturational Approach to Discourse Analysis*. New York: Norton.

DeKlyen, M., and Greenberg, M. T. (2008). Attachment and psychopathology in childhood. In J. Cassidy and P. Shaver (eds), *Handbook of Attachment: Theory, Research and Clinical Applications*. New York (2nd ed.): Guilford Press

De Schipper, J. C., and Schuengel, C. (2006). *Secure Base Safe Haven Observation list for child attachment behaviour*. Unpublished work, VU University, Amsterdam.

De Schipper, J. C., and Schuengel, C. (2010). Attachment behaviour towards support staff in young people with intellectual disabilities: Associations with challenging behaviour. *Journal of Intellectual Disability Research*, 54(7), 584–596. https://doi.org/10.1111/j.1365-2788.2010.01288.x.

Esteban L., Navas P., Verdugo M. A., and Arias V. B.(2021). Community living, intellectual disability and extensive support needs: a right-based approach to assessment and intervention. *International Journal of Environmental Research and Public Health*, 18(6), 3175. https://doi.org/10.3390/ijerph18063175.

Fletcher H. K., Flood, A., and Hare, D. J. (2016) *Attachment in Intellectual and Developmental Disability: A Clinician's Guide to Practice and Research*. New York: Wiley

Fonagy, P., Gergely, G., Jurist, E. L., Target, M. (2002). *Regolazione affettiva, mentalizzazione e sviluppo di sé*. Milano: Raffaello Cortina.

George, C., and West, M. (2001). The development and preliminary validation of a new measure of adult attachment: the Adult Attachment Projective. *Attachment and Human Development*, 3(1), 30–61. https://doi.org/10.1080/14616730010024771.

Guidano, V. F., and Liotti, G. (1983). *Cognitive Processes and Emotional Disorders*, New York: Guilford Press

Guidano, V. F. (1987). *Complexity of the Self*. New York: Guilford Press (Italian version La complessità del Sé. Torino: Bollati Boringhieri, 1988).

Guidano, V. F. (1991). *The Self in Process: toward a Post-Rationalist Cognitive Therapy*. New York: Guilford.

Hazan, C., and Shaver, P. (1987). Romantic love conceptualized as an attachment process. *Journal of Personality and Social Psychology*, 52(3), 511–524. https://doi.org/10.1037/0022-3514.52.3.511.

Hill, D. (2015). *Affect Regulation Theory: A Clinical Model*, New York: Norton and Company.

Hodes, M. W., Meppelder, M., Schuengel, C., Kef, S. (2014). Tailoring a video-feed- back intervention for sensitive discipline to parents with intellectual disabilities: a process evaluation. *Attachment and Human Development*, 16(4), 387–401. https://doi.org/10.1080/14616734.2014.912490.

Holder, J. (2000). *Parental Adaptation to the Diagnosis of a Learning Disability in Their Child: Associations with Affective Representations of Parenting*. Unpublished Doctoral thesis.

Hornby G. (1994). *Counseling in Child Disability: Skills for Working with Parents*. London: Chapman and Hall.

Horsch, A., Brooks, C., Fletcher, H. (2013). Maternal coping, appraisal and adjustment following diagnosis of fetal anomaly. *Prenatal Diagnosis*, 33(12), 1137–1145. https://doi.org/10.1002/pd.4207.

Juffer, F., Bakermans-Kranenburg, M. J., and Van IJzendoorn, M. H. (2008). *Promoting Positive Parenting: An Attachment-Based Intervention*. Hove: Psychology Press.

Juffer, F., Bakermans-Kranenburg, M. J., and Van Ijzendoorn M. H. (2014). Attachment-based interventions: sensitive parenting is the key to positive parent-child relationships. In P. Holmes, S. Farnfield, (eds), *The Routledge Handbook of Attachment: Implications and Interventions* (pp. 83–103). London: Routledge.

Juffer, F., and Steele, M. (2014). What words cannot say: the telling story of video in attachment-based interventions. *Attachment and Human Development*, 16(4), 307–314. https://doi.org/10.1080/14616734.2014.912484.

Kaminski, J. W., Valle, L. A., Filene, J. H., and Boyle, C. L. (2008). A meta-analytic review of components associated with parent training program effectiveness. *Journal of abnormal child psychology*, 36, 567–589. https://doi.org/10.1007/s10802-007-9201-.

Korff-Sausse, S. (1999). A psychoanalytical approach to mental handicap. In J. De Groef and E. Heinemann (eds). *Psychoanalysis and Mental Handicap*. London: Routledge.

Lambruschi, F. (ed) (2014). *Psicoterapia cognitiva dell'età evolutiva, procedure d'assessment e strategie psicoterapeutiche* (2nd edizione). Torino: Bollati Boringhieri.

Lambruschi, F., and Lionetti, F. (2015). Genitorialità: tra valutazione, sostegno e buone prassi. In Lambruschi, F., Lionetti, F. (eds). *La Genitorialità: Strumenti di Valutazione e Interventi di Sostegno*. Roma: Carocci Editore.

Lambruschi, F., and Muratori, P. (2013). *Psicopatologia e psicoterapia dei disturbi della condotta*. Roma: Carocci Editore.

Larson, F. V., Alim, N., and Tsakanikos, E. (2011). Attachment style and mental health in adults with intellectual disability: Self-reports and reports by carers. *Advances in Mental Health and Intellectual Disabilities*, 5(3): 15–23. https://doi.org/10.1108/20441281111142585.

Lionetti, F., Pluess, M., and Barone L. (2014). Vulnerabilità, resilienza o differente permeabilità? Un confronto tra modelli per lo studio dell'interazione individuo-ambiente. *Psicologia clinica dello sviluppo*, 18(2), 163–182. https://doi.org/10.1449/77633.

Liotti, G. (1994). *La Dimensione Interpersonale della Coscienza*. Firenze: La Nuova Italia Scientifica.

Liotti, G. (2001). *Le opere della coscienza*. Milano: Cortina.

Main, M. (1991). Metacognitive knowledge, metacognitive monitoring, and singular (coherent) vs. multiple (incoherent) model of attachment: findings and directions for future research. In C. M. Parkers, J. Stevenson-Hinde, and P. Marris (eds), *Attachment Across the Life Cycle*. London: Routledge.

Marvin, R. S., and Pianta, R. C. (1996). Mother's reactions to their child's diagnosis: Relations with security of attachment. *Journal of Clinical Child Psychology*, 25(4), 436–445. https://doi.org/10.1207/s15374424jccp2504_8.

McConachie, H., and Diggle, T. (2007). Parent-mediated early intervention for young children with autism spectrum disorder: a systematic review. *Journal of Evaluation in Clinical Practice*, 13(2), 120–129. https://doi.org/10.1002/14651858.CD003496.

Meins, E. (1997). *Security of Attachment and the Social Development of Cognition*. Hove: Psychology Press.

Meins, E., Fernyhough, C., Wainwright, R., Clark-Carter, D., Das Gupta, M., Fradley, E. and Tuckey, M. (2003). Pathways to understanding mind: Construct validity and predictive validity of maternal mind-mindedness. *Child Development*, 74(4), 1194–1211. https://doi.org/10.1111/1467-8624.00601.

Miltiades, H. B., and Pruchno, R. (2002). The effect of religious coping on caregiving appraisals of mothers of adults with developmental disabilities. *Gerontologist*, 42(1), 82–91. https://doi.org/10.1093/geront/42.1.82.

Moretti, M. M., Pasalich, D. S., and O'Donnel, K. A. (2018). CONNECT: An attachment-based program for parents of teens. In H. Steele and M. Steele (eds.), *Handbook of Attachment-Based Interventions*. New York: Guilford Press.

Oppenheim, D., and Koren-Karie, N. (2002). Mothers' insightfulness regarding their children's internal worlds: the capacity underlying secure child-mother relationship. *Infant Mental Health Journal*, 23(6), 593–605. https://doi.org/10.1002/imhj.10035.

Penketh, V., Hare, D. J., Flood, A., and Walker, S. (2014). Attachment in adults with intellectual disabilities: preliminary investigation of the psychometric properties of the manchester attachment scale – third party observational measure. *Journal of Applied Research in Intellectual Disabilities*, 27(5), 458–470. https://doi.org/10.1002/imhj.10035.

Pianta, R. C., and Marvin, R. S. (1992). *The Reaction to Diagnosis Classification System*. Unpublished materials, University of Virginia.

Platje, E., Sterkenburg, P., Overbeek, M., Kef, S., and Schuengel C. (2018). The efficacy of VIPP-V parenting training for parents of young children with a visual or visual-and-intellectual disability: a randomized controlled trial. *Attachment and Human Development*, 20(5), 455–472. https://doi.org/10.1080/14616734.2018.1428997.

Poslawsky I. E., Naber, F., Bakermans-Kranenburg, M., and van Daalen, E. (2014). Video-feedback intervention to promote positive parenting adapted to autism (VIPP-AUTI): a randomized controlled trial. *Autism,* 19(5), 588–603. https://doi.org/10.1177/1362361314537124.

Powell, B., Cooper, G., Hoffman, K., and Marvin, B. (2016). *The Circle of Security Intervention. Enhancing Attachment in Early Parent-Child Relationships*. New York: Guilford Press.

Ramchandani, P., Van Jzendoorn M. H., and Bakermans-Kranenburg, M. J. (2010). Differential susceptibility to fathers' care and involvement: the moderating effect of infant reactivity. *Family Science*, 1(2), 93–101. https://doi.org/10.1080/19424621003599835.

Ruggerini C., Rebecchi M., Seghedoni P., Arletti C., Benatti C. (2021). *La passione del possibile: Trent'anni del Charitas di Modena (1990–2020): un impegno in evoluzione*, Reggio Emilia: Consulta.

Ryle, A (1990). *Cognitive Analytic Therapy: Active Participation in Change*. Hoboken: John Wiley and Sons.

Scott, S. (2010). Randomised controlled trial of parent groups for child antisocial behaviour targeting multiple risk factors: the SPOKES Project. *Journal of Child Psychology and Psychiatry and Allied Disciplines*, 5(1), 48–57. https://doi.org/10.1111/j.1469-7610.2009.02127.x.

Schore A.N. (2003). *Affect disregulation and the Disorder of Self*, New York: Norton and Company.

Skelly, A., (2016). Maintaining the bond: working with people who are described as showing challenging behavior using a framework based on attachment theory. In Fletcher, H. K. et al. (2016). *Attachment in Intellectual and Developmental Disability: A Clinician's Guide to Practice and Research*, New York: Wiley.

Skelly, A., Collins, C., and Dosanjh, M. (2014). Clinician judged attachment narrative style and the course and outcome of psychodynamic therapy in people with intellectual disabilities. Presentation to Advancing Practice. Annual Conference of the British Psychological Society DCP Faculty for People with Intellectual Disabilities, Llandudno.

Smith, P., and McCarthy, G. (1996). The development of a semi-structured interview to investigate the attachment related experiences of adults with learning disabilities. *British Journal of Learning Disabilities*, 24(4), 154–160. https://doi.org/10.1111/j.1468-3156.1996.tb00225.x.

Sparrow, S. S., Cicchetti, D. V., and Balla, D. A. (2005). *Vineland Adaptive Behaviour Scales*, (2nd edition). Minneapolis: Pearson (Italian version Balboni, G. et al. (2016).Vineland Adaptive Behavior Scales Second Edition – Survey Forms. Adattamento italiano. Manuale. Firenze: Giunti OS)

Sroufe, L. A. and Rutter, M. (1984). The domain of developmental psychopathology. *Child Development*, 55(1), 17–29.

Waters, E. (1995). Appendix A: The Attachment Q-Set (Version 3.0). In E. Waters, B. E. Vaughn, G., Posada and K. Kondo-Ikemura (eds). *Caregiving, Cultural, and Cognitive Perspectives on Secure-Base Behavior and Working Models: New Growing Points of Attachment Theory and Research. Monographs of the Society for Research in Child Development*, 60/2–3), 234–246. https://doi.org/10.1111/j.1540-5834.1995.tb00214.x.

Wilker, L., Wasow, M., and Hartfield, E. (1981). Chronic sorrow revisited: parent vs Professional depiction of the adjustment of parents mentally retarded children. *American Journal of Orthopsychiatry*, 51(1), 63–70. https://doi.org/10.1111/j.1939-0025.1981.tb01348.x.

Young, J. E. (1990). *Cognitive Therapy for Personality Disorders: A Schema-Focused Approach*. Professional Resource Exchange, Inc.

Chapter 6

Not just telling

Narratives and the construction of shared understanding in interaction

Marilena Fatigante, Samantha Salomone, and Margherita Orsolini

In structured or semi-structured conversational settings, narratives of children with communicative and pragmatic impairments are often supported by the therapist in such a way that it is difficult to discern the child's genuine contribution to the co-telling. In this chapter, we apply Conversation Analysis to analyze the sequential development of personal narratives in the interaction between a 13-years-old girl with mild intellectual disability (with associated symptoms of Autism Spectrum Disorder) and her therapist. Narratives were examined by analysing their sequential structure from the initial assessment to later stages in the treatment. Our analyses suggested that the therapist, at the beginning of the treatment, projected her perspective, anticipating and emphasizing her own (even, emotional) reactions to the heard narrative content. After the therapist developed a deeper "listening" competence, displaying an empathic hearership, practising discourse formats that foster a sense of shared understanding and intimacy, the girl's narrative discourse changed. Narratives became more elaborate and made reference to the teller's stances and emotional reactions, and problem-solving actions.

> When somebody tells you his life – and that is principally what we shall be talking about – it is always a cognitive achievement rather than a through-the-clear-crystal recital of something univocally given.
>
> (Bruner, 1987: 692)

As Bruner (1987) has posited in an original and exemplary manner, there exist two "modes" that humans use to think and make sense of what they perceive and experience in the world. In the "Paradigmatic" or logico-scientific mode the events are apprehended and explained using scientific-like rules and hypotheses which connect certain "data" with "results", and help the knower to verify "predictions" based on those

DOI: 10.4324/9781003220367-6

hypotheses. This means that the knower's "mind" operates *via* a continuous "testing" of the hypotheses over the data in the real (and social) world. Conversely, the "Narrative" mode implies that (particularly, social) phenomena are interpreted and explained not through some logic or by reference to decontextualized rules, but rather, by reference to someone's specific goals and intentions, which account for certain actions and, in turn, for certain "consequences". In the narrative mode, the world becomes comprehensible through a plot connecting an actor, an action, a result, in a specific historical, cultural and moral space.

Bruner contends that the two modes of thought are complementary and never mutually exclusive. The narrative mode of thinking, however, does not only serve the purpose of organizing and interpreting the world around us, but also of constructing a "world inside us", and building the person we are.

From a different perspective, Harvey Sacks, the first theorist and methodologist of a systematic approach to analyzing ordinary interactions via recording and transcribing talk, called "Conversation Analysis", examined storytelling for its power to create specific interactional effects or, to "respond to" some constraints and contingencies that the ongoing talk has originated. We will turn to this issue later in the chapter. As we begin, though, the question we ask is: how do narrative and narrative studies dialogue with intellectual disability?

I Narrative as cognitive achievement

We know from Katherine Nelson's famous case study (1989) the power of early narratives to organize experience: Nelson's edited book collects contributions of several authors (including developmental psychologists, such as Bruner himself, a linguist and a psychiatrist) who analyzed the monologues that a 2-year-old girl, called Emily, produced just before falling asleep, and that had been captured on tapes. The recordings showed that left alone in her crib, Emily creatively threaded narrative plots out of scattered elements of past events she was exposed to, or of conversations she heard from her parents during the day. Narratives helped her to make sense, organize and account for the complex and often inaccessible adult world and language.

Narrative abilities in children begin, thus, to emerge early in life. They work as an efficacious "genre" (Bakhtin, 1981), which allows children to work out the discovery and mastering of the causal and conceptual links between events. Narrative discourse involves different cognitive and conceptual abilities: world knowledge is intertwined with language abilities that include lexicon, syntax, grammar but also the pragmatic rules that govern the language choices, accordingly to the listener we have and in what context we are (Rollo, 2007). It may certainly be different to tell something to an interlocutor who already knows the events told (as when children are asked by mothers or other caregivers to *retell* events that have been co-experienced; cf. Ochs and Taylor 1992; Blum-Kulka and Snow, 1992) and the narrative unfolds as a "shared remembering" (Edwards and Middleton, 1988), or, telling for a recipient who is new to the events and apprehends the story for the first time (see also Goodwin, 1979, 1981).

Authors who have engaged in the study of narratives as conceptual and linguistic schemas have elaborated several models, able to capture the most basic categories that form a narrative as a public and culturally recognized artefact.

Applying it to their research on oral narratives, Labov and Waletzky's (1967) model includes the six "Stages" that are described in Box 6.1.

Box 6.1

Table 6.1 The narrative model proposed by Labov and Waletzky (1967)

Abstract: the anticipation that a story is forthcoming	It is evoked by expressions such as "You know this reminds me of a certain episode", "let me tell you a story" or routine formulas such as "Once upon a time" in written narratives, which alert that a story will be soon delivered
Orientation: describes a setting	It prepares the recipient for the telling to follow, indicating the temporal and spatial placement of the story (such as, "yesterday I was walking in the street" or, "it was a cloudy day."), but also indicating the participants who will be involved. It gives reference to what "was going on" before a certain event would take place.
Complication: the event that disrupts a typical course of events	The specification of an unusual event triggers subsequent actions. It is usually related to Orientation by temporal connectives or adverbs which give the sense of the unexpected (and then... or, "suddenly")
Evaluation: the meaning of the narrative for the teller	It qualifies the teller's (or, the story characters') emotions and perspective. An explicit mention of adjectives such as "it was terrible" or "it was a surprise/strange/amusing/crazy, or reference to emotional reactions such as "I laughed, I was scared" may be included. Although evaluative comments are often spread throughout a narrative and are "embedded" in other stages, Labov and Waletsky stress that a successful and complete narrative will always have a discrete Evaluation stage

Resolution: the prota-gonist's attempts to resolve the crisis and return to an equilibrium	Causal conjunction relations between the actions so employed and the return to a "normal" or "routine" course of actions need to be here specified
Coda: a conclusion	In conversational narratives, the Coda signals to readers that the speaker has concluded the story and implies one or few comments that generalize what one could have "learnt" from a story, or what the story tells for the general understanding of experiences like that.

A model, particularly applied to the assessment and recognition of children's abilities to tell narratives, is the "grammar of stories", elaborated by Stein and Glenn (1979), in which the author identifies categories, partially overlapping with those mentioned by Labov and Waletsky. Models of this sort are particularly helpful in describing the story as a cognitive schema, in which events are not only linked by temporal but also and primarily causal links. The "well-formedness" of a story and the respect of a sequential logic in the different parts of it would, thus, also mean that the cognitive ability to establish coherent and plausible relations between events, actions, and personal internal states (motives, goals, desires, emotional reactions) is preserved. The assessment and the training of narrative skills *via* story grammar categories have been used particularly in tasks of elicited narratives, including the use of picture books (which the child is asked to describe), tasks of joint reading or "read-and-tell" (Baumgartner and Devescovi, 1993). Popular tools of this sort are the "Bus story" (Renfrew, 1991), used for eliciting story retelling and the "Frog story" (Mayer, 1969), used for eliciting story generation.

Structured tasks of re-production of stories provided by the researcher have also been widely used for the assessment of a range of developmental impairments and, particularly, linguistic and pragmatic impairments (Botting, 2002), autism (Tager-Flusberg, 1995; Capps et al., 2000), and learning disabilities (Roth et al, 1995). Indicators of narrative ability in these tasks are the mean length of utterance (MLU), or the number of different words and the total number of words in a given time (Miller, 1991). In all testing situations using pre-formed material, the researcher /interviewer of the child needs to remain neutral, giving minimal prompts to only solicit the child to continue. Studies (see the review by Amorotti et al., 2021) report that children with language or learning impairments, as compared to children with typical development, produce shorter narratives, with simpler syntactic constructions, less accurate and clear. Furthermore, they are more vulnerable to errors, omissions or ambiguities in the overall sequential and logical organization and connection between different story units.

As reported by Amorotti, et al. (2021), there is a dearth of studies that have employed personal narratives as assessment tools. The few studies that have done that, report that personal narratives are associated with a higher quality of narrative ability (in terms of cohesion, characterization of the teller, and others' emotional responses, length, and detail) (McCabe et al., 2008; Epstein and Phillips, 2009; Celinska, 2004).

Compared to the investigation of children with Learning disabilities or Language-Specific Impairment, studies on Intellectual disability and narrative are still scarce and scattered. Some of the studies concentrate on specific syndromes. Engaging children (between 10–16 years old) in a task of listening and retelling the Frog Stories and then applying the story grammar coding scheme to the single episodes in the story, Channell et al. (2015) suggest that children with Down Syndrome can express the key story elements (conceptual knowledge) but their narrative ability is much affected by language (particularly, syntactic) limitations, particularly for the use of verbs and connectives. Further, they appear to have most difficulties in the expression of Attempts, which implies the anticipation of the character's goals and internal states (that also means perspective-taking).

The methodological preference for structured narrative tasks implies that children are asked to do something they would not engage in spontaneously, on materials and goals that, however familiar, they did not choose. Also, the testing procedure requires that the recipient of a story is a neutral adult who most of the time already knows the story. These elements subsume a view of narrative as detached from ordinary experience, observable as monologue and privileged as a cognitive achievement rather than a tool for action and *inter*action. On the contrary, we know from the study of conversational storytelling in everyday life that telling stories is an interactive and negotiated outcome of the conversation, and always serves emotional and moral purposes, also related to the construction of self-identity (Bamberg, 2008).

Studies on mealtime conversations with children aged 3–5 and their older siblings (Ochs and Taylor, 1992; Ochs et al., 1992; Blum-Kulka and Snow, 1992; Blum-Kulka 1993; Pontecorvo and Fasulo, 1997) show that the argumentative context and the multiparty conversational framework allow children to be active and competent tellers. Engaging in family narratives also provides the children with the opportunity to sense parent-child and family *identity*, exposing them, even in the role of *bystanders* and *audience* to the telling (Goffman, 1979; Fatigante, et al. 1998), to *family culture* and values they can legitimately partake (Ochs and Taylor, 1992; Pontecorvo and Arcidiacono, 2007).

Ochs et al. (2005), observing children with autism in their home settings, showed that their language productions were far less incomprehensible and incoherent than those emerging from experimental settings with pre-determined tasks. Despite the "atypicality" of the narratives, a conversation analysis revealed a "proximal relevance" in the children's conversational contributions: what was lacking in the semantic and syntactic structure could be inferable from the closeness of other formal contextual elements, suggesting that certain formal links were maintained (Ochs, et al., 2005). Adults, who share some common ground with the child as parents do, may play the role of great supporters, helping the child to maintain a coherence that would otherwise be inaccessible by a stranger.

In the field of Disability Studies, the narrative is considered of the utmost importance as a socio-cultural achievement, allowing people with ID to "tell their story on their own" and not to "be told" by others. Telling one own's story can promote a change both in the personal experience and self-concept and the social representation of disability (see Ruggerini, et al., 2013). Supporting individuals with ID to build themselves as reliable reporters of personal experiences is also important for the argumentative and accounting purposes that are needed in everyday life as well as in the presence of critical events (e.g., experiences of neglect or abuse; cf. Gentle et al., 2013).

Narrative ability develops through social interaction, and its discourse construction in conversation is deeply influenced by the role and quality of the recipients (their sensitivity, interest and trust). Thus, observing personal narratives in conversational contexts may reveal, as suggested by Ochs et al. (2005), both some children's abilities that are not revealed by more formal evaluations with tests, and adults' interactional activities that promote children's narrative discourse. Peterson and McCabe (1994) have shown that adult prompts (e.g., questions, minimal assessments, feedbacks) correlate positively with children's increasing ability to give more contextualized details of a story. It has also been observed, though, that the adults (either parents or educators) may tend to support the child with too many initiatives and requests to tell (Bunning, et al. 2013, 2017; Bunning and Ellis, 2010). A similar tendency, resulting in explicitly directive or intrusive style, has been observed in mothers of children with Down syndrome (Roach et al., 1998) and autism (Doussard-Roosevelt et al., 2003; Wan, et al., 2012).

2 Storytelling in conversational perspective: a theoretical and methodological proposal

Conversation Analysis (CA) is an approach to the study of social interaction, whose most basic assumption is that every turn at talk never belongs to the speaker only and cannot be comprehended without reference to the sequence of actions, represented by either turns or nonverbal moves, that precedes and follows it (Schegloff, 2007). Conversation Analysis maintains that even an apparently "monological" talk such as a narrative is sensitive to the interactional setting surrounding it. In Sacks' (1992) terms, stories in ordinary interaction are *occasioned* by ongoing talk, that is, they are "triggered" by some kind of contingencies in the talk in progress such as when a participant starts to report something that s/he is "reminded" due to the current topic of discussion (Jefferson 1978). Furthermore, their significance goes always beyond narrating to simply "report" something: on the contrary, they are used for interactional purposes such as building an argument, complaining, defending a stance, displaying affiliation or agreement with someone, and the like (Stokoe and Edwards, 2006). Finally, embedded in all story fabrics is also the presentation of the teller's identity: this may be suggested in the story as, for instance, a funny character, a lonely, unappreciated individual, a vulnerable, passive subject of the happened events or, on the contrary, a determinate agent able to pursue specific goals (Ochs and Capps, 2001); in all cases, the recipient is implicitly invited to share a common view with the teller not only about the "world outside" but also about the self that s/he has selected to present (Brockemeier and Carbaugh, 2001; Bamberg, 2014; De Fina, et al., 2006 among others).

Story recipients and their visible and hearable responses have a prominent role in affecting the way the narrative will be built: whether the recipient displays (or lacks) attention and engagement and signs of "affiliation" with the teller (i.e, agreement with her/his perspective or stance) has consistent effects on whether the narrative will be delivered and how, whether it will be resumed, stopped, modified (Goodwin, 1984; Stivers 2008). Recipients' actions may align (e.g. allowing the teller to continue; Stivers, 2008), by producing minimal acknowledgement such as mh mh, and affiliation signs (by nodding; vocal uptakes such as interjections; assessments that show their endorsement of the teller's stance; Stivers, 2008; Goodwin, 1984; Heritage, 2011); affiliating is a preferred move, particularly in narratives of trouble (Jefferson, 1984). On the other hand, recipients of narrative discourse may also produce responses that block, compete with (Goodwin, 1997), or derail (Mandelbaum, 1991) ongoing narratives: "storytellings may be derailed when taking up a teller's project implemented through the storytelling would conflict with other constraints on the recipient's responses. Thus, stories are always a collaborative achievement between the storyteller and the story recipient (Goodwin, 1984; Jefferson, 1978; Mandelbaum, 1989; Sacks, 1974, 1992). Whereas this may already be taken into utmost consideration by therapists who work with children with ID, or other developmental disorders, the lack of reflexive awareness of how narrative "recipientship" works in ordinary conversations may result in interventions hindering rather than supporting the child's telling. In this regard, Fasulo and Fiore (2007) have shown that, when children with autism engage in personal, episodic storytelling, professional educators are likely to ask for clarification on details that are not the focus of the child's telling. For instance, by asking questions about "when" or "where" a certain event happened, or "what size" was a certain fish recounted in the story, educators elicit a change of orientation that generates a disruption of the sequential course of the telling and suggest uncertainty of the child's telling ability itself.

The methodological interest and rigour of CA in looking in detail at the sequence of actions, and its capability to "detect" when and how coherence between turns can be unintentionally disrupted, are useful to gather empirical conversational evidence of "responsivity" (see Ainsworth et al., 1978), a well-known and useful concept already mentioned in chapter 4, which refers to a range of the mother's or caregiver's behaviours, including: attentiveness, availability to provide the child with contiguous and contingent emotional cues to her /his initiatives or, reactions, focusing on the child's interest and agenda, showing positive affect, mirroring the child's experience and promoting infant-initiated behaviour.

Several measurement scales are available today to make an assessment of whether and how a parent or caregiver rate "high" or "low" in responsivity (for instance, the Manchester Assessment of Caregiver-Infant Interaction; cf. Wan, et al., 2012, 2013; or, the PICCOLO scale; Roggman, et al., 2013). Yet, these measures are taken as indicators of the caregiver's behavior or "style", and never assessed in relation to the specific conversational activity that the interactants perform. Being responsive to a greeting ceremony, a playful exchange, a building block game, an argument, etc. do not obviously imply the same moves. Relevantly to our case, what we ask is: what does it mean to be a "responsive" listener when the child tells a story that relates to her experience? Given that a telling is always "one's own" telling, could "silence" and signs of affiliation be types of a responsive move rather than questions or invitations to elaborate? To what extent conversational initiatives that are intended to support or encourage the child's narratives, result instead in blocking or altering them?

We have examined these issues during an intervention with a child with ID, which we describe below.

3 An analysis of therapist-child conversations aimed at promoting narrative discourse

3.1 The case

Cecilia is a girl diagnosed with mild intellectual disability who also presents symptoms of an Autism Spectrum Disorder. She was involved, at age 13, in an intervention at the University Clinic on Learning Disabilities, at Sapienza University of Rome. As the girl did not live in Rome, it was decided to share the guidelines of the intervention with an educator who was familiar with the girl and could work every week at Cecilia's home. The girl also took part in an intervention that combined stimulation of cognitive and pragmatic abilities in a monthly long session in our clinic. A specific time slot was dedicated to conversation, asking Cecilia to share what happened to her when she was home and what she would like to share with the therapist. The importance of a specific "time to *tell about you*" has been observed in several other children, particularly in their pre-adolescent or adolescent age, as supportive in the construction of their self-image and capable to prompt argumentative talk and reflexive skills (see Fatigante et al., 2015, and chapter 3 in this volume). Such conversation activity was an important part of the intervention, as Cecilia's conversational and narrative abilities were dramatically impaired at the beginning. The girl had a relatively fluent language when she interacted with her parents, but interaction with the therapist was characterized by reduced speech, long pauses, and a general inhibition to speak, despite her enthusiasm for coming to the clinic and meeting the therapist.

Cecilia did not show efficacious strategies to enter conversations, e.g., taking turns at junctures of others' contributions, maintaining the topical coherence of the conversation, or introducing a new topic. Parents reported that when she was a young child she showed atypical ways to call for attention and summoning. She also showed several deficits in emotion regulation, and severe difficulties, still present, in taking into account others' emotions and thoughts.

In a previous diagnosis issued when Cecilia attended primary school, her language and pragmatic impairment were interpreted as related to her low IQ (Verbal IQ= 79; Performance IQ=61).

During middle school, she showed several deficits in socio-emotional reciprocity, with an extremely low conversational involvement with peers. The parents reported that Cecilia's interests were few and very repetitive and that they had never noticed an interest or capability in collaborative play. Deficits in the theory of mind and emotion recognition together with difficulties in metaphor comprehension were also assessed by related tests.

Mutuality in eye gaze was very unstable, and it appeared very difficult for Cecilia to use both facial expressions and prosodic cues to display relevant and coherent affective states.

3.2 Narratives in the beginning phase

In the first meetings, the conversation that Cecilia had with the psychologists of the Clinic displayed these characteristics: Cecilia initiated talk very rarely. When she did, her speech was characterized by a few simple sentences, interposed with long (> 2,5 sec) pauses. Eye contact with the interlocutor was often missing, Cecilia looked "dull", with her gaze either maintained to some unspecified space in front of her or wandering around. What appeared utmost missing, was Cecilia's emotional participation in what she talked about. After the reading of a picture book, when she would be asked to retell the sequence of episodes and the actions of characters or when she was asked to talk about personal experiences that happened to her during the past weeks, she did not appear engaged in the conversation. In both cases, she might put a smile on her face when telling or *retelling*, but one could not appreciate whether it happened by chance, as a *habitus* marking the beginning of the conversation, or, on the contrary, whether that was marking precisely an affective connotation of the tale. Moreover, the lack of eye contact made it impossible for the interlocutor to consider whether the smile was addressed to her or whether Cecilia was pursuing co-engagement with the interlocutor and recruiting her to co-experience her telling. On the part of the psychologist, the awkward structure and rhythm of the conversation induced her to mainly use questions to solicit the child's participation. Yet, these were fashioned as so-called *polar questions* which require the addressee to either confirm (with a "yes") or deny (with a "no") the premise of the question, and did not invite any further elaboration (Heritage and Raymond, 2012). Other types of the psychologist's interventions included the repetition of Cecilia's turns formulated with interrogative intonation, to solicit Cecilia's confirmation of the psychologist's understanding but also to allow the continuation by preventing the story – and conversation – to stop at the falling intonation of Cecilia's last sentence.

Most of the narratives produced by Cecilia in these first sessions were mainly "reports" (Ochs and Taylor, 1992), that is, simple descriptions "entailing two or more temporally ordered past events" (302). Examples included going shopping with the mother, coming to the Clinic by car, going to the stables Cecilia regularly attended and cleaning her horse, etc. Examples are provided below. Due to the attention that Conversation Analysis dedicates to the importance of vocal and multimodal details (e.g., prosody, volume, lengthening of the words, emphasis etc.), transcription includes symbols that mark features of speech production.

Box 6.2

Table 6.2 Legend of transcription symbols (adapted from Jefferson, 2004)

:	*Extended or stretched sound*
__ (Underlining of characters)	Vocalic emphasis
(.)	Brief pause of less than (0.2)
(1.2)	Intervals occurring within and between same or different speaker's utterances in tenths of seconds
(())	Contextual information
(don't/won't)	Transcriptionist doubt (best guess) or (guess/other guess)
.	Falling vocal pitch
?	Rising vocal pitch
!	Animated speech tone
WORD	Extreme loudness compared to surrounding talk
° °	A passage of talk noticeably softer than surrounding talk
[	Marks the beginning point at which current talk is overlapped by other talk
*	Annotation of multimodal aspects (such as, gaze) enacted by the speaker, co-occurring with the speaker's words
§	Annotation of multimodal aspects (such as, gaze) enacted by the addressee, co-occurring with the speaker's words or actions
↓↑	Marked rising and falling shifts in intonation
=	Latching of contiguous utterances, with no interval or overlap
> <	Portions of an utterance delivered at a pace noticeably quicker (> <) or slower (< >) than surrounding talk
–	Halting, abrupt cut off of sound or word
hhh:	Audible inbreaths
hh:	Audible outbreaths from such events as laughter, or sigh
wo(h)rd(h)	Outbreaths within words

Excerpt 1

T(therapist), C(Cecilia)
  ((Cecilia said that she had gone shopping with her mother))

1	T	and then what did you do
2		besides the shopping,
3		have you also been
4		somewhere else?
5		(0.5)
6	C	no.
7		(1.0)
8		then we went back to the hotel.

Here, the therapist's effort (selected among many of the same types) is to support Cecilia's episodic memory of her personal experience (i.e., an afternoon she spent with her mother going shopping). We have consistently observed that the therapist is trying to convey to Cecilia some expectations around her reports, through expressions of emphasis and appreciation. The suggestion "besides the shopping" implies that the therapist expects that other "interesting" or "newsworthy" events happened, which Cecilia may either forget or, consider not so valuable to mention. Despite the routine content of the telling and the absence of any particular affective marking by Cecilia, the therapist responded with many emphatic evaluative comments to her descriptions, such as "great!" "super!", and markers of intensified affect.

Excerpts 2–4 provide examples of the therapist's conversational posture:

Excerpt 2

1	C	we had dinner:, at the restaurant.
2	T	uh:!
3		so you even went to the restaurant yesterday
4		**great!**
5	C	((nods))

Excerpt 3 (Cecilia refers to a television series, the Cesaroni)

1	C	I still watch the Cesaroni*(.)
2		I watch them even more than Peppa Pig, ((smiling))
3	T	**wo:w! the Cesaroni are amazing!**

Excerpt 4

1 C Peppa Pig's mum always works at the computer.
2 T really? I didn't know that at all!

In conversation, interjections such as "uh!", "oh", are labelled "change of state tokens" (Heritage, 1984), in that they signal that the interlocutor apprehends something new, of which s/he was not aware before. That means she is "changing" her state of previous knowledge. "Really"? works also as a "newsmarker" (Jefferson, 1981). This means that the therapist's conversational contributions work to intensify the "tellability" (Ochs and Capps, 2001) of the narrative, that is, the consideration that the story is worth telling. Using assessments or intensifiers, the respondent's actions turn Cecilia's report into a "story", marking the event she experienced as something non–routinary, uncanonical (Bruner, 1990). As the protagonist of an event that is deemed exceptional, Cecilia's self-image as a storyteller can also gain more value. At the same time, all these items mark that the recipient of the telling, the therapist, is intensely engaged in Cecilia's narrative and interested in getting to know about her experience and daily life.

The problem in the therapist's interventions at this point, though, was that the emphatic reactions to the girl's telling came too early in the expected development of the report. By expressing her stance immediately after the child would report something, the therapist anticipated and pre-empted the chance that the child could display her own affective or moral stance (Bruner, 1990) about the events she reported. We certainly knew that Cecilia had difficulties in elaborating on her reports and providing further details about her perception of the events she experienced, and we knew how this could be frustrating for the therapist.

Evaluative comments and empathic interjections could be viewed, then, as attempts to make the conversation more "lively", and attract Cecilia's affective perspective. However, we could not know whether the child would express the same appreciation if any, that the therapist displayed, unless the therapist would leave her more time to possibly add some (even, non-vocal) material.

3.3 Analyzing the therapist-child discourse and sharing guidelines to interact with Cecilia

At about the eight session of the treatment, we started to look at the videos, examine closely the transcripts and supervise the therapist's actions. Guidelines were proposed to the therapist, including avoidance of polar questions, and overall, the abstention from the prevailing Q-A (Question-Answer) format of interaction, which made the conversation very close to an interview, invalidating the intention to introduce Cecilia into ordinary narrative skills. When some questions would be needed, it was suggested to privilege invitations such as "tell me more", "let me understand", or propose open questions focusing on the girl's emotional responses and reflections about personal and other's viewpoints such as "how did you feel" or, "what did you think about that"? The therapist was also invited to have a greater tolerance of the girl's silence and pauses, to observe whether she would initiate further talk after the completion of turns, and to refrain from immediate and excited responses. It was also indicated to provide Cecilia with an explicit formulation of the scope of this part of the intervention, explaining that it was intended as a specific space "to tell freely", a pause in between the other activities of the sessions, which were routinely formatted as "workout".

After such initial supervision we observed 15 treatment sessions and identified some change: *stories*, which would contain some sort of problematic elements, began to emerge.

Differently from reports, *stories* are characterized by the presence of *trouble*, "a central problematic event" that elicits some forms of psychological responses, or "reactions" to that event (Stein and Glenn, 1979) by either the agents or other characters of the story. In the following, Cecilia said that she lost a password to enter her tablet, something which impeded her to have access to her photos.

Excerpt 5

1	C	a friend of my aunt is repairing ((my tablet)) (.)
2		for I could not remember the code and so she is
3		now repairing it
4	T	uh. Let me understand correctly. I mean it's been repaired
5	C	yes 'cause **I felt sorry** to lose my pictures for I could not remember the code.
6		Therefore now a friend of my aunt is fixing it
7	T	oh I see. You mean you have forgotten the password of access to the tablet.
8	C	yes because I've changed it.
9	T	uh:,
10	C	((she laughs))
11	8.	(2.0)
12	T	**too bad** when such things happen, it happens to me as well. It is often the case

13   when one changes a password (...) **I see**
14 C   right.
15 T   mmh.
16   (3.0)
17 T   **I see.**
18   (2.5)
19 T   so **you felt sorry** to lose the photos?
20 C   ((nods))
21 T   °Mh mhmhmhmh.° (.) you're right
22 C   h. ((smiles))
23 T   it **would be a pity**. you had a lot in there
24 C   right
25   (6.0)
26 C   yet, I have some in the compu:ter. but those saved on the com-
         puter aren't
27   the same as those that were on the tablet
28 T   uh. °okay° okay I see.
29   (1.0)

As it can be seen from the transcript, the therapist first acknowledged the "news" incorporated in the telling ("uh") but then she explicitly asked Cecilia to help her understand correctly the gist of the telling and what the problem was. Thus, from the very beginning, there was no more acceleration toward evaluations or expressions of affiliation with the child. Cecilia, in turn, was able to provide immediately the formulation of an emotion: "I felt sorry" and also, a clear formulation of the problematic event that provoked those undesired consequences: she could not remember the code. At the same time, she also added that attempts to resolve the problem were underway.

We can observe in Cecilia's narrative, some canonical elements constituting a narrative (Stein and Glenn, 1979) such as the specification of the Initial event, the formulation of the teller's Internal response, the Attempts that the teller herself has promoted (the aunt's friend) to overcome the problem, and the Consequences (her aunt's friend attempting to fix the computer). The therapist's interventions are far less "unspecific" than they were in the earlier sessions: she intervenes to request more specification and she carefully chooses what to "recover" in Cecilia's telling, repeating exactly her emotional reaction (see line 15). It must be noted that in line 7 Cecilia laughs, a move, that appears not so relevant and "coherent" with the regret she has just expressed (for she lost the photos). On the contrary, her laughter could be coherent with the attempt to mitigate the self-derogatory evaluation that comes with her telling: the episode might suggest that she is a person who is not able to remember a password she chose and that she cannot prevent such things to happen (via, for instance, putting a note and save the password name somewhere). The therapist, though, chooses not to align with the laughter (Jefferson, 1979; Glenn, 2003) but, rather, she emphasizes the girl's feeling of loss and regret by commenting "too bad", "you felt sorry", and "it would be a pity" (to lose the photos). These are very sensitive moves, which help Cecilia to maintain, across several turns and pauses in-between turns, a focus on the relationship between the event and the personal emotion provoked by it. Also, the therapist repeatedly displays her empathic stance minimally ("I see"), thus avoiding imbuing any judgment upon the girl's telling. It is also notable that the therapist follows the girl's telling with what is commonly expected in ordinary storytelling: a "second story" (see line 9, "it happens to me as well"), that is, a story that displays recognizable features of similarity with a narrative that has been just told: in this context, the therapist's exhibit of the second story conveys to Cecilia the meaning that she is not alone with her problems (cf. Sacks, 1992: 376–383). This move does not fully prevent the girl drop the topic and choose not to elaborate (as the long pauses demonstrate); yet, it socializes the girl to how a certain affect conveyed by the narrative just told – which implies a loss of dear objects – can be experienced and shared with others. Cecilia provides more details soon after (line 22), which justifies why it is a pity that she lost her pictures: there is nowhere else she can find them. What we also observed is that, as the therapist engaged more "locally", with interventions closely related to what Cecilia was saying and aimed to solicit or "mirror" her affective states rather than evaluating them, Cecilia started to initiate interviewing the therapist about how she responded to events similar to those that happened to her. See for instance the continuation of excerpt 5. The therapist here had just given details about her "second story", by revealing that she lost all the data she had in a small computer, for she forgot the password of access to it:

Excerpt 6 (continuation of Excerpt 5)

```
1  T    anyway I could not remember the password anymore
2  C    you don't have it on your cell phone do you?
3  T    no (.) tz
4       (2.0)
5  T    yet, I did not think to do like you did and bring it to fix, you see
6       (0.5)
7       you gave me a good idea.
```

8		I would have thought about it
9	C	((she smiles))
10		(10.0)
11	C	indeed I was desperate I didn't know what to do
12	T	u:h.
13	C	my aunt thought of it.

That Cecilia started to "reverse" her role and pose questions to the therapist meant to us two main things: one, for which she learnt the pleasure and interest in the mutual sharing of information and emotional responses with a sensitive interlocutor; secondly, she started to manage the interactional format of a conversational narrative, which also allows the addressee of the telling to ask for more specification, engage in a better understanding of the information received, and finally formulate a point of view on that. In excerpt 6, it is extremely interesting to see how Cecilia asked the therapist whether she had thought of a strategy (saving the password on her cell phone) to prevent the accident: thus, she asks her to *account* for the reasons behind her behavior. Intertwined within the narrative, then, Cecilia engages in a series of rich cognitive and discursive activities: explaining, imagining a social scenario, and engaging in problem-solving.

It can also be seen in the transcript that the therapist's tolerance of the long silence finally obtains that the girl further elaborates on her emotions, in a way that she did not do at the time of her previous telling (line 35, "I was desperate") and she also explicitly casts the aunt's actions as acting as a solution to the trouble.

At a later stage of the intervention, Cecilia surprised us with the telling of her birthday party:

Excerpt 7

1	T	and so?
2		(1.0)
3		what would you tell me Ceci ((=diminutive of the girl's name))?
4		(5.0)
5	C	I celeb[rated my birthday
6	T	[((starts to nod)) mh.
7		right.
8		(1.5)
9	T	did you celebrate it?
10	C	yes! ((smiles))
11	T	°uh:° °°so =tell me so(h)mething, °°
12		(0.5)

13		that you like to share with m[e
14	C	[hmf ((smiling))
15	T	given that I – (1.5)
16		given that we were apart
17		and I could not be th[(h)e:re,
18	C	[^^eh ehh.((laughing))
19		I celebrated it at ho:me.
20	T	mh,
21	C	I invi:ted my girlfriends,
22	T	mh.
23		(5.0)
24	C	I enjoyed it. because. (.)
25		we have, (.) ((touching her finger with the other hand as to count))
26		listened to the m[u: sic,
27	T	[((nods)) mh,
28	C	and: (1.0)
29		we, played.
30	T	^m:h
31	T	so. listened to the music, and p[layed
32		[((C looks at T))
33	C	((nods))
34		(4.5)
35	C	we were all fe:males ((smiling))
36	T	uh:. (.)so a <p[arty for wo:men>!
37		[((waving her head as to mimic a "frivolous" - feminine quality))
38	C	((laughs and bends toward T))

The girl here shows that she can supply with no solicitation, the fundamental components of a narrative including a place or setting where the event took place, the characteristics of the event, and the emotions and stance upon the events experienced.

The therapist solicits her to account and provide details on what precisely she enjoyed. She does not provide her viewpoint: although the event has been clearly defined by the girl as something amusing, the therapist abstains from making a move which would easily imbue her perspective into the telling and would lead to a closing of the sequence. Instead, she privileges turns of minimal, although responsive, acknowledgement and confirmation (see lines 6, 11, 20, 22, 27, 30).

Compared to the narratives highly supported by the therapist's questions in Stage 1 of the treatment, we also have evidence of an increased frequency and length of the pauses which leave the girl space to continue on her own (lines 23–24, 34–35).

3.4 What we have learned from the analysis of the therapist–Cecilia interaction

We interpreted the way the therapist responded to Cecilia's initial reports as an instance of the so-called *Child-Directed Communication* (Ochs et al., 2005), in which the adult assumes the child as someone who is always supposed to need support and solicitation, with little opportunity of enough time for elaborating her contribution. It is a "habitus" (Bourdieu, 1990) well exemplified by the "baby talk" register, in which the educational role of the adult is conveyed by high intonation and other language characteristics focused on eliciting the child's attention and providing stimuli that are more easily processed and memorized. Discussing these concepts with the therapist (one of this chapter's co-authors), she told us that her tendency to comment on Cecilia's ordinary reports with exaggerated affect and to ask her several questions was a way to motivate her to "tell more". The shared examination of video recordings and the close analysis of the conversational transcripts led us to identify specific advice for the therapist on how to respond to Cecilia's telling. We suggested that the therapist should wait, "take the risk" of silence, leave Cecilia the time to choose words and elaborate, and verify that her understanding of Cecilia's talk was exactly what the girl intended to convey. These were the main changes that the therapist overtly pursued. Implied in these changes was the therapist's entirely new recognition of Cecilia as someone able to reconstruct and report her memories, and as an agent entitled to select what to say and what to emphasize from certain episodes.

After such changes, Cecilia's narratives became more elaborate, the relationship between antecedents and consequences was made explicit, narratives made reference to the teller's stances and emotional reactions, and included problem-solving.

4 Conclusions

As Bruner (1990) has primarily shown, narrative supports learning and cognition: it helps to organise actions in temporal and sequential sequences, and it supports categorization processes (helping the narrator distinguish between background and focal events, to ascribe identities and states to different characters, to identify what is real, fictional or impossible). Narrative trains perspective-taking as a vehicle for the socialization of cultural values and preferences. It also encourages moral reasoning, for it is capable to elicit an evaluation or personal perspective over what is recounted. Narrative is doubly linked to cognition on the one hand, and to the construction of identity and the sense of self on the other.

The analyses reported in this chapter suggest that by interacting with children who have atypical cognitive profiles, therapists may behave as if they were addressing much younger children, who need to be stimulated and somehow "animated" (Goffman, 1979) to encourage their more active participation. We add that, even though it is seldom acknowledged, children with intellectual disabilities or pervasive developmental disorders are cast as addressees of others' initiatives rather than initiators of conversational sequences far more often than typically developing individuals (Ochs et al. 2005). Children with ID or pervasive developmental disorders are mainly invited to respond to preformed questions, prompts, hints, and are required to produce an action after the adult has done something or initiated a sequence of actions as a model to imitate. This way of interacting can be functional to specific circumscribed training contexts, aimed at facilitating or modelling performance, but it needs to be complemented with open interactional contexts in which parents and therapists act as sensitive and interested listeners who are able to wait and be patient until the child comes up at her own pace with her own response or initiative. This way, the child's narrative thinking can gradually emerge and take form through language.

In examining narratives involving an adolescent with ID, we have seen how the adult can develop a "listening" competence and learn to display an empathic hearership, practising discourse formats that can convey a sense of shared understanding and intimacy and help in the construction of a sense both of a collective (we-) and self- identity.

The fine-grained analysis of examples of therapeutic interactions with the child was recognized as very useful by the therapists working in our University Clinic. Such analysis allowed us to *see* and truly *discover* in the interaction – transcribed and commented – the richness of resources that the child and the therapist can share to ensure mutual understanding and reach more elaborate cognitive and social attainments.

We think that the analysis and the discussion of video-recorded data in therapeutic contexts addressed to children with ID has the potential to provide professionals with a set of valuable tools to become reflexive actors, observers, and "learners" of their practice.

References

Ainsworth M. S., Blehar, M. C., Waters, E., Wall, S. (1978) *Patterns of Attachment: A Psychological Study of the Strange Situation*. Oxford, England: Lawrence Erlbaum.

Amorotti, G., Cavallini, F., Corsano, P., (2021) Competenze narrative orali di bambini in età scolare con learning disabilities e developmental language disorder. *Psicologia clinica dello sviluppo*, 3, 357–388. doi:10.1449/100102.

Bakhtin, M. (1981). *The Dialogic Imagination: Four Essays*. C. Emerson and M. Holquist (trans.) Austin, TX: University of Texas Press.

Bamberg, M. (2008). Twice-told tales: small story analysis and the process of identity formation. In T. Sugiman, K.J. Gergen, W. Wagner, and Y. Yamada (Eds.), *Meaning in Action* (pp. 183–204). New York: Springer.

Bamberg, M. (2014). Narrative practices versus capital-D discoursers: ways of investigating Family. *Journal of Family Theory and Review*, 6, 132–136. doi:10.1111/jftr.12033.

Blum-Kulka, S. (1993). "You gotta know how to tell a story": telling, tales, and tellers in American and Israeli narrative events at dinner. *Language in Society*, 22 (3), 361–402. doi:10.1017/S0047404500017280..

Blum-Kulka, S., and Snow, C. E. (1992). Developing autonomy for tellers, tales, and telling in family narrative events. *Journal of Narrative and Life History*, 2 (3), 187–217. doi:10.1075/jnlh.2.3.02dev.

Bourdieu, P. (1990) *The Logic of Practice*. Stanford: Stanford University Press.

Botting, N. (2002). Narrative as a tool for the assessment of linguistic and pragmatic impairments. *Child Language Teaching and Therapy*, 18 (1), 1–21. doi:10.1191/0265659002ct224oa.

Brockmeier, J., and Carbaugh, D. (Eds.). (2001). *Narrative and Identity: Studies in Autobiography, Self and Culture*. John Benjamins Publishing.

Browder, D. M., and Spooner, F. (2006). *Teaching language arts, maths, and science to students with significant cognitive disabilities*. Baltimore, MD: Paul H Brookes Publishing Co.

Bruner, J. (1987) Life as narrative. *Social Research*, 54 (1), 11–32. https://www.jstor.org/stable/40970444.

Bruner, J. S. (1990). *Acts of Meaning*. Cambridge, MA:Harvard University Press

Bunning, K. and Ellis, M. (2010)A preliminary investigation into communication in the special needs classroom during key stage 3 English lessons. *Child Language Teaching and Therapy*, 26, 180–194. doi:10.1177/0265659010368752

Bunning, K., Smith, C., Kennedy, P. and Greenham, C. (2013) Examination of the communication interface between pupils with severe to profound and multiple intellectual disability and educational staff during structured teaching sessions. *Journal of Intellectual Disability Research*, 5, 39–52. doi:10.1111/J.1365-2788.2011.01513.x.

Bunning, K., Gooch, L., Johnson, M. (2017) Developing the personal narratives of children with complex communication needs associated with intellectual disabilities: what is the potential of storysharing? *Journal of Applied Research of Intellectual Disability*, 30 (4), 743–756. doi:10.1111/jar.12268.

Capps, L., Losh, M. and Thurber, C. (2000) 'The frog ate the bug and made his mouth sad': narrative competence in children with autism. *Journal of Abnormal Child Psychology*, 28, 193–204. doi:10.1023/a:1005126915631.

Celinska, D.K. (2004). Personal narratives of students with and without Learning Disabilities. *Learning Disabilities Research and Practice*, 19 (2), 83–98. doi:10.1177/104839500401600101.

Channell, M. M., McDuffie, A. S., Bullard, L. M., and Abbeduto, L. (2015). Narrative language competence in children and adolescents with Down syndrome. *Frontiers in behavioral neuroscience*, 9, 283. doi:10.3389/fnbeh.2015.00283.

De Fina, A., Schiffrin, D., and Bamberg, M. (2006) (eds). *Discourse and Identity*. Cambridge: Cambridge University Press.

Devescovi, A., and Baumgartner, E. (1993) Joint-reading a picture book: verbal interaction and narrative skills. *Cognition and Instruction*, 11, (3/4), 299–232. doi:10.1080/07370008.1993.9649027.

Doussard-Roosevelt, J. A., Joe, C. M., Bazhenova, O. V., and Porges, S. W. (2003). Mother–child interaction in autistic and nonautistic children: characteristics of maternal approach behaviours and child social responses. *Development and Psychopathology*, 15, 277–295. doi:10.1017/s0954579403000154.

Edwards, D., and Middleton, D. (1988). Conversational remembering and family relationships: how children learn to remember. *Journal of Social and Personal Relationships*, 5 (1), 3–25. doi:10.1177/0265407588051001.

Engevik, L. I., Næss K. A., Hagtvet B. E. (2016). Cognitive stimulation of pupils with Down syndrome: a study of inferential talk during book-sharing. *Research in Developmental Disability*, 55, 287–300. doi:10.1016/j.ridd.2016.05.004.

Epstein, S.-A., Phillips, J. (2009). Storytelling skills of children with Specific Language Impairment. *Child Language Teaching and Therapy*, 25 (3), 285–300. doi:10.1177/0265659009339819.

Farrell, M. (1996). Continuing literacy development. In B. Stratford and P. Gunn (Eds.), *Approaches to Down Syndrome* (pp. 280–299). London, UK: Cassell.

Fasulo, A., and Fiore, F. (2007). A valid person: non-competence as a conversational outcome. In A. Hepburn and S. Wiggins (Eds.), *Discursive Research in Practice: New Approaches to Psychology and Interaction* (pp. 224–247). Cambridge: Cambridge University Press.

Fatigante, M., Bafaro, S., Orsolini, M. (2015) "And you? What do you think then?" Taking care of thought and reasoning in intellectual disability. In M. O'Reilly, J. N. Lester (Eds.), *The Palgrave Handbook of Child Mental Palgrave Macmillan UK*. Health, 597–617. doi:10.1007/978-1-137-42831-8_32.

Fatigante, M., Fasulo, A., and Pontecorvo, C. (1998) Life with the alien: role casting and face-saving techniques in family conversation with young children. *Issues in Applied Linguistics*, 9 (2), 97–121.

Gentle, M., Milne, R., Powell, M., Sharman, S. (2013). Does the cognitive interview promote the coherence of narrative accounts in children with and without an intellectual disability? *International Journal of Disability Development and Education*, 60 (1): 30–43, doi:10.1080/1034912X.2013.757138.

Glenn, P. (2003). *Laughter in Interaction*. Cambridge University Press: Cambridge.

Goffman, E. (1979) Footing. *Semiotica*, 25 (1–2), 1–30. doi:10.1515/semi.1979.25.1–2.1.

Goodwin, C. (1979). The interactive construction of a sentence in natural conversation. In G. Psathas (Ed.) *Everyday Language: Studies in Ethnomethodology* (pp. 97–121). New York: Irvington Publishers.

Goodwin, C. (1981) *Conversational Organization*. Cambridge: Cambridge University Press.

Goodwin, C. (1984). Notes on story structure and the organization of participation. In M. Atkinson and J. Heritage (Eds.), *Structures of Social Action* (pp. 225–246). Cambridge: Cambridge University Press.

Goodwin, M. H. (1997). Byplay: negotiating evaluation in storytelling. In G. R. Guy, et al. (Eds.), *Toward a Social Science of Language: Papers in Honor of William Labov*. Vol. 2: Social Interaction and Discourse Structures (pp. 77–102). Amsterdam: John Benjamins.

Heritage, J. (1984) A change-of-state token and aspects of its sequential placement. In J. Maxwell Atkinson and J. Heritage (Eds.), *Structures of Social Action* (pp. 299–345). Cambridge: Cambridge University Press.

Heritage, J. (2011). Territories of knowledge, territories of experience: empathic moments in interaction. In T. Stivers, L. Mondada, J. Steensig (Eds.), *The Morality of Knowledge in Conversation* (pp.159–183). Cambridge: Cambridge University Press.

Heritage, J., Raymond, G. (2012). Navigating epistemic landscapes: acquiescence, agency and resistance in responses to polar questions. In J.P. de Ruiter (Ed.), *Questions: Formal, Functional and Interactional Perspectives* (pp. 179–192). Cambridge, U.K.: Cambridge University Press doi:10.1017/CBO9781139045414.013.

Jefferson, G. (1978). Sequential aspects of storytelling in conversation. In J. Schenkein (Ed.). *Studies in the Organization of Conversational Interaction* (pp. 219–248). New York: Academic Press.

Jefferson, G. (1979), A technique for inviting laughter and its subsequent acceptance/declination. In G. Psathas (Ed.), *Everyday Language: Studies in Ethnomethodology (pp. 79–96)*. Irvington: New York.

Jefferson, G. (1981) The abominable 'ne?' An exploration of post-response pursuit of response. In P. Shroder (Hrsg.) *Sprache der gegenwaart* (pp. 53–88). Dusseldorf. BRD: Pedagogischer Verlag Schwann.

Jefferson, G. (1984). On the organization of laughter in talk about troubles. In J. Maxwell Atkinson and J. Heritage (Eds.), *Structures of Social Action: Studies in Conversation Analysis* (pp. 346–369). Cambridge: Cambridge University Press.

Jefferson, G. (2004). Glossary of transcript symbols with an introduction. In G. H. Lerner (Ed). *Conversation Analysis: Studies from the First Generation* (pp. 13–31). Amsterdam: John Benjamins.

Labov, W. and Waletzky, J. (1967). Narrative analysis: oral versions of personal experience. In J. Helm (Ed.), *Essays on the Verbal and Visual Arts* (pp. 12–44). Seattle: University of Washington Press

Mandelbaum, S. J. (1989) Interpersonal activities in conversational storytelling. *Western Journal of Speech Communication*, 53 (2), 114–126. doi:10.1080/10570318909374295.

Mandelbaum, S. J. (1991) Telling stories. *Journal of Planning Education and Research*, 10 (3), 209–214. doi:10.1177/0739456X9101000308.

Mayer, M. (1969). *Frog, Where Are You?*New York: Dial.

McCabe, A., and Rollins, P. (1994). Assessment of preschool narrative skills. *American Journal of Speech-Language Pathology: A Journal of Clinical Practice*, 4, 45–56. doi:10.1044/1058–0360.0301.45.

McCabe, A., Bliss, L., Barra, G., Bennet, M. (2008). Comparison of personal versus fictional narratives of children with language impairment. *American Journal of Speech-Language Pathology*, 17, 194–206. doi:10.1044/1058-0360(2008/019).

Miller, J. (1991). Quantifying productive language disorders. In J. Miller (Ed.), *Research on Child Language Disorders: A Decade of Progress* (pp. 211–220). Austin, TX: Pro-Ed.

Nelson, K. (Ed.). (1989). *Narratives from the Crib*. Harvard University Press.

Ochs, E., and Capps, L. (2001). *Living Narrative: Creating Lives in Everyday Storytelling*. Harvard University Press.

Ochs, E., and Taylor, C. (1992). Family narrative as political activity. *Discourse and Society*, 3 (3), 301–340. doi:10.1177/0957926592003003003.

Ochs, E., Taylor, C., Rudolph, D. E., and Smith, R. C. (1992). Storytelling as a theory-building activity. *Discourse Processes*, 15, 37–72. doi:10.1080/01638539209544801.

Ochs, E., Solomon, O., and Sterponi, L. (2005). Limitations and transformations of habitus in Child-Directed Communication. *Discourse Studies*, 7 (4–5), 547–583. doi:10.1177/1461445605054406.

Peterson, C., and McCabe, A. (1994). A social interactionist account of developing decontextualized narrative skill. *Developmental Psychology*, 30(6), 937–948. https://doi.org/10.1037/0012-1649.30.6.937

Pomerantz, A. (1984). Agreeing and disagreeing with assessments: some features of preferred/dispreferred turn shapes. In M. Atkinson, and J. Heritage (Eds.), *Structures of Social Action: Studies in Conversation Analysis (pp. 57–101)*. Cambridge: Cambridge University Press.

Pontecorvo, C., and Fasulo, A. (1997). Learning to argue in family shared discourse: the reconstruction of past events. In L. Resnick, R., Säljö, C. Pontecorvo, and B. Burge (Eds.), *Discourse, Tools and Reasoning: Essays on Situated Cognition*. (pp. 406–442). New York, NY: Springer.

Pontecorvo, F. and Arcidiacono, F. (2007) *Famiglie all'italiana. Parlare a tavola*. Milano: Cortina (tr. Families in Italy. Talking at mealtime)

Renfrew, C. (1991). *The Bus Story: A Test of Continuous Speech*. Oxford: C. Renfrew

Roach, M. A., Barratt, M. S., Miller, J. F., Leavitt, L. A. (1998) The structure of mother- child play: young children with Down syndrome and typically developing children. *Developmental Psychology*, 34, 77–87. doi:10.1037/0012-1649.34.1.77.

Roggman, L. A., Cook, G. A., Innocenti, M. S., Jump Norman, V., and Christiansen, K. (2013). Parenting interactions with children: checklist of observations linked to outcomes (PICCOLO) in diverse ethnic groups. *Infant Mental Health Journal*, 34 (4), 290–306. doi:10.1002/imhj.21389.

Rollo, D. (2007) (a cura di) *Narrazione e sviluppo psicologico. Aspetti cognitivi, affettivi e sociali.* Roma: Carocci (tr. Narrative and psychological development. Cognitive, affective and social aspects)

Roth, F. P., Spekman, N. J., and Fye, E. C. (1995). Reference cohesion in the oral narratives of students with learning disabilities and normally achieving students. *Learning Disability Quarterly*, 18 (1), 25–40. doi:10.2307/1511363.

Ruggerini, C., Manzotti, S., Griffo, G., Veglia, F. (2013) (a cura di) *Narrazione e disabilita' intellettiva. Valorizzare le esperienze individuali nei percorsi educativi e di cura.* Milano: Hoepli.

Sacks, H. (1974). An analysis of the course of a joke's telling in conversation. In Sherzer, J. and Bauman, R. (Eds.), *Explorations in the Ethnography of Speaking* (pp. 337–353). London: Cambridge University Press.

Sacks, H. (1992). *Lectures on Conversation*. Oxford: Basil Blackwell, vol. 1 and 2.

Schegloff, E. A. (2007). *Sequence Organization in Interaction: A Primer in Conversation Analysis* I. Cambridge University Press, Cambridge.

Schiffrin, D., DeFina, A. and Nylund, A. (Eds.). *Telling Stories: Language, Narrative, and Social Life.* Washington, DC: Georgetown University Press.

Stein, N. L., and Glenn, C. G. (1979). An analysis of story comprehension in elementary school children. In R. O. Freedle (Ed.), *New Directions in Discourse Processing.* (pp. 53–120). Norwood, NJ: Ablex.

Stivers, T. (2008) Stance, alignment, and affiliation during storytelling: when nodding is a token of affiliation. *Research on Language and Social Interaction*, 41 (1), 31–57. doi:10.1080/08351810701691123.

Stokoe, E., and Edwards, D. (2006). Story formulations in talk-in-interaction. *Narrative Inquiry*, 16, 56–65. doi:10.1075/ni.16.1.09sto.

Tager-Flusberg, H. (1995) Once upon a ribbit: stories narrated by autistic children. *British Journal of Developmental Psychology*, 13, 45–59. doi:10.1111/j.2044-2835X.1995.tb00663.x.

Vygotsky, L. S. (1978). *Mind in Society: The Development of Higher Psychological Processes.* Cambridge, Mass.: Harvard University Press.

Wan, M. W., Green, J., Elsabbagh, M., Johnson, M., Charman, T., Plummer, F., and BASIS Team (2012). Parent-infant interaction in infant siblings at risk of autism. *Research in Developmental Disabilities*, 33 (3), 924–932. doi:10.1016/j.ridd.2011.12.011.

Wan, M. W., Green, J., Elsabbagh, M., Johnson, M., Charman, T., Plummer, F., et al. (2013). Quality of interaction between at-risk infants and caregiver at 12–15 months is associated with three year autism outcome. *Journal of Child Psychology and Psychiatry*, 54 (7), 763–771. doi:10.1111/jcpp.12032.

Chapter 7

Personal identity, desire, life project

Ciro Ruggerini, Stefania Musci, and Aldo Moretti

I The minority of persons with intellectual disability

In many societies and many historical periods, minorities have suffered discrimination. Laws cannot abolish discrimination but can help to overcome it because they can trigger a process of change that must be continually supported. One example could be that of the Afro-American minority of the United States. The beginning of the process of emancipation occurred with the proclamation of the end of slavery (President Abraham Lincoln in 1863), but only a century later the Civil Right Act (1965) was enacted for the recognition of all civil rights – including the right to vote. People with disabilities (about 10% of the world population) constitute the largest minority in the world (UN, 2006) and they are still subject to widespread discrimination today, even in rich Europe. The Universal Declaration of Human Rights (UN, 1948) affirmed that all "human beings are born free and equal in dignity and rights". The questions are: why was the UN Declaration of the Rights of the Mentally Disabled necessary in 1971? Why, again, was the UN resolution of 1993 necessary to approve the Standard Rules for equal opportunities for people with disabilities? And why was the approval of the UN Convention on the Rights of Persons with Disabilities necessary in December 2006?

A possible answer is the same as for the violation of the rights of all minorities: that the enunciation of a right does not in itself have the guarantee of its application in society, neither to the majority nor to minorities – such as those of the disabled.

However, a further question is needed: is the minority of people with disabilities comparable to other minorities (racial or religious)? Schroeder (2015, p. 2) has suggested an acute answer:

> While people with disabilities have made significant strides toward true integration, their progress has been suppressed by society's

DOI: 10.4324/9781003220367-7

conception of people with disabilities as broken people, damaged people, and inferior people. Civil rights are reserved for others while people with disabilities are made to make do with limited civil rights, qualified civil rights, and conditional civil rights. People with disabilities are members of a minority group but it is an orphan minority, a subordinate minority... .

The following two examples, drawn from today's reality, illustrate how appropriate this observation is.

1 An unheard adolescent

Paolo is 16 years old; he received a diagnosis of Medium-Severe Intellectual Disability, part of the Cornelia de Lange syndrome picture. His parents separate after many violent conflicts when he is 12 years old. After the separation, neither he nor his sister wishes to meet the father. His parents develop a calendar of the periodic meetings of the father with the children with the supervision of an educator (protected meetings) to guarantee the father the right of paternity.

Paolo refuses to participate in the meetings, expressing his discomfort even with physical symptoms. A psychiatrist appointed by the judge to evaluate Paolo's behavior asks to meet only his mother because she affirms that "Paolo is unable to explain what has happened and what is happening".

During a meeting with one of us, Paolo expresses himself in dysarthric language that is understandable if you have the curiosity and the patience to listen to him and accurately describes many episodes of his experience from which he drew the reasons for his refusal.

2 An elder who cannot choose

Matteo is a 73-year-old homozygous twin. He lives with his co-twin and his mother. At the age of 28, during a psychiatric hospitalization following the death of his father, he receives a diagnosis of Mild Mental Retardation. At the age of 57, he receives a Legal Protection (Support Administrator). When his mother dies at the age of 92, Matteo is 72 and asks that his mother's desire expressed in life of to be entombed rather than buried be respected. His Tutor argues that this choice is excessively expensive and, therefore, not convenient for him who also has considerable private capital.

In both cases, prejudice is active in the mind of the caretakers: in other words, they think that intellectual disability does not allow people to make decisions about their own life. This is prejudice because if they had listened to Paolo, they might have noticed that he can narrate his own experience, and Matteo has shown that he knows how to make, with minimal support, adaptive and satisfactory choices (in work, in free time and social relationships). Paolo and Matteo suffer a violation of their rights by their keepers.

The UN Convention on the Rights of Persons with Disabilities (2006) offers protection against "discrimination based on disability" and is, today, an indisputable reference.

Essential message: *laws (the UN Convention, once ratified by individual governments, is superior in authority to any law in force in that countries) are necessary to protect the citizenship rights of people with disabilities.*

2 UN Convention on the Rights of Persons with Disabilities (2006)

The general principles of the Convention (Article 3) are:

- respect for intrinsic dignity, individual autonomy, including the freedom to make one's own choices and the independence of people
- non-discrimination
- full and effective participation and inclusion in society
- respect for difference and the acceptance of people with disabilities as part of human diversity and of humanity itself
- equal opportunities
- accessibility
- equality between men and women
- respect for the development of the capacities of children with disabilities and respect for the right of children with disabilities to preserve their identity.

2.1 The person

The term "people with disabilities" is underpinned by an important conceptual change which consists in shifting "the center of gravity from functions and characteristics to being and restoring value to the ontological dimensions of the person, whose nature pre-exists and persists regardless of its qualities"(CSB, 2013). This change opens up a new model in the approach to people with disabilities based on respect for human rights, that follows the medical and social model (Oliver, 2013). The thought of the philosophers (Fulford et al., 2006) express different ways of defining the idea of a person. Among these we choose the idea that being a person consists of a set of distinctive abilities (capacity approach) because it is useful for our discussion: self-awareness and awareness of the experiences lived by oneself over time. We can trace this idea of person back to John Locke when he argued that "person" is "… a thinking, intelligent being, that has reason and reflection and can consider itself as itself, the same thinking thing, in different times and places…".

The ability to perceive one's persistence over time (self-tracking) is what makes intentional actions possible: thinking, dreaming, planning, wishing, hoping.

Therefore, each person with an intellectual disability has distinctive abilities, considering the context of common inter-individual differences: in some people inside the family, these abilities are spontaneously and brilliantly present (think, for example, of some writers or thinkers), in others these same skills must be enabled or trained.

This statement may seem obvious today but we should remember that for at least three-quarters of the last century the concept of person was not applied to those who had received a diagnosis of mental retardation; who had received this diagnosis was a biological individual, without the humanizing abilities of self-awareness; it was simply a body to be readjusted according to a medical model, unable to participate in an interpersonal dialogue because not endowed with a self able to interact with other selves.

We had to wait until 1980 to hear the expression "we are people, first!" (The Minnesota Governor's Council on Developmental Disabilities, 2020).

Essential message: *people with intellectual disabilities may find difficulties in expressing the awareness of themselves, their biography, and their project; this does not mean that these distinctive abilities are absent in them. Like every human being, they aspire to identify their meaning in life.*

2.2 Identity

The person with an intellectual disability walks, endowed with the common distinctive abilities, just like everyone, in their itinerary in life.

One of the key factors in the development of disability is the quality of the social support people receive. Cobb (1976) defined social support as "information leading the subject to believe that he or she is loved, esteemed, and belongs to a network of mutual obligation".

Based on the quality of the social support, the person with intellectual disability begins to elaborate, like everyone, on his idea of himself or rather of the different selves in which his being is articulated and his sense of identity which consists in feeling more or less an agent in his environment (agency); more or less unique, in other words, capable to differentiate himself from the definitions and expectations of others (otherness); more or less capable of finding continuity between past, present, and future (unity); more or less capable of self-reflection (Mancini, 2010).

Like everybody, the person with an intellectual disability develops, over time, his own identity, which is something different from fingerprints or physical appearance, or social security number. These are evidence of Identity, but they do not constitute its essence. The essence of Identity is the special way of being in a relationship with things or people. Identity is "a relation that no person can have to anything or anyone but himself or herself" (Fulford et al., 2006).

The acquisition of identity, starting from adolescence, allows each person to respond to questions such as "Who am I", "What is the meaning of my life", and "What is my project".

Recently the recognition that people with Intellectual Disabilities, like everyone, follow a development itinerary for the acquisition of their own Identity, is growing. In the documents of the WHO the notion of adulthood appeared only in the early 2000s (WHO, 2000), and, shortly after, the concept of Transition appeared in the literature (Barron and Hassiotis, 2008). In other words, we can say that only lately have international documents recognized that people with intellectual disabilities become adults, crossing, like everyone, the different ages of life.

The question that needs to be posed now is: does the path that leads people with intellectual disabilities to the acquisition of their own identity have characteristics that can be added to those that are common to all?

Essential message: *personal identity, one's unique being in relationships is built in the context of life; this necessarily leads each human being to identify his values and to realize them with his project; no boundary traces differences in human nature based on the characteristics of individuals.*

2.3 Identity is more complex than disability

Until a few years ago, research on the development of identity in people with intellectual disabilities has focused its attention on a single topic: are people with this diagnosis aware of it, and how much do they accept or deny it (Beart et al., 2005)?

This has led many professionals to stimulate in conversation with adults with intellectual disabilities an explicit recognition of their being "impaired". This means that the professional attempts to make explicit the physical defect in the speech of a person with a severe or moderate motor disability. If, however, the person with a disability does not speak explicitly of his or her physical defect, then they are considered to not be aware of themselves.

In more recent years this way of describing the development of Identity in people with an intellectual disability – linked exclusively to the awareness of belonging to a diagnostic category – has been considered artificial because it expresses the point of view of researchers but not that of people with an intellectual disability.

The research of Dorozenko et al. (2015) takes exactly this perspective by involving people with intellectual disabilities as co-researchers who can not only express but also discuss their point of view. The results can be summarized with the help of the fact that people with intellectual disabilities focus on describing themselves and their ordinary social roles: they describe themselves as a member of a family, in a relationship with friends or a beloved one, as the owner of a small animal, as a person who goes on vacation or organizes their free time, as a member of an association or a church. As an important part of the construction of their identity, they also indicate a salaried job, living in their own house, and the possibility of enjoying a retirement pension. The label of intellectual disability does not seem to be the central point of the development of their identity; what is central is interpersonal relationships and the social roles covered.

In the path of their life, people with intellectual disabilities find that they have experienced de-humanizing ideologies or myths in the words and the relationships with specialists or with people in their context; for example, the ideology that people with intellectual disabilities are intrinsically different, so that their friendship or intimate relationships, their desire to be of help to others or the desire to show their skills do not belong to their humanity.

The particularity of the identity development process in people with intellectual disabilities is that they can experience a process of dehumanization that defines them as "incompetent and a burden on society", instead of supporting the development of their humanity. The effort in building their own identity is therefore double: they have to free themselves from an identity assigned by society (ascribed identity) and then develop a positive non-stigmatized identity.

The systematic review of the English literature from the years 1980 to 2017 (Forber-Pratt et al. 2017) on the theme of identity development in people with disabilities reinforces this conclusion: the development of identity is a social process strongly intertwined with the feedback received from significant people in context (social support); among these, the actions of the operators of social agencies such as schools, social services, and health services have special importance.

Article 8 of the UN Convention explicitly indicates the need to fight stereotypes, prejudices, and harmful practices: society should, in short, be rehabilitated to assist people with certain characteristics.

Essential message: *the identity of people with disabilities is built on interpersonal relations and the roles covered in society; both people with disabilities and the people who make up their context must be aware of the effects of de-humanizing myths and values.*

2.4 Self-determination

A teenager or an elderly person who has received a diagnosis of a mental disorder would probably not be denied the possibility of choice as in the case of Paolo and Matteo; it would probably seem more appropriate in such situations to offer dialogue to examine the issue on the mat. The Convention states that, even for people with disabilities, a similar attitude is needed. The Convention establishes, in fact, the need to "take appropriate measures to provide access to persons with disabilities to the support they require in executing their legal capacity".

The person with an intellectual disability has the same rights and duties as all citizens, including the choice between possible options that may affect their life. However, they may need support to make some choices or decisions. After the UN Convention, a broad discussion took place on the process of Supported Decision Making in the light of the socio-ecological concept of disability discussed in the first chapter.

A summary of the current data (Shogren, et al., 2017) indicates that a support process is possible and is influenced by personal factors (such as, for example, beliefs about the ability to make decisions) and by context (such as, for example, the possibility to access to relevant information, the attitude of the supporter in the decision, the degree of respect of people in the context for personal preferences, the attitudes of family members regarding decision making by people with disabilities). People with disabilities can, therefore, determine their Self if they are supported, when necessary, in their decisions. The Mental Capacity Act (Bild, 2005) establishes 5 principles:

Principle 1: A presumption of capacity. Assume a person has capacity unless proved otherwise.
Principle 2: Individuals being supported to make their own decisions. Do not treat people as incapable of deciding unless all practicable steps have been tried to help them.
Principle 3: Unwise decisions. A person should not be treated as incapable of deciding because their decision may seem unwise.

Principle 4: Best interest. Always do things or make decisions for people without the capacity in their best interests.
Principle 5: Less restrictive opinion.

Before doing something to someone or making a decision on their behalf, consider whether the outcome could be achieved in a less restrictive way. How the tutors of Paolo e Matteo have responded to their requests in our days is therefore illegal. The construction of a Life Project according to the Guidelines illustrated in the following sections – in which the essential core of the process is the alignment between the wishes of the subject, the opportunities of the context, and the possibility of support – offers an operational model of this process.

Essential message: *people with intellectual disabilities have the right to choose (and can do so!) even though they may need support to make decisions that are useful for the full development of their being.*

2.5 Development

"Growth" means a quantitative increase of the size of a person; "development" means a qualitative increase, an expansion of a person's complexity. The development of the being lasts a lifetime if the conditions are right because it is based on a neurobiological organization designed for continuous adaptation to new situations. Once this has been established, it is necessary to clarify what is the direction of this increase in complexity and who sets the goal (Berrios, 2015).

The Convention identifies this goal in the enhancement of personal resources and the participation in inclusive contexts and the decision-maker of the goal in the subject himself – through the support to his empowerment.

Essential message: *the person with disabilities is the helmsman of his vessel that he directs, together with his crew, towards his destination, under the sky of human rights.*

3 Implement a human rights model for disability

The content of this chapter is focused on the implementation of a human rights-based disability model in adulthood.

3.1 Premises

Some premises are necessary:

Premise 1. The development of each of us is influenced by three orders of systems (Bronfenbrenner, 1979) that interact with each other. These systems are:

- the macrosystem is made by the concepts of culture, politics, and economy that prevail in society. At the beginning of this chapter, we examined how the macrosystem shapes the quality of the environment in which support for the person with disabilities is activated. The UN Convention is today the key component of this system. Each of its articles (Box 7.1) illuminates a space where coherent actions at the mesosystem and microsystem levels should occur. For example, Article 19 indicates the right to "Living independently and being included in the community". This is the space (of independent life) indicated by the Convention. But how, in what ways, and when this should happen?
- the mesosystem includes the community to which a person belongs, including the agencies and services that make it up. Agencies and services have the task to transform the indications of the Convention into coherent support actions.
- the microsystem includes the restricted social context: family, group of friends, colleagues, or leisure time. People of the microsystem have the task to act together with agencies and services to facilitate inclusion and development paths. The actors of the mesosystem and microsystem have the task, in short, of implementing (making operational) the indications of the Convention.

Box 7.1 Articles of the UNCRPD (United Nations Convention on the Rights of Persons with Disabilities) (United Nations, 2006)

Article Definition

01	Purpose
02	Definitions
03	General principles
04	General obligations
05	Equality and non-discrimination
06	Women with disabilities
07	Children with disabilities
08	Awareness-raising
09	Accessibility
10	Right to life

11 Situations of risk and humanitarian emergencies
12 Equal recognition before the law
13 Access to justice
14 Liberty and security of person
15 Freedom from torture or cruel, inhuman or
    degrading treatment or punishment
16 Freedom from exploitation, violence and abuse
17 Protecting the integrity of the person
18 Liberty of movement and nationality
19 Living independently and being included in the
    Community
20 Personal mobility
21 Freedom of expression and opinion, and access to
    Information
22 Respect for privacy
23 Respect for home and the family
24 Education
25 Health
26 Habilitation and rehabilitation
27 Work and employment
28 Adequate standard of living and social protection
29 Participation in political and public life
30 Participation in cultural life, recreation, leisure and sport

Premise 2. The implementation of rights requires that the operators of the mesosystem agencies and the components of the microsystem share cultural tools or compasses that guide their actions. These tools consist of two constructs: the Quality-of-Life construct and the Support System construct (Schalock, 2020).

The Quality-of-Life construct defines "personal well-being" as a construct applicable to everyone's life, including people with intellectual disabilities (Schalock et al, 2002). The construct comprises 8 domains, it has been developed gradually over the last ten years of the last century and is, today, recognized as valid in assistance systems all over the world.

The domains of the construct are indicated in Box 7.2.

The Quality-of-life construct indicates the goal of human development for every human being. Verdugo et al. (2012) underline that there is a close connection between areas of the Quality of Life and articles of the UN Convention, and this could practically mean that respect for human rights allows people with intellectual disabilities to enjoy a good quality of life.

All the areas of Quality of Life are important for all people of all ages, even though in certain stages of life some areas acquire greater importance than others. Up to the age of adolescence, the goals of personal growth are prevalent in both typical and atypical development. Starting from this point, however, the area of self-determination begins to take priority importance. In adolescence, the general development plan expects the need to mature, for every person, an individual life plan inspired by personal goals and values.

To this longitudinal perspective is added the urgency of current needs, typical of the age, such as interactions in a social network of acquaintances, relationships with friends and peers, and the need to cover roles in the community (community roles) in which a concrete sense of belonging (community integration) develops. This aspect of the development is often denied to disabled adolescents because typically developing peers usually don't prefer to go out with them, they don't invite them to parties, or to go to the cinema. For this reason, the telephone of people with disabilities sometimes never rings, and this is a factor that highly threatens their well-being and introduces very negative consequences for their cognitive, linguistic, and emotional development.

People with disabilities need support to carry out their development path, the intensity of which is very variable (see chapter 1). The term support refers to a wide range of resources and strategies. The construct of a support system was developed gradually from the mid-1980s.

This support can be natural (for example a friendship) or specialized (for example provided by medical specialists). In any case, however, supports contribute to improving the quality of life if they respect the choices and autonomy of the person to whom they are addressed and if they facilitate participation in inclusive environments. The elements of a support system are, therefore: the construct of Quality of Life; an existential condition in which personal choice and autonomy are possible; the possibility of accessing inclusive living environments; the possibility of receiving natural or specialized support. The Quality of Life construct is at the core of the different elements and indicates the direction of the support actions.

Premise 3. The Quality of Life construct, therefore, provides a frame reference for the development of social policies and the evaluation of good practices and outcomes (at the macro-system level). The construct of support systems provides a framework to design person-referenced support strategies. In creating the individual's support plans the two constructs should be aligned (Croce, 2013; Schalock, 2020). The core of a support plan is the personal goal. The person himself sets his target for each of the Quality of life areas (see Box 7.2) and the people in his context (at the mesosystem and microsystem level) identify the intensity of support needed, the strategies to be implemented and the operating methods to achieve it.

Box 7.2 Quality of Life Domains and Exemplary Indicators (Shalock et al, 2002)

Quality of Life Domain	ExemplaryIndicators
Personal Development	- Education status - Personal competency (cognitive, social, practical)
Self-Determination	- Autonomy/personal control
Interpersonal Relations	- Interactions (e.g., social networks) - Relationship (e.g. family, friends, peers)
Social inclusion	- Community integration - Community roles
Rights	- Human (respect, dignity, equality) - Legal (citizenship, access, due process)
EmotionalWell-Being	- Contentment (satisfaction, enjoyment) - Lack of stress (predictability and control)
PhysicalWell-Being	- Health status - Activities of daily living (self-care, mobility)
MaterialWell-Being	- Employment status - Personal possessions

3.2 Guidelines for a life project definition

All pre-adolescents and adolescents feel they are called to a new evolutionary task which consists in identifying their role in the social context. This is a different role from the one held up to that moment in the family environment. The new task requires a project, a desire, an idea of the future. This requires at least two preconditions.

The first is that the adolescent can think about himself in the future, and this can happen if he experiences the possibility to activate autonomous thoughts. As seen in chapter 5 (Attachment and intellectual disability: promoting secure attachment in the relationship) the child develops the ability to think through the experience of the interaction with significant adults and when these figures (the adults) consider the child "gifted with a mind". This is important but not sufficient because it is essential to add to this condition the concrete experience of being involved in a dialogue on the issues of daily, social and cultural life; a dialogue in which the child's expressions are taken into account.

The second condition is that families should believe that children with intellectual disabilities can follow their path toward adulthood. This condition is also essential according to an innovative Italian experience on the life project begun in the seventies with people with Down syndrome (Moretti and Felicioli, 2011; Felicioli and Moretti, 2022).

The two conditions operate in all adolescents but in those with intellectual disabilities their life quality is likely less optimal: it is possible that an adolescent with an intellectual disability is less determined in formulating his dream and that his family members are less determined in granting him opportunities that arise.

In our country (Italy), guidelines have been drawn up to help the construction of the life plan for people with intellectual disabilities to guide family members and operators in this difficult transition phase (AIRIM, 2010). Guidelines developed in other countries (for example in England: NICE, 2015) have the same content. The Italian Guidelines are based on a very large international literature and are continuously updated and fine-tuned (Francescutti et al., 2016; Cavagnola et al., 2020).

We present these Guidelines below and provide an example of their use. The Guidelines are based on the Quality of Life and Support System constructs, and provide indications to those who work in the mesosystem and those who cooperate between the mesosystem, the subject, and his family (microsystem).

The Guidelines trace a path that will be overviewed below:

- **Diagnostic Classification and Assessment:** these phases permit collecting pieces of information about the characteristics of the neurobiological system (brain), intellectual and adaptive functioning (mind), and personal biography including values and expectations (person). Specifically, in these phases the cognitive and socio-emotional profile (see chapter 3, section 4) is very important, because it answers the question about the types of contexts and activities that can support learning, promotes active experiences, and keeps a good fit with the person's preferences and desires.
- **Planning supports:** this phase is composed of different elements. The first element requires an analysis that includes the person's desires and the actual resources and opportunities of the context. We can define this moment as "ecological balance". A second element consists of the definition of a "personal life project". A third element is the "Personal Supports Plan Based on the QOL Supports Model" coherent with the personal objectives.

An "ecological balance" is achieved by answering a series of questions that we have collected in Box 7.3. These questions can also be relevant for typical development. The answer to the different questions generates a current portrait (or profile) of the person and their perspectives. Similar questions are used in the English Guidelines (NICE, 2015).

Box 7.3 Questions for the ecological balance (Cavagnola et al., 2020)

Ecological area	Questions
Preferences and wishes of the disabled person (important things from her point of view)	* What the individual likes * What the individual wants * What the individual states is important to
What is important for the person (the caregiver's point of view and the context to which the person belongs)	* What do we think is necessary for this person? * What are the important skills for this person to reach a good quality of life? * What skills would be helpful to improve his quality of life?
Behaviours that are contextually problematic for the environment and dysfunctional for the person (which challenging behaviours limit his active participation)	* The challenging behaviours produce self-injurious behaviour (SIB) or damage to other people or things? * Does The SIB limit the person's development and well-being? *, Do the SIB reinforce social stigmatisation and marginalisation?
Performance/skills of the person not required by the environmental contexts	* Does the person have abilities that are currently unexpressed? * The person has a skill we had the opportunity to encounter in the past or that emerged during the assessment, which is currently not being exercised or valued by the environment?
The balance between the performance of the person and the demands of the ecosystems (identifying significant skills the person already expresses)	* Does the person exhibit skills that we consider particularly useful in the life she leads within that system (family, service, community centre, etc.)? * What strikes us most positively among the skills exhibited by the person? * What skills make her more adequate and capable than what is typically required in daily life?
Health conditions that can limit the person's active participation and hinder the pursuit of the best quality of life	* Is there a lifestyle that represents a risk factor for physical illness? * Are there any side effects of therapies that can affect the quality of life?

Below we describe an example drawn from the "ecological balance" of 13-year-old Sonia. Sonia lives with her parents and three sisters. She received a diagnosis of intellectual disability when she was in primary school and a diagnosis of celiac disease. Her parents have a high-level of education (college). When Sonia was 11 years old, she started a pharmacological treatment with methylphenidate. Sonia received multiple evaluations in several centers, but the assessment always highlighted her weaknesses in cognitive and adaptive functioning. In the last evaluation made at the age of 11, she obtained a Total IQ of 40 on the Wechsler Test (results of the following lower-order composite scores: Verbal Comprehension Index: 68; Perceptual Reasoning Index: 54; Working Memory Index: 46; Processing Speed Index: 47); at the Questionnaire on Adaptation Skills (ABAS – II) (Harrison and Oakland, 2000) the scores in all conceptual, social, and practical areas were placed very far from the means of the same age sample (under 3 standard deviations). Since the clinical documents described Sonia only for her set of deficits, her parents decided to ask her to participate, for many years, in a long training of verbal language, movement, and attention. With the onset of adolescence, parents felt the need to introduce an idea of the future. In some meetings with them and with an educator who knows Sonia well (because she spends two afternoons per week with her), we explained the contents and logic of the Italian guidelines on the project of life and discussed the questions listed in Box 7.3. Some paragraphs of Sonia's ecological balance are reported at the end of the chapter.

The description of Sonia's parents provided a lot of information that could be added to those coming from the standard tests (Wechsler and ABAS-II) and provided a broad description of the cognitive and socio-emotional profile. The information concerns some cognitive functions (problem-solving, visual memory, spatial orientation) and the circumstances that activate them (for problem-solving: strong motivation, or explicit teaching); the reflection of the difficulties of verbal language and insufficient self-regulation in relationships; Sonia's emotional reactions to difficulties and novelties, attitude, and aspirations (taking care of children younger than her). If prompted appropriately, many parents could provide this kind of information that can orient the observations and the intervention. The personal life project is linked to the ecological balance, which is a kind of map of a "field" from which one draws the personal life project. The life project considers three types of goals:

- Personal Goals: the targets are the expectations and the desires of the disabled person to ensure the highest grade of personal satisfaction. If we consider, for example, Sonia's ecological balance, we notice that sometimes the personal goals are indicated and at other times they are suggested. Sonia certainly wishes to be included in a social network of friendships and feels that she could have the chance to take care of younger children by becoming an aide or kindergarten teacher.

- Functional Goals: the target is the functioning of the person in his ecosystem and is tailored towards the best possible adaptation. In Sonia's case, this could mean, for example, improving some of her social skills as she is, sometimes, inadequate in relationships (like keeping friendships that are also desired) and increasing her knowledge of children in preschool age.
- Clinical Goals: the targets are the condition of disease and the identification of purposes of prevention, healing, reduction and/or control of symptoms and, more generally, a condition of psychophysical well-being. In the case of Sonia, this could mean, for example, increasing knowledge in the field of celiac disease and the ability to self-manage it.

The notion of a "life project" introduces in Sonia's story the idea that it is necessary to plan a transition to adulthood for her too. In children with typical development, it is not necessary to explicate this, since it is assumed that this transition is written in nature and foreseen in the social organization. Typically developing children know that they will be able to meet a school that has already arranged curricula, and after school, a world of work that will be able to welcome them. For children with atypical development, the transition must be planned case-by-case.

The first step is to introduce the idea that there is a future for them. It is like indicating that there is a horizon in which a distant point is signed towards which we must tend, and this should make the actions of the various agencies synergistic: schools, extracurricular services, the world of work. The idea of the future introduces a longitudinal perspective. This idea is functional to the assistance system but also to the person who can perceive himself as the helmsman of his vessel in navigation (not stationary in a warehouse with no exit!). However, the longitudinal perspective cannot absorb every action to promote development. We must add a cross perspective that intersects the present time. An idea of the future opens the horizon but does not satisfy every need in life. There is a present time to live: it is the time of learning new skills, participating in new experiences, building relationships with friends and love, assuming responsibility, and experimenting with pleasure. The programming of the supports, therefore, develops in two directions: longitudinal, towards the horizon, and transversal, in the current domains of living. The third element is the "Personal Supports Plan Based on the QOL Supports Model" (see Table 7.1 below).

Table 7.1 Supports Plan for Sonia

QOL Domain	Personal Goal	Support Needs	Support Strategies	Implementation Questions (who, what, when, and how)
Personal Development	(2) Increase knowledge about the development of preschool children Increase cooking abilities increase competence in other activities (sporting, artistic, etc.)	An adequate teaching method The opportunity to cook with a family member or with an expert figure	Frontal or field lessons Explicit teaching of food preparation processes	Support teacher at high school family, friends, professional figures
Self – Determination	(1) Gain a job with preschool children	A teacher or aide for support during the internship	Allow Sonia to experience herself in real situations	Support teacher at high school
Interpersonal Relations and Social inclusion	(3) Develop new extra-family relationships Improve adaptive skills that facilitate relationships with peers (relationship style, autonomy in clothing, use of public transport)	Participation in new contexts of social interaction involvement in group psychotherapy targeting emotional and social awareness	Increase awareness of the response that our behaviour can cause in other people talking about emotions and social behaviours in conversation Practising problem-solving and reflective thinking on life situations in which dysfunctional behaviours occurred	Psychologist Speech therapist Parents: Should work out strategies with specialists to respond to Sonia's narratives when they are confused Identify an organised peer group able to include Sonia.

QOL Domain	Personal Goal	Support Needs	Support Strategies	Implementation Questions (who, what, when, and how)
Rights	(7) Respect and dignity	Support in identifying situations of violation of respect and dignity	Teaching the school community the origin and meaning of individual differences and the concept of learning	Parents and Teachers
Emotional Well-Being	(4) Increase Emotional Awareness Enhance the perception of self-efficacy	Family members and teachers organise learning and social opportunities	Enhancement of social roles Involvement of Sonia's father in teaching board games to play at home participation in artistic and creative works (e.g. drawing)	Parents and Teachers
Physical Well-Being	(5) Increase the ability to manage celiac disease	Familiar teaching	Keeping the acknowledge of celiac disease updated	Doctors and family components
Material Well–Being	(6) Have personal items (photographs, books, board games) and spaces at home (personal room, other spaces in the apartment, or the garden) Possibility to spend a weekly amount of money	Support in choices and decision	Attribution of responsibility	Parents and others in the family

To illustrate this model, we can consider the elements of Sonia's biography, for which a plausible (but not necessarily definitive) goal is to become an operator with preschool children at a young adult age (indicated as (1) in Table 7.1). Once established, the goal in the area of development ((2) in the table) becomes that of increasing the knowledge related to the development of preschool children but also that of increasing competences in activities carried out with pleasure. These goals aim to acquire new skills (these are constructive goals).

Sonia's other goals are to increase interpersonal relationships and to have a role in a community of friends ((3) in the table). To reach these goals, Sonia should modify some of her social behaviours reflecting on her own experience and/or going through training in her verbal skills (these goals are focused on decreasing maladaptive behaviours).

The ecological balance also highlighted that Sonia's self-esteem needs to be strengthened ((4) in the table), and this can be achieved in the family with the support of the members and in school with the support of teachers (this is an environmental modification).

Sonia was able to understand well the restrictions related to celiac disease ((5) in the table); she has taken on a conscious and active role (agency capacity) and this also increased her self-esteem. Furthermore, she had the right to own personal objects and spaces ((6) in the table) and the right to have personal respect ((7) in the table).

4 Evaluating the outcomes of a support plan based on Quality of Life

We can consider three types of measures analysing the effectiveness of the support actions that have been undertaken: Clinical, Functional, and Personal.

Clinical outcomes measure the variation of clinical indexes identified in the assessment phase. For example: considering the number of crises at a certain time in an antiepileptic therapy; quantifying the persistence over time or the variation in the intensity of the symptoms in therapy for mental disorder co-occurring with the condition. However, the description of the medical, neurological, and psychiatric disorders associated with the condition of intellectual disability is not the goal of our text.

Functional outcomes measure the change in indices of cognitive or adaptive functioning. These types of results should refer to the integrated use of quantitative and qualitative measures.

Personal outcomes assess whether the goals set in the support program regarding the wishes and expectations of the disabled person have been met.

Pietro's story shows the outcomes that can be generated when opportunities are aligned with desires.

We met Pietro at the age of 13 when he was in the second secondary school. He received a diagnosis of Mild Intellectual Disability due to partial agenesis of the corpus callosum. On the Wechsler Scale, he achieved a Verbal Comprehension Index of 47 and a Perceptual Reasoning Index of 68. Compared to the same age sample he scored more than two standard deviations under the mean on 6 sub-scales of the Adaptive Behavior Assessment System (ABAS-II, Harrison and Oakland, 2000); and at 3 sub-scales (Communication, Free Time, Use of the Environment) he had obtained scores ranging between minus 1 and minus 2 standard deviations. He had difficulty in understanding written text but above all in calculating. Pietro was isolated in his class, the only thing his mates knew of him was his neurobiological alteration, he was known as "the boy with the agenesis of the corpus callosum". When Pietro was experiencing difficulties, he reacted by adopting aggressive or provocative behaviours towards his classmates (e.g.: throwing their backpacks out of the window if feeling humiliated by their observations about his learning difficulties).

In our meetings with Pietro, we were curious about his interests and his plans, in other words, about his person. So, we discovered that Pietro had a great interest in the activities of his parents' farm and in tractors. He was able to build tractors with cardboard and to design, drawing it on a plan, the farm that he would have liked to run in adulthood. In the meeting with Pietro, we recognized him as a person and we completely neglected the anomaly of his brain and his learning difficulties. After these meetings, we asked Pietro and his parents to introduce him to his schoolmates and teachers as a person who desires and plans. In other words, we tried to modify the reductive representation that mates and teachers had of him.

Our environmental modification project was useful, his classmates began to approach him differently. Pietro also began to meet friends who had the same interests as him in his free time. Slowly, the aggressive and oppositional behaviours at school disappeared and his teachers began to think about teaching content consistent with his projects. Pietro enrolled in a high school of agriculture, where he had a support teacher. There he expanded his interest in agriculture and agricultural machinery. He finished agricultural school with an essay on a particular brand of tractors. The recognition of his being a person and the alignment of the opportunities offered by the context allowed a positive change in each of the areas of quality of life.

At the age of 21, he received a new assessment on intellectual functioning from social service workers to ensure public support in his search for a job. The WAIS Scale assigned him the following scores: Verbal Comprehension Index: 53; Perceptual Reasoning Index: 61; Working Memory Index: 52; Processing Speed Index 58; Full-scale IQ: 43. Based on this evaluation, Pietro receives a diagnostic classification of Intellectual Disability with Mild Severity. Pietro, with the help of his parents, wrote a resume and a motivation letter in which he describes his work experiences and his personal qualities as follows:

> … I am a shy boy, sensitive but generous with others and respectful of the rules. During the internships, which I completed with personal and with the owner's satisfaction (in an agricultural consortium for customer assistance; in a nursery for greenhouse work; in an agricultural company for agricultural work; in an oven for customer assistance and preparation of pizza), I managed to establish good interpersonal relationships by fulfilling with high satisfaction the tasks entrusted to me. In my free time, I like to use the play-station, I go to the gym and a sports club where I play football. I like to hang out with friends and in general share my experiences with others. My great passions are football and the use of digital technologies. I am enthusiastically preparing to enter the world of work, to be with others, and have my financial independence.

The Quality of Life construct is measurable with standardized instruments (for example the Personal Outcomes Scale, van Loon et al., 2017; and the San Martin scale, Verdugo et al., 2014).

In our last meeting with Pietro and his family, we asked them to fill in the Personal Outcomes Scale questionnaire (POS) to have a standardized index of the current level of quality of life. The scores obtained in the questionnaire were the following: Personal development= 17; Self-determination= 16; Interpersonal relationships= 15; Social integration= 11; Rights= 16; Emotional well-being= 17; Physical well-being= 16; Material well-being= 12. We must consider that the expected average score at each of the subscales is 12. The questionnaire gave us the chance to look at Pietro's existential situation and it highlighted two areas of weakness (social integration and material well-being) for which Pietro should have adequate support. Considering, for example, the area of material well-being, the relatively low score (compared to that obtained in the other areas) is because of Pietro's affirmation that "only sometimes does he have the opportunity to save money", "he owns few valuables and/or he would like to have more", "he doesn't have a paid job", "he has his room but can't always lock it". The questionnaire, therefore, reinforces Pietro's request to reach an active role in the world of work and urges both community agencies (such as social services) and family members to move in this direction.

5 A new sky

The UN Convention on the Rights of Persons with Disabilities constitutes a new sky (macrosystem) under which the life path of disabled people takes place.

The quality of the sky affects the quality of the soil and every form of life: the Irish turf or the sandy desert; in the same way, the cultural conceptions that make up the macrosystem determine different ways of welcoming people with disabilities: from segregation to inclusion. The UN Convention has introduced a new paradigm in assistance that restores the right of citizenship of disabled people and, above all, the right to be recognized, just like everyone else: as people capable of desiring, choosing, and imagining their life projects. If we don't want to keep the concept of being a person as a slogan (an empty consideration), it is desirable (necessary) to have not only ethical principles in the sky but also have on earth a smart, complex methodology, truly oriented to the values and expectations of the person with intellectual disability.

The Guidelines for the construction of the Life Project, the Quality of Life construct and the Personal Supports Plan Based on the QOL Supports Model are what connect the "heaven of law" to life experiences: the macrosystem to the mesosystem of assistance agencies and to the family microsystem.

Box 7.4 Sonia's Ecological Balance

* **Sonia's preferences and wishes.** When asked what she likes to do, Sonia replies: "cooking, listening to music, playing cards, drawing, keeping small children, riding a bicycle, and doing things with my aunts, such as watching TV series."

When asked: "what do you want to do?" Sonia replies: "carrying out outdoor activities, playful and fun activities, activities with younger children, activities with other people."

When asked: "what is important to you?" Sonia replies: "being with my friends is important; when they appreciate me, it is important to go to school; it is important to be with my friend Elisa."

* **What is important for Sonia according to her parents?** Sonia has a particular aptitude for keeping younger children. She loves caring for them

and letting them play: she often says she wants to be a teacher or baby-sitter. Sonia loves cooking, especially when she is with her friends. She is highly motivated when given a responsible task and loves being with her peers and interacting with them. She generally loves contact with people, even bigger or smaller than her. We believe that it is vital for Sonia to feel accepted and to be part of a group (class, friends, catechism, sport, etc.).

* **Challenging behaviours.** Sonia tends to exasperate certain attitudes, such as coarse laughter, physical movements, and tone of voice. She may do this to be accepted and included in the group of her peers. However, her exasperation makes her sometimes grotesque and ridiculous. Another difficulty is that she cannot elaborate on a fluent and articulate speech that makes sense to the listener. For example: "the man of the thing who can play the guitar told me." For those who know the content, the sentence means: "Giovanni, Michela's boyfriend, who knows how to play the guitar, told me ... ". In her relationship with others, Sonia is particularly nagging. If she wants to get something, she asks for it countless times, exasperating her interlocutor. This attitude occurs both in the presence and even on the phone.

Another limit is the difficulty she finds in sharing her intentions with others. For example, for a long while, Sonia had wanted to invite one of her friends home, and when this eventually happened, she started watching television, leaving her friend alone. Sometimes Sonia is likely to feel "not listened to" or not considered by the group in which she is, so she interferes inappropriately in an ongoing speech to impose herself. We also believe that the fear of exploring the new can be included in challenging behaviours. Sonia finds herself in trouble when she must face something she has never experienced before. This produces in her a reaction of not being involved. However, in cases where Sonia is encouraged or helped by others to do something, she overcomes the resistance and is extremely happy. An example: Sonia's family went on a trip to the Apennines. "We took Sonia and her sisters on the track for bobs. Her sisters immediately took the sledges and began to descend. Sonia was particularly nervous. She asked us to help her put on gloves, which usually is difficult for her. Later, we realised she wasn't nervous about putting on the gloves. Rather she was afraid of "the novelty",: while for her sisters taking the sledge in their hands and trying to get off did not create problems; for Sonia, the fact of having to do something new was a cause of great anxiety. Sonia watched her sisters get on and off the sledge for a while, then she tried sleighing on her own, and taking her time, she measured with herself and started to do exactly what her sisters were doing.

* **Does Sonia have abilities that are currently unexpressed?** We think the logical skills are quite unexpressed. For example, seeing an

instrument hanging over the roadway, Sonia said that *it could be a camera* and immediately added *to slow down; otherwise, we could get a fee and have less money to fix the house* or the *Japanese restaurant.* Rapid and pragmatic-oriented logic. Among Sonia's attitudes, there is finding creative solutions and solving problems. For instance, one day, Sonia found a pack of coloured rubber bands and a small plastic crochet hook to make the bracelets in the playroom. "Mom, will you help me?". At that moment, her mother didn't have time because she was cooking. After a while, her mother heard her talking to the voice composer on the phone: "Google, can you show me a tutorial on how to make bracelets?". Sonia watched the tutorial on YouTube for making bracelets with her elastic bands.

* Skills that Sonia already expresses. Sonia has a particular aptitude for digital tools. Since she was young, even though she couldn't read, she could orient herself on the mobile phone, change settings, or search for information. Sonia still has difficulty with fine dexterity, so she finds it more accessible to write on the keyboard than on paper; she often uses the vocal composer as she makes many spelling mistakes. Sonia also has a strong aptitude for observing and memorising what she sees about places, icons, and people or environments. For example, she can describe – with extreme accuracy – the clothing of a person whom she met for only a few minutes, and she pays much attention to details. Furthermore, she notes insignificant changes in people or places. Sonia also has a terrific long-term memory. She remembers objects or events that happened a long time ago. She amazes us with her ability to create connections between a thing she saw and an experience she had years before. These mental connections are fast, relevant, and extremely precise, almost as if a cue in the present opened a quick link with something from the past. Sonia can wonderfully orient herself in new places or in which she has been only once.

* Is there a lifestyle that constitutes a risk factor or a physical disease? Sonia is celiac, and this has not affected her life at all, making her feel "special" and thus attracting the "envy" of the little ones who always want some of her gluten-free food.

References

AIRIM (Associazione Italiana per lo Studio delle Disabilità Intellettive ed Evolutive) (2010). *Linee Guida per la definizione degli Standard di Qualità nella costruzione del Progetto di vita per le persone con Disabilità Intellettiva.* https://el.unifi.it/pluginfile.php/956088/mod_resource/content/1/LG%20DIS%20INTELL.pdf

Barron, D.R.A., Hassiotis, A. (2008). Good practice in transition services for young people with learning disabilities: a review. *Advances in Mental Health and Learning Disabilities*, 2, 18–22.

Beart, S., Hardy, G. and Buchan, L. (2005). How people with intellectual disabilities view their social identity: a review of the literature. *Journal of Applied Research in Intellectual disabilities*, 18, 47–56. doi:10.1111/j.1468-3148.2004.00218.x.

Berrios, G.E. (2015), The history and epistemology of the neurodevelopmental disorders, *Spazi e Modelli*, 12, (1),47–48.

Bild (2005). *Mental Capacity Act.* www.bild.org.uk.

Bronfenbrenner, U. (1979). *The Ecology of Human Development.* Cambridge: Harvard University Press.

Cavagnola, R., Alzani, L., Carnevali, D., Chiodelli, G., Corti, S., Fioriti, F., ... Miselli, G. (2020). Neurodevelopmental disorders and development of project of life in a lifespan perspective: between habilitation and quality of life. *Annali dell'Istituto Superiore di Sanità*, 56 (2), 230–240.

Cobb, S. (1976). Social support as a moderator of life stress. *Psychosomatic Medicine*, 38(5), 300–314. doi:10.1097/00006842–197609000–00003.

Comitato Sammarinese di Bioetica (CSB)(2013). *L'approccio Bioetico alle Persone con Disabilità.* http://www.superando.it › files › 2013/05

Croce, L. (2013). Assessment, employment e capability nell'approccio alle persone con disabilità intellettiva. Il ruolo delle narrazioni. In C. Ruggerini, S. Manzotti, G. Griffo, and F. Veglia (Eds.), *Narrazione e disabilità intellettiva* (pp. 149–157). Trento: Erickson

Dorozenko, K., Roberts, L. and Bishop, B. (2015).The identities and social roles of people with an intellectual disability: challenging dominant cultural worldviews, values and mythologies. *Disability and Society*, 30, 1345–1364 http://www.tandfonline.com/10.1080/09687599.2015.1093461

Harrison, P.H., and Oakland, T. (2000). *ABAS-II. Adaptive behavior assessment system second edition.* Los Angeles: Western Psychological Services (Italian version Ferri, R. et al. ABAS – II. Firenze: Giunti OS).

Felicioli, F., and Moretti, A. (2022). *Storia ed analisi dei processi di accompagnamento alla vita indipendente e tracciamento di line guida.* Unpublished work.

Forber-Pratt, A.J., Lyew, D., and Mueller (2017). Disability identity development: a systematic rewiew of the literature. *Rehabilitation Psychology*, 62 (2):198–207. doi:10.1037/rep0000134.

Francescutti, C., Faini, M., Corti, S. and Leoni, M. (2016). *Disabilità: servizi per l'abitare e sostegni per l'inclusione.* Rimini: Maggioli Editore.

Fulford, K.W.M., Thornton, T., and Graham, G. (2006). *Oxford textbook of philosophy and psychiatry.* Oxford: Oxford University Press.

Mancini, T. (2010). *Psicologia dell'Identità.* Bologna: Il Mulino.

Moretti, A., and Felicioli, F. (2011). *D.O.N.N.E (Dare Opportunità Non Negando Esperienze).* Pisa: Edizioni Del Cerro.

National Institute for Health and Clinical Excellence (2015). *Transition from children's to adults' services for young people using health or social care service.* NICE guidelines (NG43).

Oliver, M. (2013). The social model of disability: thirty years on. *Disability and Society*, 28 (7), 1024–1026. doi:10.1080/09687599.2013.818773.

Schalock, R.L., Brown, I., Brown, R., Cummins, R.A., Felce, D., Matikka, L., ... Parmenter, T. (2002). Conceptualization, measurement, and application of quality of life for persons with intellectual disabilities: report of an international panel of experts. *Mental Retardation*, 40 (6), 457–470.

Schalock, R.L. (2020). *The quality of life supports model: components and applications, 17ᵗʰ international conference on positive behavior supports*. Miami, Florida, March 12, 2020.

Schroeder, F.K. (2015). *People with disabilities: the orphan minority*. Jacobus tenBroek Disability Law Symposium March 26, 2015.

Shogren, K.A., Wehmeyer, M.L., Lassmann, H. and Forber-Pratt, A.J (2017). Supported decision making: a synthesis of the literature across intellectual disability, mental health, and aging. *Education and Training in Autism and Developmental Disabilities*, 52 (2), 144–157.

The Minnesota Governor's Council on Developmental Disabilities (2020). *Parallels in Times. A History of developmental disabilities*. https//:mn.gov>mnddc> parallels.

United Nations (1948). *Universal declaration of human rights*. http://www.un. org/en/documents/udhr.

United Nations (1975). *Declaration on the rights of disabled persons*. http://www2. ohchr.org/English/law/res3447.htm.

United Nations (1993). *Standard rules on the equalization of opportunities for disabled persons*. United Nations General Assembly, New York.

United Nations (2006). *Convention on the rights of persons with disabilities*. http://www.un.org/disabilities/convention/conventionfull.shtml.

Van Loon, J.H.M., van Hove, G., Schalock, R.L., and Claes, C. (2017). *POS – personal outcomes scale, versione italiana. protocollo*. (Adattamento Italiano A. Coscarelli e G. Balboni, Vannini Editoria Scientifica)

Verdugo, M.A., Gomez, L.E., Arias, B., Santamaria, M., Navallas, E., Fernandez, S. and Hierro, I. (2014). *Scala San Martin*. Fundacion Obra San Martin.

Verdugo, M.A., Navas, P., Gòmez, L.E. and Schalock, R.L. (2012). The concept of quality of life and its role in enhancing human rights in the field of intellectual disability. *Journal of Intellectual Disability Research, 56(11), 1036–45*. doi:10.1111/j.1365-2788.2012.01585.x.

World Health Organization. (2000). *Healthy ageing: adults with intellectual disabilities: summative report*. https://apps.who.int/iris/handle/10665/66367.

Subject and Authors Index